DOMESDAY AND FEUDAL STATISTICS.

KENNIKAT PRESS SCHOLARLY REPRINTS

Dr. Ralph Adams Brown, Senior Editor

Series on

ECONOMIC THOUGHT, HISTORY AND CHALLENGE

Under the General Editorial Supervision of

Dr. Sanford D. Gordon

Professor of Economics, State University of New York

DOMESDAY AND FEUDAL STATISTICS

WITH A CHAPTER ON

AGRICULTURAL STATISTICS

BY

A. H. INMAN

Sunt geminæ Somni portæ quarum altera fertur
Cornea quâ veris facilis datur exitus umbris
Altera candenti perfecta nitens elephanto
Sed falsa ad cœlum mittunt insomnia manes
VERG.

KENNIKAT PRESS
Port Washington, N. Y./London

DOMESDAY AND FEUDAL STATISTICS

First published in 1900
Reissued in 1971 by Kennikat Press
Library of Congress Catalog Card No: 77-137948
ISBN 0-8046-1450-4

Manufactured by Taylor Publishing Company   Dallas, Texas

KENNIKAT SERIES ON ECONOMIC THOUGHT,
HISTORY AND CHALLENGE

PREFACE.

THE Analysis of Domesday set forth in some six Tables in this volume rests on the computations of Sir H. Ellis, and Messrs. F. Maitland and C. Pearson, the first of which is *generally* reliable, and practically accords with that of an independent authority (Sharon Turner).

Most essential service has recently been rendered by Professor Maitland, whose calculations of certain factors have made advance in the knowledge of our ancient Record practicable : it is not easy to overestimate the debt due to the labour of this author, but it must also be borne in mind that a computation of *Hides* and *Carucates* is a matter of much difficulty. The method used has been re-marked in these pages in a note, but direct reference should be made to the computer's own remarks in *Domesday Book and Beyond*; although there are theories in that volume scarcely compatible with the witness of the " Survey," and other evidences, it is nevertheless full of interest, and should be possessed by all who have an interest in England's greatest *record*.

There is no reason to challenge the figures obtained from the *History of England during the Middle and Early Ages*, and it is believed that the Analysis of the several additions of the three above-named writers, yield *generally* correct information ; there are also in this volume independent computations from Domesday and other sources, which claim *practical* rather than *minute* accuracy.

With regard to the Statistics of Feudal Tenures, it may be observed that the Baronial Charters of 1166 are incomplete, that the deficiencies can to some extent be supplied from the *Pipe Roll* of 1167-8, and that further additions (given separately), are available from other sources : these returns are corroborated by those of the *Pipe Roll* of 1253-4, and the *Enrolled Accounts of the Exchequer* for the Inquisitions of 1346-7 (as computed by a mediæval and contemporary scribe), so that the correctness of the *general* result is a matter scarcely to be affected by criticism, save of the records themselves. This, of course, is to be understood rather of the plain facts elicited, than of any deductions from them containing elements of estimation ; the latter, to a certain extent, are inevitable in the earliest (1166-8) case, and the method, acceptable or otherwise, is set forth, but as a *modus*, necessitated by the defect of contemporary evidences.

A considerable amount of space is allotted to tabular illustration, and, it is believed, that the mere *arithmetical* results are free from conspicuous errors, although no attempt has been made to *exactly* determine long series of fractions; nor can pages, so largely concerned with mere figures, attempt to compete in interest, for the *general* reader, with *theories*, elaborated by verbal art, and displayed in becoming detail.

A Statistical Index, before the *text* (the former perhaps also of service in demonstrating any too condensed details of latter), recapitulates and classifies some of the more important *data*, but rarely repeats those given only in the Tables, a list of which (arranged) precedes it : both, of course, are for convenience of reference, *etc.*, and the former, owing to necessary brevity, does not always *quite* convey the sense, more precisely given in the pages alluded to.

Some sort of apology may be esteemed necessary in the presentation of pages mainly concerned with prosaic details ; the reply must be, that in any acknowledged science, *speculations*, and other the usual *impedimenta* of *extraordinary* genius should be put to the *ordinary* tests of *observation* and *experiment*, and that there are no (or scarcely any) practical systems of knowledge, where so many *theories*, alike unproved and improbable, are permitted to survive, thrive, and increase, as in the accepted School of History. The *practical* Sciences have formulated their systems, *not* without labour, and by careful examinations and comparisons ; the modern historian, it is true, has dismissed the wonders, signs, and portents of the mediæval world, but taking into consideration the usages and relative opportunities of the different ages, he often displays so vast an inexperience of the ordinary *phenomena* of the physical world, as to convict himself of a *credulity* much less excusable than that of an *antecessor*, whom it is his frequent pleasure to decry.

It may be permitted to notice some of the novelties in these pages : for example, it appears that the number of *Liberi Homines* and *Sochemanni* in Lincoln, and Norfolk (presumably also Suffolk), have been greatly overestimated, the figures in Domesday giving no direct clue as to the actual number of those classes ; again it seems to amount to a matter of demonstration that the *Carucates* of Norfolk (supposedly also Suffolk), were usually neither Fiscal Units nor Teamlands.

A theory is current that the total "Service" of the Military Fees of England was equivalent to the number of *Milites* due from the feudal tenants *in exercitu ;* such a doctrine has nothing *a priori* in its favor, save facility of computation, nor has it (so far as I am aware), any *general* support from records, but very much the reverse.

There is, of course, no attempt here to develope the History of the Feudal System in England ; the publication of some recent volumes of the *Rolls Series* allowed their editor the opportunity of *suggesting* (and little *more*), at considerable length, certain views, scarcely probable in themselves, and which could not have been put forward at all, had a few elementary *data*, concerning the military tenures of this country, been available for general reference.

The view that *one* plough could, and did, *till* annually 120 acres of arable land, has been long established, and is, of course, completely at variance with any known practice of Agriculture in this country ; as theories of this Art are usually held with a tenacity justly proportioned to their propounder's inexperience of the details of husbandry, it is scarcely probable that the *numerou*s examples drawn from English *records* in these pages, can *possibly* diminish the confidence of those who *allege* historical evidences in support of what passes for Scholarship—to any actually acquainted with the practice of Agriculture, the appeal to records (which uphold such) is entirely superfluous.

The curiosities of Domesday can very well be studied in Sir H. Ellis' *General Introduction* and *Index of Matters* (Vol. III), nevertheless in writing on our ancient Record, it has (contrary to the practice of many of its exponents), been esteemed necessary to traverse it, entry by entry, for certain matters exemplified in this volume. This remark applies but partially to *Little Domesday*, whose *technical* manorial details have been almost unperused (valuable as they may be for the three counties therein contained), nor is there the least pretension towards exhausting — in any way — the contents of that unrivalled witness of Anglo-Saxon customs.

In conclusion, it should be stated that Mr. N. J. Hone, of Surbiton, is responsible for the evidence from unprinted materials in Chapter II, having made professional searches (to instructions, in particular records), on divers matters ; references to these are given in their place, so that they can easily be tested for *general* accuracy ; this the writer (who is responsible for the remaining extracts, etc., from records and works of authority) does not doubt.

Wardrew House,
Gilsland,
Oct. 22, 1900.

EPITOME

DOMESDAY STATISTICS.

CHAPTER I (pp. 1—24).

Population and Counties, p. 1. Main Statistical Table, p. 5.
Population 1086 and 1377, p. 5. Units of Assessment and
Measures, p. 5. Plough Team, p. 6. Comparative Values of
Implements and Oxen, p. 6. Ploughland, p. 7. Area *not* tilled
by one plough, p. 7. *Oxford Arithmetic*, p. 8. *College Farming*,
p. 9. *Valets* and *Valuits*, p. 10. *Villani*, p. 10. *Opera*, p. 10.
Bordars and Cottars, p. 11. Illustrations of same from *D. B.*,
p. 11. *Servi*, p. 12. Sokemen, p. 12. Popular estimate of
Liberi Homines, and Sokemen (1086) not in accord with *D. B.*
evidence, p. 12. *Liberi homines*, p. 12. Radknights, p. 13.
Tenants in chief, p. 13. *Coliberti* and *Buri*, p. 13. *Geburi*
not *Coliberti*, p. 13 *Geburi* as *Villani*, p. 16. Other Classes,
p. 16. *Porcarii* and *Bovarii*, p. 16. Remarks on Comparative
Table I, p. 17. Land to one team, p 17. Land of one team
in demesne, and in villeinage, p. 18. Oxen per plough in
Wales, *t.* Hen. II, p. 18. Teams of less than 8 oxen, p. 22.
Teams of 8 oxen, p. 22. Rotations, p. 23. Method of Tables,
p. 23. Population varies as Teams, p. 24. Slender results
from other *unlike* Factors, p. 24.

FEUDAL STATISTICS.

CHAPTER II (pp. 25—109d).

Anglo-Saxon Charters, p. 26. Norman Charters, p. 26.
Heptarchic Hides, p. 28. 120 statute acres arable *not* the
land of one family, p. 29. Owners of land T.R.E. and
T.R.W., p. 30. Modern theories of ancient landownership

EPITOME

DOMESDAY STATISTICS.

CHAPTER I (pp. 1—24).

Population and Counties, p. 1. Main Statistical Table, p. 5. Population 1086 and 1377, p. 5. Units of Assessment and Measures, p. 5. Plough Team, p. 6. Comparative Values of Implements and Oxen, p. 6. Ploughland, p. 7. Area *not* tilled by one plough, p. 7. *Oxford Arithmetic*, p. 8. *College Farming*, p. 9. *Valets* and *Valuits*, p. 10. *Villani*, p. 10. *Opera*, p. 10. Bordars and Cottars, p. 11. Illustrations of same from *D. B.*, p. 11. *Servi*, p. 12. Sokemen, p. 12. Popular estimate of *Liberi Homines*, and Sokemen (1086) not in accord with *D. B.* evidence, p. 12. *Liberi homines*, p. 12. Radknights, p. 13. Tenants in chief, p. 13. *Coliberti* and *Buri*, p. 13. *Geburi* not *Coliberti*, p. 13 *Geburi* as *Villani*, p. 16. Other Classes, p. 16. *Porcarii* and *Bovarii*, p. 16. Remarks on Comparative Table I, p. 17. Land to one team, p 17. Land of one team in demesne, and in villeinage, p. 18. Oxen per plough in Wales, *t.* Hen. II, p. 18. Teams of less than 8 oxen, p. 22. Teams of 8 oxen, p. 22. Rotations, p. 23. Method of Tables, p. 23. Population varies as Teams, p. 24. Slender results from other *unlike* Factors, p. 24.

FEUDAL STATISTICS.

CHAPTER II (pp. 25—109d).

Anglo-Saxon Charters, p. 26. Norman Charters, p. 26. Heptarchic Hides, p. 28. 120 statute acres arable *not* the land of one family, p. 29. Owners of land T.R.E. and T.R.W., p. 30. Modern theories of ancient landownership

AGRICULTURAL STATISTICS.

CHAPTER III (pp. 109e—161).

FORTY-THREE TABLES
CHRONOLOGICALLY ARRANGED.

FORTY-THREE TABLES CHRONOLOGICALLY ARRANGED —*contd.*

THE ABOVE FORTY-THREE
TABLES ARRANGED BY SUBJECT MATTER.

Subject.	Reference Numbers.	En-tries.
Agriculture .	B, K to O, Q, R, T, U, LL to OO, QQ	15
Domesday .	A to T	20
Feudal Service .	V to Z, AA to KK	16
Measures, and } *"Measures"* }	A, G, N, S, II, LL, OO . . .	7
Population .	A, D, E, M, PP	5
Præ-Domesday .	A to C	3
Yorkshire .	B, C, N, PP	4
	Total . .	70

STATISTICAL INDEX OF TEXT, ARRANGED
CHRONOLOGICALLY AND BY SUBJECTS,
BUT NOT INCLUDING DETAILS OF ABOVE
FORTY-THREE TABLES—194 REFERENCES

AGRICULTURE (*Nos. 1—30*).

Date.	Ref. Nos.	Matter.	Statistics.	Pages
A. S.	1	*Gebur* has of plough oxen ...	2	10
A. S.; etc.	2	Ploughs	1, 2, 4, and 8 oxen	22
11th cent.	3	Plough ox; Cost of ...	2/6	7
1124	4	Seed Wheat for 1 acre ...	2 seedlips	149
,,	5	,, Barley ,, ,, ...	3 ,,	149
,,	6	,, Oats ,, ,, ...	4 ,,	149

STATISTICAL INDEX OF TEXT—*contd.*

AGRICULTURE *(Nos. 1—30)—contd.*

STATISTICAL INDEX OF TEXT—*contd.*
DOMESDAY (*Nos. 31—80*).

Date.	Ref. Nos.	Matter.	Statistics.	Pages
c. 1065	31	*Liberi Homines,* Sokemen, *Homines, Fratres,* Thanes, Burgesses, and Radknights (Ellis)	6,000 to 7,000	30
,,	32	A.S. Landowners, excluding *Liberi Homines,* and Sokemen	*c.* 13,000	30
1065-1086	33	Landowners A. S. to A. N.	3 : 2	30
1086	34	Recorded Population ...	283,242	2
,,	35	,, ,, extended to all England	*c.* 300,000	117
,,	36	Villeins, bordars, cottars and coscez, *servi ;* of total population	$\frac{4}{5}$	1
,,	37	Total population *(England)*	1,800,000	5
,,	38	,, capital tenants ...	*c.* 1,400	68
,,	39	Tenants *in capite,* and Mesne Lords	9,000 to 10,000	30, 102
,,	40	Church lands ; Value of (in 21 counties) to total	$\frac{3}{10}$	63
,,	41	Hides in *D. B.* in 34 counties (as from *Prof. Maitland*)	*c.* 67,000	35
,,	42	Places—Number of	15,000 to 18,000	31
,,	43	Population *per* place ...	*c.* 100	31
,,	44	Counties in *D. B.*	34	1

STATISTICAL INDEX OF TEXT—*contd.*

DOMESDAY (*Nos. 31—80*)—*contd.*

Date.	Ref. Nos.	Matter.	Statistics.	Pages
1086	45	*Milites* (Ellis)	137	102
,,	46	,, *(actually found)* ...	700+	103
,,	47	Villeins—their holdings ...	*nil*, 7 acres to 2 Hides	10
,,	48	,, some at Hanwell and West Bedfont	2 fiscal Hides	10, 131
,,	49	Villeins—average holdings, Middlesex	1 fiscal virgate	10
,,	50	Villeins—Cambridge, in Ely Manors	$10\frac{1}{2}$ acres	10
,,	51	Villeins—average holdings, England *(estimated)*	20 to 21 acres	11
,,	52	Villeins—plough oxen	*nil* to $3\frac{1}{2}$ teams to 3 villeins	148
,,	53	Villeins — average plough oxen not less than ...	2	13, 122
,,	54	Bordars—holdings	*nil* to 2 bovates	11
,,	55	,, plough oxen ...	*nil* to 8 oxen	11
,,	56	Coscez, ,, ,, ...	*nil* to 4 oxen	11
,,	57	Cottars, ,, ,, ...	*nil* to 6 cottars per team (8 oxen).	11

STATISTICAL INDEX OF TEXT—*contd.*

DOMESDAY (*Nos. 31—80*)—*contd.*

Date.	Ref. Nos.	Matter.	Statistics.	Pages
1086	58	*Coliberti* and *Buri* (*Ellis*) ...	920	16
,,	59	,, ,, ,, of which found	891	16
,,	60	*Coliberti* and *Buri* on *royal* Manors, in 48 entries ...	552	16
,,	61	*Coliberti* and *Buri* on *church* Manors, in 32 entries ...	311	16
,,	62	*Coliberti* and *Buri* on *lay* Manors, in 6 entries ...	28	16
,,	63	*Coliberti* and *Buri ;* the above 891 in *but*	86 entries	16
,,	64	Proportion of demesne to total Teams (*9 counties*) ...	$\frac{3}{10}$	145, 147
,,	65	Estimate of demesne to total Arable	$\frac{2}{5}$	147
,,	66	Land *tilled* by one team ...	64 acres	130
,,	67	Teamlands (demesne and villeinage combined), Ely Manors, Norfolk	52 to 53 acres	125, 126
,,	68	Teamlands (demesne and villeinage combined), Ely Manors, Suffolk	52 to 53 acres	125, 126
,,	69	Number of oxen *per* team by Domesday scheme ...	8 oxen	6, 146, 147
,,	70	Ploughs, all England, estimated	84,130 (8 oxen)	117, 121

STATISTICAL INDEX OF TEXT—*contd.*

DOMESDAY (*Nos. 31—80*)—*contd.*

Date.	Ref. Nos.	Matter.	Statistics.	Pages
1086	71	Ploughs in co. Northants (*see No.* 11)	2,422 (8 oxen)	33
,,	72	Examples of *one* to *seven* oxen, 1 *team*, and *nine* to *ten* oxen in *D. B.*, but not of ...	8 oxen	146, 147
,,	73	Ploughs (8 oxen each, *D. B.*) in the 34 recorded counties	*c.* 78,000	121, 122, 146
,,	74	Ploughs (8 oxen each, *D. B.*) in 30 counties	70,606	4, 117
,,	75	1000 acres arable supports of recorded population	47 +	123, 124
,,	76	1000 acres arable tilled by	*c.* 16 teams (8 oxen each)	123
,,	77	1 acre arable, average rent value	2d.	140
Wm. I to Ed. I or Ed. II.	78	Some Rochester Manors; Teams, latter to former period	2 : 1	152
,,	79	Some Rochester Manors; demesne Teams, latter to former period	1 : 1	152
,,	80	Some Rochester Manors; villeinage Teams, latter to former period	9 : 4	152
		See also : Nos. 1 to 2; 82; 84 to 87 ; 162 to 165 ; 181 to 184 ; and 192.		

STATISTICAL INDEX OF TEXT—*contd.*

FEUDAL SERVICE (*Nos. 81—161*).

Date.	Ref. Nos.	Matter.	Statistics.	Pages
996-1026	81	Military service (cited by *J. F. Baldwin*)	*militiæ statutum*	109
t. Wm. I	82	*Possible* reference to *escuage* or its *antecessor*, before	A.D. 1086	81
,,	83	Dean of Evreux, *bent with age* (*1066-89*), holds of paternal inheritance	1 knight's fee	104
1086	84	Total capital tenants by knight service (*ut de corona*), probably	300—	68
1086-1166	85	Knights' Fees, in the *D. B.* Hides of *Prof. Maitland*	*c.* 50,000	79
1086— 12 Car. II }	86	Value of Knight's Fee ...	£2 to £200 p. a.	45
t. Wm. I	87	John holds Teusham of the Abbot of Ely, as	2 knight's fees	109
1088	88	The Bishop of Durham has (not necessarily all feudal tenants) as retainers	100 *milites*	42
1103	89	Earl Flanders' service to the King of France	10 knights	107
1109	90	Aid to marry the daughter of *Hen. I*	3/- per Hide	83
Hen. I—II	91	Flemish Knights for England	500 and 1000	100*a*
,,	92	Horses *per* Knight	3	100*a*
1107-8	93	Bigot Roger (*ob. 1107* or *1108*) had feft in	115 fees	108, 109

STATISTICAL INDEX OF TEXT—*contd*

FEUDAL SERVICE (*Nos. 81—161*) — *contd.*

Date.	Ref. Nos.	Matter.	Statistics.	Pages
t. Hen. I	94	Bayeux Fees	120 fees	102
,,	95	,, Service, for 40 days	40 knights	102
Hen. I—II	96	Wages of *miles*	4d. (?), and 8d. to 1/-	100*a*
1163	97	Earl Flanders' service to the King of France	20 knights	107
11 Hen. I	98	Earl Richard leads *in exercitu*	20 knights and 40 *servientes*	99
1166-1168	99	Number of tenants *in capite*, *ut de corona*, by Knight service	*c.* 300	51
,,	100	Of *c.* 300 tenants, 11 hold of fees as on p. 51	$\frac{1}{4}$	51
,,	101	Of *c.* 300 tenants, 34 hold of fees as on p. 51	$\frac{1}{2}$	51
,,	102	*c.* 206 tenants hold	2 fees +	52
,,	103	*c.* 94 ,, ,, ...	2 fees & 2—	52
,,	104	*c.* 125 ,, ,, ...	5 ,, —	67
,,	105	*c.* 155 ,, ,, ...	10 ,, —	67
,,	106	*c.* 145 ,, ,, ...	10 ,, and 10 +	67
,,	107	Church capital tenants ...	*c.* 39	67
,,	108	Lay ,, ,, ...	*c.* 261	67

STATISTICAL INDEX OF TEXT—*contd.*
FEUDAL SERVICE (*Nos. 81 — 161*)—*contd.*

Date.	Ref. Nos	Matter.	Statistics.	Pages
1166-1168	109	Total Fees, England ...	7173+	65
,,	110	Old feoffment, as given	4903 fees	65
,,	111	New ,, ,, ,,	483 ,,	65
,,	112	Returns by sheriff, as given	745 ,,	65
,,	113	*Super dominicum*, ,, ,,	315½ ,,	65
,,	114	Deficiency, *not* returned, estimated at	700 to 800 fees	54
,,	115	Total "Service," England, estimated	6676+	64
,,	116	Estimate of Fees (*Pearson*) .	6400	53
,,	117	Number of Fees, of "Services" of more than 100 Knights	11 cases	99
,,	118	Average Lay Fee	5 to 6 *D.B.* Hides	43
,,	119	Scope of Church Fee ...	12,000 acres	65
,,	120	Church fees to total, as by *service*	$\frac{1}{6}$ to $\frac{1}{7}$	63
,,	121	Scope of Lay Fee	2,500 acres	65
,,	122	Charters—names in ...	*c.* 4000	103
,,	123	,, names holding less than 1 fee	*c.* 1600	103

STATISTICAL INDEX OF TEXT—*contd.*

FEUDAL SERVICE (*Nos. 81—161*)—*contd.*

Date.	Ref. Nos.	Matter.	Statistics.	Pages
1166-1168	124	$36\frac{3}{5}$ fees of Simon de Beauchamp (all of old feoffment), held by	85 tenants	103
,,	125	Charters; " Service " stated	*c.* 146 cases	57
,,	126	Many Examples in Multiples of	5 fees	67
,,	127	A meaningless phrase—feudal service of	1000 Hides	46
,,	128	Honor of Totnes consisted of $49 + 19\frac{4}{15} + \frac{11}{15}$, that is	75 fees	55
t. Hen. II	129	Normandy—no. of Fees ...	1500, or 1830	102
,,	130	,, —Service ...	581, or 652	102
,,	131	Bayeux — ,, ...	20 knights	102
,,	132	Bayeux fees	*c.* 120	102
Hen. II— } *III*	133	Fees of Bishop of Durham .	10, 70 and 150	43
7 John to t. Hen. III	134	Variations of Fees as to Hides and Carucates (*see* Nos. 136, 150)	$2\frac{1}{2}$ to 159 carucates per fee	43, 44
1211	135	Army of Ireland, greatest number of knights of feudal tenant	10	111
1242	136	Hides per fee, a case of (*see* Nos. 134, 150)	32	75

STATISTICAL INDEX OF TEXT—*contd.*

FEUDAL SERVICE (*Nos. 81—161*)—*contd.*

Date.	Ref. Nos.	Matter.	Statistics.	Pages
38 Hen. III	137	Number of capital tenants (*ut de corona*), by Knight Service (*auxilium*) ...	*c.* 450	51
,,	138	Fees omitted in above record	775+	51
38 Hen. III	139	Total fees (*render*)	6734 +	51
,,	140	Number of Fees, of " Services " of more than 100 knights	9 cases	99
,	141	Of 5959 fees (returned) with *c.* 439 tenants *in capite* (ut de corona) of all the fees, 9 feudatories hold	$\frac{1}{4}$	51
,,	142	Of 5959 fees (returned) with *c.* 439 tenants *in capite* (ut de corona) of all the fees, 29 feudatories hold	$\frac{1}{2}$	51
,,	143	*Re* above, 204 tenants hold	2 fees +	51
,,	144	,, ,, 235 ,, ,,	2 fees and 2 fees —	51
,,	145	The Luterell fee (*see Nos.* 148, 151), assessed to an *auxilium* at	12½ fees	89, 90
t. Hen. III	146	Estimated number of *Bannerets* and *Bachelors* ...	1000 to 1500	99
Hen. III—Ed. II	147	Period of service *in exercitu* .	40 days	102
5 Ed. I	148	The Luterell fee, discharged by service *in exercitu* (*see* also *Nos.* 145, 151) of ...	2 Knights	88

STATISTICAL INDEX OF TEXT—*contd.*

FEUDAL SERVICE (*Nos. 81—161*)—*contd.*

Date.	Ref. Nos.	Matter.	Statistics.	Pages
1284	149	Pact with a *miles* for quittance of service of 1 fee (recognised *in exercitu*), in the Welsh war, for ...	£20	100
t. Ed. I	150	Hides per fee, a case of (*see Nos.* 134, 136)	2	78
10 Ed. I	151	The Luterell fee (*see Nos.* 145, 148), in default of service *in exercitu*, and *presumably* no fine having been taken, pays Scutage, 35 years after said army, on ...	12½ fees	95
t. Ed. I	152	The Bishop of Durham has in the Scotch war (not necessarily as his service, *i.e.* 10)	26 Banerets, 140 Knights	42
1300	153	The same has at Caerlaverock	160 *men at arms*	42
4 Ed. II	154	Expenses of 1 *miles* for the Scotch war	60 marcs +	100
1346	155	Fees found at this date (36 counties)	*c.* 6000	69
20 Ed. III	156	Fees in Cornwall	165¾	70
,,	157	English Earls, Bannerets, and Knights, at Calais ...	*c.* 1063	98
,,	158	English Esquires, at Calais	*c.* 3000	98

STATISTICAL INDEX OF TEXT—*contd.*

FEUDAL SERVICE (*Nos. 81—161*)—*contd.*

Date.	Ref. Nos.	Matter.	Statistics.	Pages
4 Hen. IV	159	Returns at £1 *per* fee of tenants " in capite," by Knight Service (*30 counties*), and of capital socagers (£20 land as for 1 fee)	£1075	70
,,	160	Cornwall Fees held " in capite " (*i.e. demesne*) ...	½ fee	70
1630-2	161	Knighthood Money (*i.e.* distraint, *t. Car. I*)	£100,000 or £173,537 9s. 6d.	97
		See also: Nos. 33; 38 to 40; 45 to 46; 176; 179; and 193 to 194.		

MEASURES AND "MEASURES" (*Nos. 162—180*).

Date.	Ref. Nos.	Matter.	Statistics.	Pages
1086	162	Hide, Scope of	*c.* 400 acres	41
,,	163	1 fiscal *sulung* perhaps ...	160 fiscal acres	39
,,	164	1 ,, jugum ,, ...	40 fiscal acres	39, 153
,,	165	Cornish fiscal Acre	*c.* 10 normal fiscal acres	38
1125-1128	166	Old measure of *presumably* seed for 1 acre	1 *achersetum*	161

STATISTICAL INDEX OF TEXT—*contd.*

MEASURES AND "MEASURES" (*Nos. 162—180*)—*contd.*

Date.	Ref. Nos.	Matter.	Statistics.	Pages
Hen. II— *John*	167	A quarter (sometimes of 8 bushels), as compared with quarter in No.173, not more than	$\frac{1}{2}$	159
,,	168	This smaller quarter approximates to	1 horse load	160
14 John	169	The King's carthorses have 1 bushel each (old, small measure), of which the quarter sells at	10d. to 1/-	160
c. 1240	170	1 Hide=4 Virgates= ...	48 acres	37
,,	171	,, = ,, = ...	256 acres	38
t. Hen. III	172	A farm horse has of oats (query in Measure as in No. 173)	$\frac{1}{6}$ bushel	160
Hen. III to *Hen. VII*	173	1 Quarter = 8 bushels of 64 lbs. (old Troy) each, each lb. made up of	7680 wheat grains	158
t. Ed. I	174	Bedfordshire — demesne carucates,—average of ...	$91\frac{1}{5}$ acres	141
1279	175	$5\frac{1}{2}$ Hides Arable + 5 Hides of Meadow, Pasture, and Marsh + (*query*)=	11 rateable Hides	140
t. Ed. I	176	Allowance of a *destrier* in oats	$\frac{1}{2}$ bushel	160
,,	177	Allowance of a cart-horse in oats	$\frac{1}{4}$ bushel	160

STATISTICAL INDEX OF TEXT—*contd.*

MEASURES AND "MEASURES" *Nos. 162—180—contd.*

Date.	Ref. Nos.	Matter.	Statistics.	Pages
t. Ed. I	178	Kentish *iugum*	40 acres	153
1560	179	Weight (rider and total armour) carried by a certain *destrier*	361 lbs. modern avoird.	160
1900	180	1 lb. *avoirdupois* of well dried wheat grains	7000	159
		See also—Nos. 4 to 6; 15 to 16; 21; 41; 47 to 51; 54; 67 to 69; 72; 85; 90; 119; 121; 126 to 127; 134; 136; 150; 182 to 183; and 192.		

POPULATION (*Nos. 181—188*).

Date.	Ref. Nos.	Matter.	Statistics.	Pages
Heptarchy.	181	Population of England ...	*c.* 1,500,000 to 2,000,000	29
,,	182	Part of England; land of ...	250,000 families	29
t. Bede	183	Isle of Wight; land of ...	1,200 families	29
1086	184	,, ,, recorded population	1,124	29
1347	185	England and Wales; population	*c.* 4,000,000	5, 121

STATISTICAL INDEX OF TEXT—*contd.*

POPULATION (*Nos. 181—188*) —*contd.*

Date.	Ref. Nos.	Matter.	Statistics.	Pages
1377	186	England and Wales; population	c. 2,700,000	5, 121
1688	187	Houses in England and Wales	1,300,000	115
1696	188	Population in England and Wales	5,500,000 to 7,000,000	115
		See also: Nos. 31 to 39; 43; 45 to 46; 58 to 63; 75; 84; 99; 107 to 108; 122 to 123; 137; 141 to 144; 146; 157 to 158; 161; and 190.		

PLACES AND PARISHES—ENGLAND (*Nos. 189—190*).

Date.	Ref. Nos.	Matter.	Statistics.	Pages
1371	189	Parishes in England (less Cheshire)	8,600	31
,,	190	Population *per* parish ...	c. 300	31
		See also: Nos. 42 to 44.		

PRÆ-DOMESDAY.

See Nos. 1 to 2; 31 to 33; 81 to 83; and 181 to 183.

STATISTICAL INDEX OF TEXT—*contd.*

SOCAGE (*No. 191*).

Date.	Ref. Nos.	Matter.	Statistics.	Pages
4 Hen. IV	191	Cornwall; Socage *in capite* . See also No. 159.	*nil*	70

YORKSHIRE (*Nos. 192—194*).

Date.	Ref. Nos.	Matter.	Statistics.	Pages
1086 onwards	192	Liberty of Ripon; acres in .	*c.* 40,000	63, 127
20 Ed. III	193	Fees, W. R., Yorks	*c.* 150	69
4 Hen. IV	194	„ „ „ held *in capite* (*i.e. demesne*) ...	*c.* 12	69
		See also : Nos. 88; 133; 145; 148; and 151 to 153.		

SUMMARY OF INDEX AND TABLES.

(But not including detailed statistics in latter).

STATISTICAL INDEX.

	Direct Entries.	Under other Heads.	Table Entries	Total Entries.
Agriculture	30	42	15	87
Domesday	50	16	20	86
Feudal Service	81	10	16	107
Measures and "Measures"	19	29	7	55
Population	8	35	5	48
Places and Parishes ...	2	3	—	5
Præ-Domesday	—	11	3	14
Socage	1	1	—	2
Yorkshire	3	7	4	14
Totals ...	194	154	70	418

TABLES FROM THOMAS RUDBORNE'S
WINCHESTER HISTORY,

Under the year 1083, but presumably written in the reign of Henry the Sixth.*†

3	grains of barley, dry and round	*make*	1 inch (*pollex*).
12	inches	,,	1 foot (*pes*).
3	feet	,,	1 yard (*ulna*).
5½	yards	,,	1 perch (*pertica*).
20	(*sic*) *1 by 4 perches	,,	1 acre (*acra*).

*† The author may of course have used older materials, but Section II seems inconsistent with a date earlier than Hen III (*vide* p. 159), and the Escuage Tables could scarcely apply prior to Ed. I (the amount being fixed, *vide etiam* p. 96); all the items however [saving that one noted (*2) as not understood], appear proper to the 15th cent.

*1. This is an obvious error, presumably of the pen.

TABLES FROM THOMAS RUDBORNE'S
WINCHESTER HISTORY—*contd.*

1 penny (*denarius*) [called *Starelyng*, round without clipping, will weigh 32 grains of wheat, in the midst of the ear (*spica*)]	*weighs*	32 wheat grains.
20 pence	*weigh*	1 ounce.
12 ounces, according to the English currency (*cursus*)	,,	1 lb., *i.e.*, 20/-
8 lbs. of wheat	*make*	1 gallon (*lagena*).
8 gallons [make a bushel (*modius*), according to the measure (*mensura*) of London]	,,	1 London measure.
8 bushels (*modii*)	,,	1 quarter
250 lbs. of sterlings *2 (*sic*)	,,	1 bushel (*bussellus*).

4 virgates (*virgæ*) *3 make 1 *Hide*	*being*	64 acres of land.
5 *Hides* make 1 Knight's Fee	,,	320 ,, ,, ,,

Each Knight's Fee	will give for Scutage	40/-
{ ,, ½ ,, ,, *i.e.*, { 160 acres of land	,, ,, ,, ,,	20/-
{ ,, ⅓ Knight's Fee, *i.e.*, { 106½ (*sic*) acres of { land	,, ,, ,, ,,	12/- (*sic*).
1¼ Hides, *i.e.*, 24 *4 (*sic*) acres of land ...	,, ,, ,, ,,	10/-
⅕ Knight's Fee, *i.e.*, 64 acres of land ...	,, ,, ,, ,,	8/-
1/10 Knight's Fee, *i.e.*, 33 (*sic*) acres of land	,, ,, ,, ,,	4/-
1/16 Knight's Fee, *i.e.*, 20 acres of land ...	,, ,, ,, ,.	24*d.* ¾ (*sic*).

*2. The explanation of this entry is unknown to the writer.
*3. Suppose a clerical error for *virgata*.
*4. A slip of the pen, or printer, for four score.

CHAPTER I

DOMESDAY STATISTICS

"Cæterum tota vita ita fortunatus fuit, vt exteræ & remotæ gentes, nihil magis, quam nomen eius timerent. Prouinciales adeo nutu suo substrauerat, vt sine ulla contradictione primus censum omnium capitum ageret, omnium prædiorū redditus in tota Anglia notitiæ suæ per scriptum adiiceret, omnes liberos homines cuiuscunq; essent, suæ fidelitati sacramento adigeret."

[Willielmi Malmesburiensis, curâ H. Sauile.]

D OMESDAY BOOK gives much information which can be displayed in statistical tables—to wit, as to population, ploughteams, ploughlands, hidage, past and present values: it should be borne in mind that thirty-four counties are enumerated ; of the remaining six, Monmouth was then in Wales, Northumberland and Durham are not found: in the Yorkshire "Survey" Cumberland and Westmoreland are slightly noticed, and most of North Lancashire, the remainder of that county being found under Cheshire. For fuller information as to the recorded population, reference can be made to Ellis' "Introduction to Domesday Book" (1833), from which the underwritten figures are taken: in the thirty-four counties (as then

Population and counties.

1

constituted) is a total of 283,242 recorded folk, of which, in rough percentages :

					%
Villans	...	...	108,456	...	38
Bordars	...	...	82,624	...	29
Servi	...	...	25,156	...	9
Sokemen	...	...	23,090	...	8
Liberi Homines	...	...	12,384	...	4
Burgesses	...	...	7,968	...	3
Mesne Lords	...	...	7,871	...	3
Cottars	...	...	6,819	...	2½
Tenants-in-chief	...	...	1,400	...	½
Homines	...	...	1,287	...	2⁄5

making a sum of 277,055, or some 98 % of the whole, the most prominent of the remainder being 995 presbyters, 920 coliberti, 749 *bovarii*, 565 radknights, 467 female servants, 427 *porcarii*, 354 Frenchmen, 207 of the establishment of Bury St. Edmund's Monastery, 178 paupers, 159 censarii, 137 milites, 111 Welshmen, 111 fishermen, and 108 salt-workers. It should be noticed that almost four-fifths of the population are comprised under villans, bordars, cottars, and servi, and in the following table (p. 3) it will be seen that in more than three-fourths of the thirty-four counties, nine-tenths of the population are composed of villans, bordars, cottars, servi, sokemen, and liberi homines.

The county constitution table is intended to show features peculiar to districts : in each shire the whole of the recorded population is accounted for, save from 5 % to 0 %, and all classes are noted which amount to or exceed 1 % in all of the thirty-four counties.

COUNTY CONSTITUTION TABLE.

	Villans.	Bordars and Cottars.	Servi.	Sokemen and Lib. Hom.	Total.	Tenants-in-Chief and Mesne Lords.	Oxherds.	Burgesses.	Homines.	Presbyters.	Radknights.	Censarii.	Porcarii.	Female Servants.	Coliberti.	Frenchmen.	Welsh.	Mon. St. Edmund's.	At Tutbury Market.	Total.
England ...	38	$31\frac{1}{2}$	9	12	91															
Beds ...	47	30	12	$2\frac{1}{2}$	$91\frac{1}{2}$	$8\frac{1}{2}$	..	..	..	..	..	..	..	..	..	..	..	..	..	100
Berks ...	$41\frac{1}{2}$	$40\frac{3}{4}$	$12\frac{1}{2}$	..	$94\frac{3}{4}$	$4\frac{1}{5}$	..	..	..	..	..	..	..	..	..	..	..	..	..	$98\frac{19}{20}$
Bucks ...	$53\frac{1}{2}$	$24\frac{1}{2}$	$15\frac{1}{2}$	$\frac{1}{3}$	$93\frac{4}{5}$	$5\frac{2}{5}$	..	..	..	..	..	..	..	..	..	..	..	..	..	$99\frac{1}{5}$
Cambs ...	$36\frac{1}{2}$	$41\frac{1}{2}$	$10\frac{1}{2}$	4	$92\frac{4}{5}$	$5\frac{3}{4}$	..	..	..	..	..	..	..	..	..	..	..	..	..	$98\frac{11}{20}$
Cheshire ...	34	27	8	2	71	7	$7\frac{1}{3}$	$2\frac{1}{2}$	1	$1\frac{1}{5}$	6	..	..	..	..	$1\frac{3}{4}$	..	..	..	$96\frac{31}{40}$
Cornwall ...	32	$43\frac{1}{3}$	$21\frac{1}{3}$	..	$96\frac{1}{2}$	2	..	..	..	..	..	..	..	..	..	..	..	..	..	$98\frac{1}{2}$
Derby ...	$60\frac{1}{2}$	$23\frac{2}{3}$	$\frac{2}{3}$	$4\frac{1}{4}$	89	$3\frac{1}{3}$	..	$4\frac{2}{3}$	..	$1\frac{2}{3}$	..	$1\frac{1}{3}$	..	..	..	..	..	..	..	100
Devon ...	$46\frac{1}{3}$	$28\frac{1}{3}$	19	..	$93\frac{1}{2}$	$2\frac{4}{5}$	..	$1\frac{1}{2}$	..	..	..	..	$1\frac{3}{4}$	..	..	..	..	..	..	$99\frac{1}{2}$
Dorset ...	$33\frac{1}{3}$	$42\frac{3}{4}$	16	..	92	$4\frac{1}{3}$	..	2	..	..	..	..	..	..	..	..	..	..	..	$98\frac{1}{3}$
Essex ...	$25\frac{1}{2}$	50	11	$5\frac{1}{4}$	$91\frac{1}{2}$	$3\frac{5}{6}$	..	$3\frac{3}{4}$	..	..	..	..	..	..	..	..	..	..	..	$99\frac{1}{12}$
Gloucester	$43\frac{1}{2}$	$21\frac{1}{2}$	$24\frac{1}{2}$	$\frac{1}{4}$	90	$3\frac{1}{5}$	..	$1\frac{1}{5}$	..	..	$1\frac{2}{3}$	..	..	1	$1\frac{1}{5}$	..	..	..	..	$98\frac{4}{15}$
Hants ...	37	38	$16\frac{1}{2}$	..	$91\frac{1}{2}$	4	..	$2\frac{3}{4}$	..	..	..	..	..	..	1	..	..	..	..	$99\frac{1}{4}$
Hereford ...	$39\frac{3}{5}$	$26\frac{4}{5}$	13	$\frac{1}{4}$	$79\frac{4}{5}$	6	2	..	4	..	$1\frac{1}{3}$	..	..	$1\frac{4}{5}$	..	..	..	..	..	95
Herts ...	37	$39\frac{1}{2}$	$11\frac{1}{3}$	1	$88\frac{3}{4}$	5	..	$2\frac{3}{4}$	..	1	..	..	..	..	..	1	..	..	..	$98\frac{1}{2}$
Hunts ...	$66\frac{1}{3}$	$16\frac{3}{4}$	..	$\frac{3}{4}$	84	4	..	10	..	$1\frac{1}{2}$	..	..	..	..	..	..	..	..	..	$99\frac{1}{2}$
Kent ...	54	$28\frac{1}{2}$	$9\frac{1}{3}$	$\frac{1}{3}$	$92\frac{1}{3}$	$1\frac{5}{6}$	..	$5\frac{1}{2}$	..	..	..	..	..	..	..	..	..	..	..	$99\frac{1}{2}$
Leicester ...	$39\frac{1}{3}$	20	6	$28\frac{1}{4}$	$93\frac{3}{8}$	$3\frac{5}{6}$	..	1	..	..	..	..	..	..	..	..	..	..	..	$98\frac{1}{5}$
Lincs ...	$30\frac{1}{2}$	16	..	$45\frac{1}{2}$	92	2	..	$5\frac{1}{4}$	..	..	..	..	..	..	..	..	..	..	..	$99\frac{1}{4}$
Middlesex	$50\frac{3}{4}$	$35\frac{3}{4}$	5	..	$91\frac{1}{3}$	4	..	2	$1\frac{1}{2}$	..	..	..	..	..	..	..	..	..	..	$98\frac{5}{6}$
Norfolk ...	$17\frac{1}{2}$	37	$3\frac{2}{3}$	$33\frac{1}{2}$	$91\frac{2}{3}$	$1\frac{4}{5}$	..	$5\frac{4}{5}$	..	..	..	..	..	..	..	..	..	..	..	$99\frac{1}{3}$
Northants	$46\frac{4}{5}$	$24\frac{2}{5}$	$9\frac{3}{5}$	$12\frac{3}{5}$	$93\frac{1}{4}$	4	..	1	..	..	..	..	..	..	..	..	..	..	..	$98\frac{1}{4}$
Notts ...	$45\frac{4}{5}$	$19\frac{1}{3}$	$\frac{1}{2}$	$26\frac{2}{3}$	$92\frac{1}{4}$	$3\frac{1}{3}$	..	3	..	1	..	..	..	..	..	..	..	..	..	$99\frac{7}{12}$
Oxon ...	$52\frac{1}{3}$	28	$14\frac{1}{5}$	$\frac{2}{5}$	$94\frac{5}{6}$	$4\frac{2}{5}$	..	..	..	..	..	..	..	..	..	..	..	..	..	$99\frac{1}{4}$
Rutland ...	$84\frac{3}{4}$	$12\frac{2}{5}$	..	$\frac{3}{5}$	98	$1\frac{1}{4}$	..	..	..	1	..	..	..	..	..	..	..	..	..	100
Salop ...	$35\frac{1}{3}$	$23\frac{1}{4}$	17	$\frac{1}{4}$	76	4	$7\frac{1}{2}$	$7\frac{2}{5}$	..	1	$3\frac{1}{3}$	..	..	1	..	..	$1\frac{1}{3}$	..	..	$96\frac{1}{2}$
Somerset	$38\frac{1}{2}$	$37\frac{1}{3}$	$15\frac{1}{3}$	..	91	$3\frac{1}{4}$	..	$3\frac{1}{2}$	..	..	..	..	..	..	$1\frac{1}{2}$	..	..	..	..	$99\frac{1}{4}$
Staffs ...	$54\frac{1}{3}$	$28\frac{2}{3}$	$6\frac{2}{3}$	$\frac{2}{5}$	90	$5\frac{1}{3}$	..	$1\frac{1}{2}$	..	..	..	..	..	..	..	..	..	..	$1\frac{1}{3}$	$98\frac{1}{6}$
Suffolk ...	$13\frac{2}{3}$	$30\frac{1}{3}$	$4\frac{1}{2}$	$41\frac{1}{4}$	90	$3\frac{1}{4}$	..	$3\frac{3}{5}$	..	..	..	..	..	..	..	..	..	1	..	98
Surrey ...	54	$27\frac{3}{5}$	11	..	$92\frac{2}{5}$	$3\frac{2}{5}$	..	4	..	..	..	..	..	..	..	..	..	..	..	$99\frac{4}{5}$
Sussex ...	$56\frac{2}{3}$	$31\frac{1}{3}$	4	..	92	$5\frac{1}{4}$	..	$2\frac{1}{2}$	..	..	..	..	..	..	..	..	..	..	..	$99\frac{3}{4}$
Warwick ..	$53\frac{1}{4}$	27	13	$\frac{1}{3}$	$93\frac{2}{5}$	$3\frac{1}{2}$	..	..	..	1	..	..	..	..	..	..	..	..	..	$97\frac{9}{10}$
Wilts ...	$30\frac{2}{5}$	44	15	..	89	$4\frac{1}{3}$	..	3	..	..	..	..	..	..	$2\frac{1}{2}$	..	..	..	..	$98\frac{5}{6}$
Worcester	$32\frac{4}{5}$	$38\frac{2}{3}$	$14\frac{1}{3}$	$\frac{1}{13}$	$86\frac{1}{4}$	$3\frac{3}{8}$	$1\frac{1}{2}$	$3\frac{1}{4}$	..	$1\frac{1}{4}$	..	..	..	$2\frac{1}{5}$	..	..	..	..	..	$97\frac{3}{4}$
Yorks ..	63	$22\frac{3}{4}$	..	$5\frac{1}{2}$	$91\frac{1}{4}$	4	..	$1\frac{3}{8}$	..	$1\frac{3}{4}$	..	..	..	..	..	..	..	..	..	$98\frac{3}{8}$

MAIN STATISTICAL TABLE.

	(Census Ancient Counties.) Area, 1891.	ELLIS. Recorded Population, 1086.	MAITLAND.				PEARSON.	
			Hidage,* 1065-86.	Danegeld, *circa* 1150.	Ploughteams, 1086.	Potential Ploughlands, 1086.	Valets in Pounds, 1086.	Valuits in Pounds, 1065.
Beds ..	298,494	3,875	1,193	1,106	1,367	1,557	1,096½	1,474½
Berks ..	462,224	6,324	2,473	2,056	1,796	2,087	2,383¾	2,378½
Bucks ..	475,694	5,420	2,074	2,047	1,952	2,244	1,813½	1,785¼
Cambs ..	549,749	5.204	1,233	1,148	1,443	1,676		
Cheshire ..	657,068	2,349	512					
Cornwall ..	868,208	5,438	155	227	1,187	2,377	662	729½
Derby* ..	658,876	3,041	679	*1121	862	762	461¼	631¼
Devon ..	1,667,097	17 434	1,119	1,040	5,542	7,972	3,220¾	2,912
Dorset ..	632,272	7,807	2,321	2,482	1,762	2.332	2,656½	2,564½
Essex ..	987,028	16,060	2,650	2,364	3,920	..	4,784½	4,098
Gloucester	795,734	8,366	2,388	1,941	3,768	..	2,827¼	2,855½
Hants ..	1,037,764	10,373	2,588	1,848	2,614	2,847		
Hereford ..	537,363	5,368	1,324	938	2,479			
Herts ..	406,161	4.927	1,050	1,101	1,406	1,716	1,541¾	1,894¾
Hunts ..	234,218	2,914	747	713	967	1,120	864¾	890¾
Kent ..	995,344	12,205	1,224	1,058	3,102	..	5,140½	3,953½
Leicester ..	527,124	6,772	[? 2,500]	1,000	1,817	..	736¼	491¼
Lincs ..	1,693,547	25,305	4,188	2,660	4,712	5,043		
Middlesex	181,301	2,302	868	856	545	664	754¼	910¾
Norfolk ..	1,308,440	27,087	[? 2,422]*	3,301	4,853	..	4,154½	2,219¼
Northants	641,992	8,441	1,356	1,195	2,422	2,931	1,843	1,407¼
Notts* ..	539,752	5,686	567	*1121	1,991	1,255		
Oxon ..	483,614	6,775	2,412	2,498	2,467	2,639	3,242¼	2,789¾
Rutland ..	97,273	862	37	116	[239]			
Salop ..	859.516	5,080	1,245	1,179	1,755			
Somerset ..	1,043,485	13,764	2,951	2,775	3,804	4,812	[4,161¼]	
Staffs ..	749,601	3,178	499	451	951	1,398	[516¾]	
Suffolk ..	952,709	20,491	[ ]	2,350				
Surrey ..	485,128	4,383	1,830	1,798	1,142	1,172	1,524¼	1,417¼
Sussex ..	933,269	10,410	3,474	2,170	3,091	..	3,255¼	3,467
Warwick ..	577,462	6,574	1,338	1,280	2,003	2,276	1,359	953¾
Wilts ..	880,248	10,150	4,050	3,896	2,997	3,457		
Worcester	480,560	4,625	1,189	1,013	1,889	..	991	1,060¼
Yorks ..	3,882,848	8,055	10,095	1,655	[2,959]			
	27,506,622 acres.	283,242	34 counties, *circa* *67,000	30* counties, 47,628	30 counties, 70,606	21 counties, 52,354	23 counties, 49,658 li	21 counties, 45,744 li

* The Hides are avowedly overestimated (*D. B. and Beyond*, p. 409), including dormant ones and duplicates (D. B. sometimes states a total, and then repeats same Hides in particulars), to distinguish which *both* reading and counting are often necessary: the writer holds that the Norfolk carucates have no reference to Hidage (see note, p. 12); Yorks, Suffolk, and Rutland are omitted in the Danegeld total, but Derby and Notts together equate 1,121 *Hides* (here *carucates*).

The main statistical table is a compilation, the acreage being from the census of 1891 (ancient counties), the population from Ellis, the valets and valuits from pp. 665-669 of Pearson's "English History," and the rest from Professor Maitland's "Domesday Book and Beyond," with small additions.

As to population, some of the boroughs of 1086 (notably London and Winchester) are omitted in D. B. (Domesday Book), and presumably a considerable proportion of the inhabitants of West Yorkshire, and all in North Lancashire : however, the same persons are sometimes mentioned more than once, and females occur notably as ancillæ. In the present state of our knowledge, 2,000,000 total population would be an extreme figure for the forty counties of modern England for 1086 : it is probable, from the poll-tax returns of 1377, that at that date the population might well lie between $2\frac{1}{2}$ and 3 millions, and prior to the Black Death (1348-49) 4,000,000 and upwards, whereas 1,800,000 might be a reasonable postulate from D. B. for 1086.

The hides in the table include the carucates of the Danish districts and the sulungs of Kent, and are estimated for the thirty-four recorded counties ; for 1065-1086 they must be regarded as units of assessment, not in any obvious connection with area or value, and the underwritten equations seem to prevail in D. B. :

```
1 hide     = 4 virgates = 120 fiscal acres.
1 carucate = 8 bovates  = 120    ,,
1 sulung   = 4 juga*    = 120    ,,
```

* See, note p. 39.

The above terms were also used as mediæval areal measures, and when normal the same equations held ; the variations are well known, *e.g.*, 1 carucate might contain 64 acres (8 per bovate), or 1 hide, 5 virgates of 28 acres each, and so forth, so that it is necessary to know the mensuration in use at a given date in any particular manor when dealing with actual quantities (and yet at the same date in the same manor one equation might not be sufficient for all the lands in it—*e.g.*, Ramsey Chartulary).

Plough-team.

The plough-team is often (if not always) in D. B. at the rate of eight oxen per plough, but there seem to have been actual ploughs of one, two, and four oxen, etc. : the enumeration of ploughs by the rate of eight oxen, of course, predicates no similar uniformity in practice. To record actual husbandry would have been difficult, but to assume a like number of oxen per plough a proceeding eminently rational for statistical purposes : it has been argued that the ploughs (as recorded) varied, which does not greatly flatter the wisdom of the compilers of our national record, and seems to be inconsistent with evidence like the following :

Fo. 304*a*.—Bilton : 13 villans with 2 ploughs, and 5 oxen.
Fo. 312*a*.—Borell : 2 villans with 6 oxen.
Fo. 314*a*.—Naburn : 3 oxen ploughing there.
Fo. 319*a*.—Stainton : 2 villans and 3 bordars ploughing with 2 oxen.
Fo. 323*b*.—Dringoe : 1 villan with 2 oxen.
Fo. 325*a*.—Newsholme : Ralph has now $\frac{1}{2}$ plough and 1 villan with 2 oxen.

Comparative values of implements and oxen.

Fo. 328*a*.—Aluengi : 1 villan and 2 oxen.*

* In the fourteenth century a plough might be valued at 1s., and a single ox at about 15s. ; if this comparison even

that is to say, if D. B. counts a plough of two or four oxen as one whole plough on its system of record, the authors of this theory are burdened with the explanation of expressions as above.

The ploughland leaves some room for estima- Plough-land. tion, but Professor Maitland's figures show that it usually varies not widely from the teams ; in some cases, as in the wasted Yorkshire manors, his surmise that the potential were the actual ploughlands of King Edward's day seems natural, but it does not meet an entry like the following from that county (fo. 299a) : " land to 42 ploughs, $7\frac{1}{2}$ there now, and formerly 46 teams." Again, he quotes as an instance of inexplicable divergence the Rutlandshire entries (fo. 293b and 294a, and " Domesday Book and Beyond," p. 471) of 48 ploughlands and 127 teams ; but in the first place he seems to have omitted to note the teamlands were 14 plus 48, and in the second that the villen- age teams were probably those of small burgesses wealthy enough to have oxen in excess of the re- quirements of co-operative agriculture (a similar entry occurs on fo. 316b, Tateshalle), and rather comparable to farmers of the present day with arable from 1 to 30 acres and a pair of horses.

Having just noted the fact of actual normal Area *not* tilled by hides of 120 acres, and roughly allowed a plough- one team to a ploughland, the inference may seem to plough. follow that a plough tilled 120 acres arable ; but

approximately holds for the eleventh century, when the ox is taken at 2s. 6d., it seems inconceivable that the return of teams should be made from the actual implements in use rather than from the oxen.

that is exactly what is not suggested, and which, I believe, can be demonstrated did not occur. Should any practical agriculturist honour my pages by his perusal, he must bear in mind there are who believe that not 120 acres, but even 180, of arable were tilled in one year by one plough ; certain it is he will be as little able to credit such unheard of practices in his art as the real existence of the dragons etc., of our monastic chroniclers. Whilst those abstracted from terrestrial affairs may conceive such astounding husbandry, he can never have been so fortunate as to have seen or heard of it (saving steam-ploughing) in any ordinary tillage routine of this country, nor will he allow the speculations of scholars the colour of superior knowledge. For what of credence would be given to the mathematician who persistently found a product of five from the addition of two and two, or to the classical instructor who rendered *tenet* and *valet* as *tenuit* and *valuit;* just so when writers on matters rural inform their readers of the non-existence of the mediæval harrow, or gravely repeat that in ploughing an acre three miles (two leucæ) are traversed, or that from $\frac{7}{8}$ to all 1 acre could be ploughed before mid-day.*

Oxford arithmetic.

* But the profundity of the erudite mind is best discovered in a statement of the Regius Professor of Modern History at Oxford (p. 123, "Social England," vol. i.), where for every perch of " 16½ feet," for a furrow of " eleven inches broad," the "plow" is made to traverse the distance in " 4 or 4½ " rounds : with such a furrow of course 22 inches would be done per round, making just 9 journeys to and fro. It is to be hoped that the promoters of the Agricultural Education

The first may possibly be an instance of *college* College
farming, as it occurs in Professor Rogers' "History farming.
of Agriculture," and is repeated in that singular
unbending of University erudition to popular
requirements ("Social England") by the writer
on "Agriculture": though no one should be so
exacting as to seek particular knowledge of so
base an art from scribes of scholarly attainments,
it may be pointed out that the Bayeux Tapestry
and Loutrell Psalter (*c. 1340*) give undeniable
pictorial representations of harrowing; again, D. B.
(fo. 163 and 166) notes the practice—also the
Burton Chartulary (*1114*), and, indeed, almost
every custumal of any length, works which historical writers might well condescend to.

The second is quoted on p. 58 (Taylor's
"Analysis of Glos'ter Domesday Book," 1889)—
now, if the ploughing of an acre is too hard
a problem in arithmetic to design on paper, any
ploughman could testify he goes about 10 miles
per acre—*i.e.*, with a furrow of 8 inches 12 miles,
with a 12-inch one 8 miles, or 8 to $5\frac{1}{3}$ leucæ.

The last occurs on p. 377, note 4 ("Domesday
Book and Beyond"), where the author corrects
Miss Lamond's rendering of *a noune*, from 3 p.m.
to 12 mid-day — the technical point I cannot
pretend to discuss, but on p. 415 (vol. i., Ramsey

Extension System from our fountains of learning may com-
mence at home, by giving those pioneers who are to enlighten
the supposed darkness of the rural mind, such an elementary
knowledge of arithmetic, as to place them on somewhat more
even terms with the average *carucarius* in matters of simple
addition, division, etc.

Cart.), it may be observed, "apud dinariam" occurs in point of time before " ad nonam."

Reserving the discussion of how much land may or may not be assigned to a plough for the sequel, let it be noted that the *valets* and *valuits* of 1086 and 1065 seem to represent the yearly profits of manors from whatever cause arising, and that the term *villani* is used to distinguish the whole class of villans, bordars, etc., holding by base tenure from the *liberi homines*, and that tenants in villenage were free, except as against their lord. The Villan* proper would seem to have held from 7 acres (Wiceford, fo. 192*a*, D. B., 17 villans each of 7 acres) to 2 hides (Hanwell and West Bedfont D. B., co. Middlesex), with rights of pasturage ; let it be observed that these may be assessed rather than areal quantities, and that, in the case of villans of 1 and 2 hides (if areal), these were not all arable land, and may have been partly held at a rent. Seebohm (p. 102, " English Village Community ") allows the average villan 20 to 21 acres in 1086, but considers the A.S. gebur of 30 acres and 2 oxen, to answer to the normal villan of the same amount : according to the Middlesex Domesday an average villan is rated at 1 virgate ; in the I. E. (Cantab.) at $10\frac{1}{2}$ acres ; the later custumals give examples of holdings of 3, 5, $7\frac{1}{2}$, 10, 15, 20 acres, and virgates for the classes embraced by the D. B. villans, bordars and cottars, and precise definition of each

Valets and *Valuits.*

Villani.

Opera.

---

* Villans usually owe week work and precations, sokemen the latter ; in 1321 (*Hist. Pet.*) free tenants as opposed to socagers appear to owe no *works* of any kind ; see note, pp. 147-9.

grade is difficult. The estimate of 20-1 acres of workland for an average villan seems at any rate ample ; possibly the Middlesex villans assessed in quantities exceeding ½ hide may answer to the thirteenth-century class who held both at work and at rent, bearing in mind that Yorkshire, Middlesex, and Surrey were, in proportion to their teams, the counties most highly rated to *gheld*.

The bordar* occurs in each county, the cottar*
in but 18, nevertheless these terms are sometimes interchangeable ; the whole class may be broadly assessed up to 10 acres, and where both occur together, the former considered the larger tenant. The bordar frequently had an ox or oxen, (some-times also the cottar as distinct from the bordar); and custumals demonstrate that owners of 3 to 5 acres might have an ox or more, and subsequently I shall show that the holder of a virgate in the thirteenth century may often be rated at 4 oxen. The disappearance of the name (as a name) bordar is to be noted ; also the presence of the class in towns, and the use of the terms ½ villans and

Bordars and Cottars.

---

* Bordars occur as *paying rent*, D. B. 52*a*, from 20 masuræ, 14s. ; 167*b*, 38 with 7½ pls., pay 8s. ; 264*b*, 1 renders 2s. ; as to *amount of land* from nothing up to 2 bovates (by 1 man), see 353*b* ; and 84*b*, 2 held $\frac{v}{4}$ freely, and now hold ; 139*b*, 46 hold 8 ac. each ; 190*a*, nine each 5 ac.—together 2 pls. ; and the following 20 references (a selection only) from as many counties demonstrate they often *had separate plough oxen*, 14*a*, 17*b*, 52*b*, 70*b*, 82*b*, 94*a*, 117*a*, 120*a* (13 to 1 pl., lowest in list), 160*b*, 177*b*, 180*a* (1 bordar 1 pl., highest found), 205*b*, 215*b*, 222*a*, 241*b*, 250*b*, 259*b*, 274*b*, 285*b*, 331*b* ; on 186*a*, 12 *work* one day per week : Coscez and Cottars some-times also had pls., thus Coscez 71*b*, two, 1 pl. ; 72*a*, four, ½ pl. ; 72*b*, 6 and 1 cottar, ½ pl. ; 74*b*, four, 1½ pls. ; 74*b*, eight, 1 pl. ; Cottars, 97*b*, six, 1 pl.

Illustra-tions of same from Domesday.

$\frac{1}{2}$ bordars, giving ground to suppose that occasionally full villans and bordars may be fractionally composed: in such a case (fo. 324*a*, D. B.) as 30 villans and 3 ploughs it is equally hard to imagine more than 30 men, less than 24 oxen, or as much as 900 acres of land (*i.e.*, the " so-called " normal villan of 30 acres × 30).

Servi.

The servi were a class personally unfree, notable in S.W. England : in that name they soon disappeared, becoming presumably free labourers and cottars.

Sokemen.

The sokemen* make a particular figure in E. England, and were under a lord with varying liberties as regarded their land—sometimes they had one lord for soke and another for commendation, and though not rarely performing base services may be referred to the class of liberi homines as opposed to tenants in villenage: at least on one occasion the I. C. Cant. enumerates as villans the sokemen* of D. B. (Wilberton, co. Cambs). In the absence of precise figures Seebohm's estimate of 22-3 acres as an average holding is noted ; in the custumals the smaller freemen seem often of less importance than holders of virgates in villenage.

The liberi homines* as a sub-class are inconsider-

Popular estimate of *liberi homines,* and sokemen, discordant with Domesday.

* The population assigned to these classes is probably quite unreliable, and members thereof must appear more than once in the record ; the *villani* may be roughly rated at 3 per team (8 oxen) : taking the **9067** freemen and sokemen (Ellis) of *Norfolk* they can only be assessed at a like no. of teams as the **4731** villans, on the supposition that neither the lords nor other of the community had plough oxen. If the **7723** villans of Lincs. are taken at above rate, there will be but 1½ oxen each left for **11,504** sokemen (4712 teams in the

able out of Norfolk and Suffolk; Seebohm assesses *Liberi homines.* their holdings at 42 acres; sokemen and liberi homines may occasionally have been interchangeable terms, at the same time noting that the latter is used also for the whole class of superior tenantry, viz., tenants in chief, mesne lords, liberi homines, and presumably radknights and drenghs as distinguishing them from tenants in villenage.

The radknights, comprising the radchenistri and *Radknights.* radmanni, were as peculiar to the W. Midlands as the sokemen and liberi homines to the E. shires; they amount to 2 % of the recorded population, and may possibly be regarded as the antecessors of tenants by serjeantry.

The tenants in chief (about $\frac{1}{2}$ % of the popula- *Tenants in chief.* tion) held their lands directly of the King (*sine medio*) and the mesne lords (some $2\frac{4}{5}$ % of population) held of the former, or of other vassals holding of the King's tenants.

For the rest, it must suffice that the coliberti* *Coliberti and Buri.* seem to have equated the buri,* and to have ranked

---

co.) on the same theory; as the lords and others could scarcely have owned less than $\frac{1}{3}$ of the teams in either county it seems clear that freemen and sokemen are indeterminable both as to numbers and extent of holding. The application of the 4 ox per plough theory as in D. B. (Seebohm) is strikingly refuted here : the evidence for the rest of England (excepting Lincs., Norf., and Suff.) demonstrates the average villan could not have had less than 2 oxen.

* Prof. Maitland (p. 37, "D. B. and Beyond") endeavours *These do* to equate this class with the A.S. *geburi,* in order to appreciate *not corre-* the *villani;* whilst admiring his sympathetic leanings to the *spond with* latter, such are scarcely the results of studies in Domesday *Geburi.* Book. The geburs occur in the Laws of Ine ; as servile tenants of Tiddenham (10th cent.), and in a like condition

COMPARATIVE TABLE

Population by Teams (30 Counties).			Population by Teams (21 Counties.)			Hides by Gheld (30 Counties).		
		255			230			180
Norfolk	... 5·5		Lincs ... 5·370			Cornwall	... ·7	
Lincs ...	... 5·3				130	Norfolk	... ·73	
		{ 200	Cornwall	4·58				100
		{ 150	Dorset...	4·4		Dorset ...	... ·93	
Cornwall	... 4·5				100	Herts ...	... ·95	
Dorset ...	... 4·4		Middlesex	4·2				50
		100	Hants ...	3·968		Bucks ...	... 1·01	
Middlesex	... 4·2				50	Middlesex	... 1·01	
E-sex ..	... 4·0		Surrey ...	3·8		Surrey ...	... 1·02	
Kent ...	... 3·9				25	Oxon ...	... 1·03	
			Somerset	3·6		Warwick	... 1·04	
Hants ...	... 3·9		Cambs...	3·6		Wilts ...	... 1·04	
Surrey ...	... 3·8		Derby ...	3·5		Hunts ...	... 1·05	
		50	Berks ...	3·5		Salop ...	... 1·05	
Leicester	... 3·7		Herts ...	3·5		Somerset	... 1·06	
Somerset	... 3·6		Northants	3·4				25
Cambs	... 3·6				25	Beds ...	... 1·08	
Derby ...	... 3·5		Wilts ..	3·38		Cambs ...	... 1·08	
Berks ...	... 3·5		Staffs ...	3·342		Devon ...	... 1·08	
Herts ...	... 3·5		Warwick	3·2		Derby ...	... 1·13	
Northants	... 3·4		Devon ...	3·145		Northants	... 1·13	
Staffs ...	... 3·3				50	Notts ...	... 1·13	
Sussex ...	... 3·3		Hunts ...	3·0		Staffs ...	... 1·15	
		25	Notts ...	2·8		Essex ...	... 1·12	
Wilts ...	... 3·3		Beds ...	2·8		Kent ...	... 1·16	
Warwick	... 3·2		Bucks ...	2·78		Worcester	... 1 17	
		50	Oxon ...	2·746				25
Devon ...	... 3·145				100	Gloucester	... 1·22	
Hunts ...	... 3·0					Berks ...	... 1·23	
Notts ...	... 2·8							{ 50
Beds ...	... 2·8							{ 100
Salop ...	... 2·8					Hereford	... 1·41	
Bucks ...	... 2·78					Hants ...	... 1·43	
		100				Lincs ...	... 1·6	
Oxon ...	... 2·74		Population=155,512			Sussex ...	... 1 6	
Worcester	... 2·4		Teams=43,932					200
		150	Mean=3·54			Leicester	... [2·5]	
Gloucester	... 2·2		New mean=442½					550
Hereford	... 2·1		(Mean×125)					
		180						

Population=251,485	Entries.		Population=155,512 (dup)	Entries.		Hides, 54,000	Entries.	
	% line			% line		Gheld, 47,628 florins	% line	
Teams=70,606	100 in 255		Teams=43,932	100 in 230		Mean=1·134	100 in 550	
Mean=3·56	93¼ ,, 180		Mean=3·54	95 ,, 130		Comparative or new	96¾ ,, 200	
New mean=445	86⅔ ,, 150		New mean=442½	85¾ ,, 100		mean=453½	76⅔ ,, 100	
(Mean×125)	73¾ ,, 100		(Mean×125)	54¼ ,, 50		(obtained by	70 ,, 50	
	43¾ ,, 50			28½ ,, 25		400×1·134)	33⅓ ,, 25	
	30 ,, 25							

NO. I.

Valets by Valuits (20 Counties).			Teamlands by Teams (21 Counties.)			Population by Teamlands (21 Counties).		
		200			205			300
Leicester ...	1·50		Notts ...	·63		Lincs ...	5·0	
Warwick ...	1·425		Derby ...	·88				230
		150			100	Notts ...	4·4	
Northants ...	1·31		Surrey ...	1·02				150
		100			50	Derby ...	3·96	
Kent ...	1·30		Oxon ...	1·069		Surrey ...	3·7	
		50	Lincs ...	1·07		Hants ...	3·643	
Essex ...	1·17		Hants ...	1·08				{ 100
Oxon ...	1·16				25			{ 75
		25	Beds ...	1·13		Middlesex ...	3·46	
Devon ...	1·106		Warwick ...	1·13		Dorset ...	3·39	
Surrey ...	1·07		Bucks ...	1·14				{ 50
Dorset ...	1·04		Wilts ...	1·15				{ 25
Bucks ...	1·02		Hunts ...	1·15		Cambs ...	3·10	
		25	Berks ...	1·16		Berks ...	3·0	
Berks ...	1·002		Cambs ...	1·16		Wilts ...	2·9	
Gloucester ...	·99		Middlesex ...	1·21		Northants ...	2·88	
Hunts ...	·96		Northants ...	1·21		Herts ...	2·87	
		50	Herts ...	1·22		Warwick ...	2·84	
Sussex ...	·94				25			{ 25
Worcester ...	·935		Somerset ...	1·27				{ 50
Cornwall ...	·908		Dorset ...	1·30		Somerset ...	2·83	
		100			50	Hunts ...	2·602	
Herts ...	·81		Devon ...	1·43		Oxon ...	2·5	
Beds ...	·74				100	Beds ...	2·48	
Derby ...	·73		Staffs ...	1·47				75
		150			205	Bucks ...	2·41	
Middlesex ...	·628		Cornwall ...	2·0				100
		200			300	Staffs ...	2·2	
						Cornwall ...	2·2	
						Devon ...	2·1	
								130

Valets = 41,159 li.
Valuits = 38,652 li.
Mean = 1·0647
New mean = 447
(*i.e.*, mean × 420)

Teamlands = 52,354
Teams = 43,932
Mean = 1·192
New mean = 441
(Mean × 370)

Teamlands = 52,354
Population = 155,512
Mean = 2·97
New mean = 445½
(Mean × 150)

Entries.
%	line
100	in 200
85	,, 150
65	,, 100
45	,, 50
20	,, 25

Entries.
%	line
100	in 300
95	,, 205
81	,, 100
71½	,, 50
47½	,, 25

Entries.
%	line
100	in 300
95	,, 230
90	,, 150
62	,, 100
33½	,, 50
33½	,, 25

between the villans and servi ; that the ancillæ
(most frequent in the W. Midlands) are regarded
as female slaves ; that the burgesses as a class are
incompletely returned, that the censarii were a
small class of free rent-paying tenants, and that the
porcarii* and bovarii* may be considered both as
servile herds, and free farmers of swine and oxen.

Other classes.

Turning to the relationship to one another of
the figures in the Main Statistical Table, it is

(pedigrees) in co. Herts (Earle's Land Charters), the *coliberti*
and *buri* being not (I believe) found in either place : Ellis
adds these 2 (latter) classes at **920**, and references to **891**
may be found in D. B. 38*a* and *b*, 39*a* and *b*, 41*a*, 44*a*, 57*b*,
58*a*, 64*b*, 65*a*, 66*a* and *b*, 67*a* and *b*, 68*a*, 71*a*, 75*a*, 77*b*, 86*a*
and *b*, 87*a* and *b*, 90*a*, 91*a*, 96*b*, 101*a*, 103*b*, 120*a*, 149*a*,
154*a*, 163*a* and *b*, 164*a* and *b*, 165*a*, 166*a*, 174*b*, 179*b*, 181*b*,
182*a* and *b*, 239*b*, 254*a*, 260*a*, in **86** entries only (and to **19**
coliberts of 1065 on 38*a* and 163*a*) ; of these **552** occur on
royal manors in **48** entries, **311** on church ones in **32**, and but
28 on **6** lay estates. The A.S. *Rectitudines* (10th or 11th
cent.) describe the gebur as on a thane's manor, and there
seems small room to doubt his correspondence with the villein
of D. B. (see note, pp. 147-9) ; the above shows that the *coliberti*
(tho' numerous) were not a widely spread class, and scarcely
to be found on lay estates.   They seem to have as many or
more oxen than the villans [38*a*, 163*a* (*bis*), 164*b*] ; on fo.
38*b* six hold 1 Hide ; they sometimes pay rent or produce
[38*a* and *b*, 39*a*, 165*a*, 174*b* (*bis*), 179*b* (*bis*)], and on the
Estates of Westminster Abbey (174*b*), 6 coliberti sow 12 ac.,
and render 11s. 2d., whereas 8 villans and 10 bordars sow
4 ac., and 10 vill., and 10 bord., 6 ac. ; altogether their
position as a class is of much uncertainty—they do not occur
where *Censarii* are found, save in Dorset (Ellis).

Geburi as *villani.*

* The *porcarii* seem to have been the higher class and
sometimes pay a rent in pigs ; the *bovarii* often appear to
replace the *servi* on the demesnes of Cheshire and Salop
Manors, where they were presumably unfree ploughmen ;
a *liber bovarius* occurs on 183*a*.

Porcarii and Bovarii.

obvious that 28 separate divisions might be con- Remarks on Comparative Table I.
structed ; of which 15 are set forth in the three
following comparative accounts ; no extreme mathe-
matical accuracy being postulated in a matter where
rough correctness is all that at present can be
looked for.   In the first table it will be noted that
the comparison of like items gives satisfactory
results ; thus the hides of 1065 seem distinctly
the antecessors of those which furnished the ghelds
of the middle of the twelfth century, and the
valuits of 1065 differ not widely from the valets
of 1086, bearing in mind the absence of Yorks in
the former class, and of most of the carucated
counties in the latter.   In these (Derby, Leicester,
Lincs, Norfolk, Notts, Rutland, Suffolk, Yorks,
and part of Cheshire) greater changes occurred
than in hidated England, which the tables do not
adequately set forth ; nor are the wasted Yorkshire
manors to be discovered in the comparison of
Teamlands with Teams, the incompleteness of
which table gives it a better appearance than it
otherwise would have.   In a country ploughed up
to the maximum an excess of teams over teamlands
would be expected, for the reason instanced above ;
according to the witness of D. B. the majority of
counties had surplus arable.*   It seems that no
definite amount of land was in view by the expres-
sion of land to one team, which would indicate Land to one team.
different quantities respectively on the demesne
and village ; the distinction is often made, and
the difference should not be overlooked, for on the
land of the lord the land of one plough would
include the assistance of the tenant, and on the

---

* That is more teams, could have been used with advantage.

2

land of the villein the assistance rendered by the plough there was land to, must be subtracted in an areal estimate. Putting aside the probability that the tenant in villeinage worked his own land usually with less than 8 oxen, and taking D. B.'s view of a full team, suppose the demesne plough could till x acres per ann., and that the team of the men (8 oxen) could work $a + b$ acres (where $x = a + b$); then $x + a$ would be the land of one plough on the demesne; and $(a + b) - a$ on the arable set to the villeins. This I believe was in the minds of the men of the hundreds when they state there could be so many more ploughs on the demesne and villeinage respectively; the matter would not stand exactly as above in actual practice where the occurrence of smaller ploughs of the men, would disturb the balance. Clearly a plough of 4 oxen* would do far more than half the tillage of one of 8, and one of 2 beasts more than a quarter of it (smaller and lighter implements are predicated); however, when in the returns, mention is made of land to 2, 3, 4 or more oxen, an artificial and roughly proportional comparison may be all that was in view, rather than details of practice, *e.g.*, land to 2 oxen may mean about half the amount of land to 4 oxen, though the varying quantities of demesne and villeinage would further complicate each case. No frequenter of the towing-path would ever be likely to suppose

Marginal note: Difference of teamland, of demesne, and *villeinage*.

Marginal note: Oxen per plough in Wales, *t.* Hen. II.

---

* Probably common enough on *villein* lands ; cf. *Gerald de Barri* (*t.* Hen. II.) who states that the Welsh yoke 4 oxen in a plough more often than two : *Wm. de Malmesbury* (*t.* Hen. I.), writing of Wm. II., and Anselm, states, *Vt aratrum sanctæ ecclesiæ, quod in Anglia duo boves validi & pari fortitudine ad bonum certantes, id est, rex et archiepiscopus Cantuariensis debeant trahere nunc ove vetula cum tauro indomito iugata.*

COMPARATIVE TABLE NO. II.

Acres by Population (30 Counties).			Acres by Teams (30 Counties).			Valuits by Hides (20 Counties).	
Norfolk	48	200	Oxon	196	{ 200 / 170	Kent ... 3·23	820
Essex	61		Gloucester	211			600
Lincs	66		Hereford	216		Devon ... 2·60	
		100	Beds	218			300
Oxon	71				100	Cornwall 1·826	
Berks	73		Hunts	241		Herts ... 1·80	
Northants	75		Bucks	243			200
Somerset	75		Essex	251		Essex ... 1·54	
		50	Worcester	254			{ 100 / 50
Beds	78		Berks	257		Beds ... 1·23	
Middlesex	78		Northants	264			25
Leicester	78		Norfolk	270		Hunts ... 1·20	
Kent	79		Notts	271		Gloucester 1·19	
Hunts	80		Somerset	274		Oxon ... 1·156	
Dorset	80				50	Dorset 1·12	
Herts	82		Warwick	288			250
		25	Herts	289		Middlesex 1·05	
Wilts	86		Leicester	291		Northants 1·04	
Bucks	87				25		50
Warwick	88		Wilts	293		Sussex ... 1·0	
Sussex	89		Devon	300		Berks ... ·96	
		25	Sussex	301		Derby ... ·93	
Notts	94		Kent	314			100
Gloucester	95				25	Worcester ·89	
Devon	95		Middlesex	331		Bucks ... ·86	
		50			50	Surrey ... ·77	
Hunts	100		Dorset	358		Warwick ·71	
Hereford	100		Lincs	359			200
		75	Cambs	380		Leicester ·196	
Worcester	103				100		400
Cambs	105		Hants	397			
Surrey	105		Surrey	403			
		{ 100 / 200	Salop	489			
Cornwall	159				200	Valuits=38,652 li.	
Salop	169		Cornwall	731		Hides=33,240	
		415			300	Mean=1·163	
Derby	216		Derby	762		New mean=453½	
		645			600	(Mean×390)	
Staffs	235		Staffs	788			
		740			655		
					670		

Entries.			Entries.			Entries.	
	% line			% line		% line	
Acres=21,918,531	100 in 740		Acres=21,918,531	100 in 670		100 in 820	
Population=251,485	96⅔ ,, 645		Teams=70,606	96⅔ ,, 655		95 ,, 600	
Mean=87·15 acres	93¼ ,, 415		Mean=310½	93⅓ ,, 600		90 ,, 400	
New mean=435¾	86⅔ ,, 200		New mean=434 7/10	90 ,, 300		85 ,, 300	
(Mean×5)	76¾ ,, 100		(Mean×¾)	86⅔ ,, 200		75 ,, 200	
	46⅔ ,, 50			66⅔ ,, 100		50 ,, 100	
	13⅓ ,, 25			26⅔ ,, 50		35 ,, 50	
				13⅓ ,, 25		20 ,, 25	

COMPARATIVE TABL[E]

Teams by Hides (30 Counties.)

County	Value	
		300
Surrey ...	·6	
Middlesex	·6	
		200
Berks ...	·73	
Leicester	·726	
Wilts ...	·74	
Dorset ...	·8	
Sussex ...	·9	
Bucks ...	·9	
Hants ...	1·010	
		100
Oxon ...	1·023	
Lincs ...	1·1	
Beds ...	1·1	
Derby ...	1·3	
Cambs ...	1·2	
Herts ...	1·3	
Hunts ...	1·3	
Somerset	1·3	
Salop ...	1·4	
Essex ...	1·5	
Warwick	1·5	
Gloucester	1·6	
Worcester	1·6	
		100
Northants	1·8	
Hereford	1·9	
		200
Staffs ...	1·9	
Norfolk	2·0	
		300
Kent ...	2·5	
		445½
Notts ...	3·7	
		820
Devon ...	5·0	
		1,250
Cornwall	7·7	
		2,200

Teams by Valets (23 Counties).

County	Value	
		200
Kent ...	·6	
Dorset ...	·66	
Middlesex	·72	
Berks ...	·75	
Surrey ...	·75	
Oxon ...	·76	
		100
Essex ...	·82	
Herts ...	·91	
Somerset	·91	
Sussex ...	1·07	
Bucks ...	1·10	
Hunts ...	1·10	
Norfolk	1·12	
Beds ...	1·3	
Gloucester	1·3	
Northants	1·3	
Devon ...	1·4	
Warwick	1·5	
Staffs ...	1·8	
Cornwall	1·8	
Worcester	1·9	
Derby ...	1·9	
		200
Leicester	2·5	
		300

Valets by Hides (22 Counties).

	County	Value
965		
	Cornwall	4·27
950		
	Kent ...	4·208
510		
	Devon ...	2·87
{ 200 / 300		
	Essex ...	1·80
	Norfolk	1·71
100		
	Herts ...	1·47
	Somerset	1·41
	Northants	1·358
	Oxon ...	1·34
100	Gloucester	1·18
	Hunts ...	1·15
	Dorset ...	1·14
100		
	Staffs ...	1·03
	Warwick	1·01
{ 200 / 300	Berks ...	·96
	Sussex ...	·93
	Beds ...	·91
	Bucks ...	·87
	Middlesex	·86
	Surrey ...	·83
400	Worcester	·82
610	Derby ...	·67
227		

Teamlands by Hides (21 Counties).

County	Value	
		4,20[0]
Cornwall	15·3	
		1,80[0]
Devon ...	7·1	
		40[0]
Staffs ...	2·8	
		30[0]
Notts ...	2·21	
Northants	2·16	
		{ 20[0] / 10[0]
Warwick	1·70	
Somerset	1·63	
Herts ...	1·63	
		5[0]
Hunts ...	1·5	
Cambs ...	1·36	
Beds ...	1·30	
		5[0]
Lincs ...	1·20	
		10[0]
Derby ...	1·12	
Hants ...	1·10	
Oxon ...	1·09	
Bucks ...	1·08	
Dorset ...	1·0	
Wilts ...	·85	
Berks ...	·84	
		20[0]
Middlesex	·76	
Surrey ...	·64	
		30[0]

Teams = 52,615
Valets = 49,991¾
Mean = 1·05
New mean = 441
(Mean × 420)

Hides = 36,412
Valets = 49,255½
Mean = 1·352
New mean = 446
(Mean × 330)

Teamlands = 52,354
Hides = 35,691
Mean = 1·467
New mean = 440
(Mean × 300)

Teams: 70,606
Hides: c. 54,000
Mean: 1·31
New mean: 445½
(Mean × 340)

Entries.	
%	line
100	in 2,200
96⅔	,, 1,250
93½	,, 820
90	,, 445½
75½	,, 200
43½	,, 100

Entries.	
%	line
100	in 610
95⅔	,, 400
78½	,, 200
30⅔	,, 100

Entries.	
%	line
100	in 965
95½	,, 950
91	,, 510
86½	,, 227
81¼	,, 200
31¼	,, 100

Entries.	
%	line
100	in 4,200
95	,, 1,800
90	,, 400
85⅝	,, 300
66⅔	,, 200
33¾	,, 100
14⁴⁄₇	,, 50

O. III.

Acres by Hides (34 Counties.)

		250
erks ...	187	
xon ...	199	
iddlesex ...	208	
eicester ...	213	
Vilts ...	217	
		200
ucks ...	231	
urrey ...	252	
eds	254	
ussex ...	268	
orset ...	272	
unts ...	313	
		100
loucester ...	336	
omerset ...	354	
ssex ...	369	
erts ...	385	
orks ...	385	
uffolk ...	395	
unts ...	401	
Vorcester ...	404	
incs ...	405	
ereford ...	407	
Varwick ...	433	
ambs ...	449	
orthants ...	471	
		100
orfolk ...	543	
		{ 200 / 300
alop ...	692	
ent ...	797	
		500
otts ...	953	
erby ...	961	
hester ...	1,278	
		1,000
evon ...	1,490	
taffs ...	1,493	
		2,000
utland ...	2,629	
		3,000
ornwall ...	5,601	
		5.750

	Entries. %	line
cres=27,506,622	100	in 5,750
ides=*c.* 67,000	88	,, 1,000
lean=410	80	,, 500
lew mean=451	73⅓	,, 250
(Mean × 11/10).	60	,, 200
	38	,, 100

Population by Hides (30 Counties).

		220
Surrey ...	2·39	
Wilts ...	2·51	
		200
Berks ...	2·6	
Bucks ...	2·6	
Middlesex ...	2·7	
Leicester ...	2·7	
Sussex ...	3·0	
Oxon ...	3·1	
Beds ...	3·3	
Dorset ...	3·4	
Gloucester ...	3·5	
		100
Worcester ...	3·9	
Hants ...	4·0	
Hunts ...	4·0	
Hereford ...	4·1	
Salop ...	4·1	
Cambs ...	4·2	
Derby ...	4·5	
Somerset ...	4·7	
Herts ...	4·7	
Warwick ...	5·0	
		100
Lincs ...	6·0	
Essex ...	6 1	
Northants ...	6·2	
Staffs ...	6·4	
		200
Kent ...	10·0	
Notts ...	10·0	
Norfolk ...	11·2	
		610
Devon ...	15·6	
		1,040
Cornwall ...	35·1	
		2,950

	Entries. %	line
Population=251,485	100	in 2,950
Hides=*c.* 54,000	96⅔	,, 1,040
Mean=4·657	93⅓	,, 610
New mean=442½	83⅓	,, 220
(Mean × 95)	76⅔	,, 200
	33⅓	,, 100

Teams by Danegeld (30 Counties).

		250
Surrey ...	·635	
Middlesex	·64	
Dorset ...	·71	
Wilts ...	·769	
		200
Berks ...	·87	
Bucks ...	·95	
Oxon ...	·988	
		100
Beds ...	1·236	
Cambs ...	1·257	
Herts ...	1·277	
Hunts ...	1·356	
Somerset ...	1·371	
Hants ...	1·414	
Sussex ...	1·424	
Norfolk ...	1·470	
Salop ...	1·489	
Warwick ...	1·557	
Essex ...	1·658	
Lincs ...	1·772	
		100
Leicester ...	1·817	
Worcester	1·864	
Gloucester	1·941	
Northants	2·024	
Staffs ...	2·108	
		{ 200 / 300
Derby } ...	{ 2·545	
Notts } ...	{ 2·545	
Hereford ...	2·643	
		445
Kent ...	2·932	
		460
Cornwall ...	5·23	
		1,140
Devon ...	5·329	
		1,160

	Entries. %	line
Teams=70,606	100	in 1,160
Danegeld=47,628	96⅔	,, 1,140
Mean=1·4824	93⅓	,, 460
New mean=444¾	90	,, 445
(Mean × 300)	80	,, 250
	66⅔	,, 200
	36⅔	,, 100

that eight men rowing in a " best " boat would be able to cover the Putney-Mortlake course in half the time of a single sculler ; to a lesser degree this applies to tillage.   Cott. Jul. A **Teams of less than 8 oxen.** (eleventh century) gives a pictorial sketch of 2 ploughmen, 1 plough, 4 oxen ; the Utrecht Psalter and Harl. 603 two of A.S. tillage, both showing 1 man, 1 plough, 2 oxen; Cott. Tib. B. V. (eleventh century) 2 men, 1 plough, 4 oxen ; the Bayeux Tapestry 2 men, 1 plough, 1 beast ; the Royal MS. (thirteenth century) 1 man, 1 plough, 2 oxen ; the Chron. Roff. and Loutrell Psalter (both fourteenth century) respectively 1 man, 1 plough, 2 oxen ; and 2 men, 1 plough, and 4 oxen: most of these are to be found in books, viz., Larking's D. B. of Kent; Utrecht Psalter ; Bayeux Tapestry, and Green's Hist. Eng. (illustrated edition).   Nevertheless it seems equally **Teams of 8 oxen.** certain that in England the normal demesne plough consisted of the holder and driver, 8 oxen (or 8 animals partly oxen and partly horses), and 1 implement ; not necessarily proving the absence of a lighter plough worked by less oxen on the land of the lord, for some occasions.   The ploughs of the tenantry seem usually to have consisted of 8 oxen (as joined) when at work on the demesne ; the above illustrations indicate this not to have been the custom for working land in villenage, and I know no MS. evidence to the contrary.

Notably in Cornwall, the teamlands vary much from the teams, the correct explanation (alternate husbandry*) of which is noted by Professor Mait-

* D. B. 9*a*, pasture whence they ploughed 9 ac. ; 80*b*, was pasture, now sowable.

land ; where portion of what is estimated as arable Rotations. is in grass, plainly less aration is demanded than on a 2 or 3 course shift. As a rule, (1) wheat, (2) barley and oats, (3) bare fallow would seem to have been the rotation ; or a shift of (1) wheat, barley, oats, (2) bare fallow ; and though there is no great amount of precise evidence, the comparison of Teamlands and Teams on the whole support the above.

To bring the fifteen tables into fair comparison Method of the following method has been used ; in each table Tables. find a mean, and multiply same by a variable figure to produce a new mean, in such a way that the new means of each of the fifteen tables will be nearly alike ; the new mean is then used for the construction of the comparative lines, the results from which are appended in percentages. Thus taking population by teams in 30 counties (Comparative Table I.) the mean is 3·56 (Population by Teams); the new mean is most conveniently taken as between 440 and 450 ; and therefore the old mean 3·56 is multiplied by 125, product being 445. To 445, additions and subtractions of 25, 50, 100, 150, 180, and 255 have been made ; the results of which are now divided by the former multiplier (125), enabling lines of 25, 50, etc., to be drawn in the actual table as shown; with the needful variations this convention has been used in all the fifteen tables, in order to discover their relative superiority.

The first table plainly shows that to state that William the Conqueror made the land to be assessed on an entirely fresh set of units, or that he so devastated the whole country that the value was greatly reduced twenty years after his landing, would not be supported by evidence, for the hides and valuits of 1065 roughly answer to those of *circa* 1150 and 1086 respectively in the comparisons as made ; setting aside the comparison of like with like, the only table really satisfactory is Population varies as Teams. that of Population by Teams, where (as should be expected) a clear relation is established.

Except in the first table (5 divisions), the comparisons are slender; the remaining 10 divisions appear in Tables II. (3 divisions) and III. (7 divisions); the tables having been grouped by comparative results : Density (Table II.) gives the best yield, and the supposed relationship (1085) of Hides, Teams, Values, and *Valuits* (1065) is Slender results from other *unlike* Factors. demonstrated to have but slight grounds of support, for plainly the results from these items will not compare with the very artificial one of Acres by Recorded Population.   In a country like England, both of 1085 and 1900, there can be no very near kinship between the acres and population county for county, as plainly the flat agricultural districts will be more densely inhabited than the hills and moors ; hence *a fortiori* as to the remaining 9 divisions which yield an inferior result.   The areas of counties in Maitland's *D. B. and Beyond* are from the Agricultural Returns, 1895, and his results from them used here, though the figures in the Main Statistical Table in this book are from the Census Table, 1891—the difference is not great.

CHAPTER II

FEUDAL STATISTICS

" Eodem anno rex Angliæ pater transfretauit de Normannia in Angliam, & apud Wodestocke fecit *Gaufridum* filium suum, Comitem Brittanniæ, militem : qui statim post susceptionem militaris officii, transfretauit de Anglia in Normanniā, & in confinibus Franciæ & Normanniæ militaribus exercitiis operam præstans gaudebat se bonis militibus æquiparari & eo magis ac magis probitatis suæ gloriam quæsiuit, quo fratres suos, *Henricum* videlicet regem, & *Richardum* Comitem Pictauiæ in armis militaribus plus florere cognouit. Et erat eis mens vna, videlicet, plus cæteris posse in armis : scientes, quod ars bellandi, si non præluditur, cum fuerit necessaria non habetur. Nec potest athleta magnos spiritus ad certamen afferre, qui nunquam suggilatus est. Ille qui sanguinē suum vidit ; cuius dentes crepuerunt sub pugno ; ille qui supplantatus aduersarium toto tulit corpore, nec proiecit animum proiectus ; qui quotiens cecidit, contumacior surrexit, cum magna spe descēdit ad pugnam. *Multum enim adiicit sibi virtus lacessita;* fugitiua gloria est mens subiecta terrori. *Sine culpa vincitur oneris immensitate, qui ad portandam sarcinam impar, tamen deuotus occurrit. Bene soluuntur sudoris præmia, ubi sunt templa Victoriæ.*"

[A.D. 1178 ; Rogeri de Hoveden* Annalivm, curâ H. Sauile.]

---

* Rog. de Houeden — Justice Itinerant, A.D., 1189-90 ; *I Ric. I., Rot. Pip.*

IN Saxon† charters from the 7th century onwards grants are made as the land of so many
manentes, cassati, tributarii, and the terms
mansæ, mansiunculæ, hida londe, sulungs occur as
well as ploughlands, yoklets, and acres, some
avowedly and others presumably by way of estimation: plainly not all equating each other, tho' some
of them synonymous.   Now it so happens that
sometimes the numerical estimate agrees with that
of Domesday ; for example before 988 Woldham
came to the Bishop of Rochester for 6 Sulungs
(Reg. Roff.) which estimate is repeated 1086
(D. B. *s.v.* Oldham) ; in 948 Edred restored to
the church at Winchester 100 mansæ at Downton
and Ebbesburn (K. 421) which by Domesday was
100 Hides in the time of Cnut, and the same less
3 in 1065 (fo. 65*a*).   Edgar in 972 (K* 570)
granted to Pershore perpetual freedom in their
choice of abbot, in which deed upwards of 300
mansæ in Glos'ter and Worcester are named, and
tho' in 1086 the Abbot had not actual possession,
he had rights over a similar number of Hides
(D. B.) ; in 725 Ine granted 12 manentes to
Glastonbury in Sowey (K* 74) which had 12 Hides
in 1086 ; in 984 Ethelred's charter to the nuns of
Shaftesbury names "twen tiwe hiwe at tissebiri,"
where a like number 1086 ; in 998 (Reg. Roff.)
are some 6 Sulungs at Bromley (with further estate
in Andrede's Wood) by measure, and in 1086, ten
teamlands and 6 Sulungs at the former place, and
should any dislike of the above by reason of their

† In Norman charters, the land of a plough (*caruca*), frequently ; no indication of a *carucata ad gheldum* (*Ord. Vit.*) *:* the
term Saxon is loosely used for the people of England (from
whatever source deriving), before the advent of Duke William.

scantiness and dates, reference to the paper on the Præ-Domesday Hide of Glos'ter by the editor of the Journal of the Bristol etc. Arch. Soc. should give full satisfaction for that county. Not that it is meant to say that all the land in Domesday, or any considerable portion thereof, can be accounted for in A.S. Charters, but that in so hard a comparison there are striking instances of similarity ; not much do these deeds tell of actual Husbandry, but Seebohm (p. 139 *Eng. Vill. Comm.*) cites Abba's Will A.D. 835 (K. 235) in support of the 120 acre theory, which said testator bequeaths a $\frac{1}{2}$ Sulung with 4 oxen, 2 cows, and 50 sheep thereto, but as may be discovered from Domesday Sulings were fiscal as well as areal units, and should this half one mean 60 acres, at least 20 in grass would be wanted for the support of the stock named. Again teamlands in A.S. deeds were (at any rate some times) of estimate ; thus A.D. 774 (K. 121) " et huius terræ estimatio v. aratorum " and A.D. 738 (K. 85) " id est decem aratorum iuxta æstimationem prouinciæ eiusdem "; further A.D. 1016-1020 (K. 732) in Godwin's marriage contract " on Búrwaramerse other half 100 acres and thereto 30 oxen, and 20 cows and 10 horses, and ten theowmen " and on fo. 12*b* (D. B.) under Burwarmaresc, the lands is 12 pls., 4 in demesne, and 44 villans with 5 bordars have 10 pls., which is not disagreeable (*i.e.* 4 dem. pls.) to the above, and also Add. Ch. 19,796 in the Abbot of Evesham's lease of A.D. 1017-1023, for 3 lives of 3 Hides to inware and other half to outware, but 1 man, 6 oxen, 20 sheep, and 20 acres sown to corn are to revert to the Minster on the termination of the agreement for Norton, which plainly shows the Hide not necessarily entirely arable, as is frequently supposed. In a grant of A.D. 812 by Cenwulf King of the Mercians (K. 199) occur "mediam partem unius mansiunculæ id est an ioclet" and " hoc est terræ particula duarum manentium id est an sulung," suggesting

$$1 \text{ mansiunculus} = 2 \text{ yoklets}$$
$$1 \text{ sulung} \qquad = 2 \text{ manentes}$$

or perhaps that the mansiunculus and manens here equate the yoklet and suling respectively. The Burghal and County Hidages are set forth in Prof. Maitland's *D.B. and Beyond*, and the Tribal Hidage therein named is here given, from Earle's *Land Charters* which dates the Saxon writing as of the 10th or 11th century.

HIDAGE OF PART OF ENGLAND AT THE TIME OF THE HEPTARCHY.

1.	Myrcna landes	30,000	20.	Hwinca	7,000
2.	Wocen sætna	7,000	21.	Ciltern sætna	4,000
3.	Westerna	7,000	22.	Hendrica	3,500
4.	Pecsætna	1,200	23.	Unecungga	1,200
5.	Elmed sætna	600	24.	Avo Sætna	600
6.	Lindes farona, with		25.	Færthinga	300
	Hæthfeldlande	7,000	26.	Bilmiga	600
7.	Suth Gyrwa	600	27.	Widerigga	600
8.	North Gyrwa	600	28.	East willa	600
9.	East Wixna	300	29.	West willa	600
10.	West Wixna	600	30.	East engle	30,000
11.	Spalda	600	31.	East Sexana	7,000
12.	Wigesta	900	32.	Cant Warena	15,000
13.	Herefinna	1,200	33.	Suth Sexena	7,000
14.	Sweordora	300	34.	West Sexena	100,000
15.	Gifla	300		Two Hundred Thousand and	
16.	Hicca	300		Two and Forty Thousand	
17.	Wiht Gara	600		Hides and Seven Hundred	
18.	Nox Gaga	5,000		Hides (242,700)	
19.	Oht Gaga	2,000			
	That is, 66,100 Hides				

Why this early estimate is to be regarded as mere exaggeration I am entirely at a loss to discern,

for (for aught I can find) England might well
have had a population of 1½-2 millions at the time
of the Heptarchy, which would be answerable to
the quantities in the table: for the ancient meaning
of the word Hide (see King Alfred's trans. of
Bede) would seem to be the land of one family,
hence a population of 1½ millions or a little less
might correspond to 250,000 families (bearing in
mind that the table presumably falls far short of
the 40 modern English counties); for example
Bede names the Isle of Wight as the land of 1,200
families, and the recorded population of 1086 is
1,124 by Ellis' cast. True it is that in 1065 the
Hide is a fiscal unit, which is not to say that it at
no time had been closely allied with reality, nor,
because this artificial Hide of D. B. is computed at
120 fiscal acres, is it to be therefore imagined that
each head of a family in Heptarchic days had that
amount of arable. For I would suppose that never
in the History of England could ¼ of the heads of
families have been masters of so many ploughed
acres with suitable rights of wood, pasture and
meadow for the extremely simple reason that 5
men would be but a scanty allowance for the
working of such a tenement (by theory 2 men
would be ploughing the greater part of the year,
and if two 4 ox teams were used 4 of them). And
plain it seems to be that this vision of fraternal
harmony (at the rate of 120 acres of arable) would
necessitate an overwhelming majority of the population in a dependent condition; that is to say, as
labourers not necessarily servile, but under conditions of subjection as employed persons. This of
course does not include such a supposed stipulation

120 statute acres *arable, not* the land of one family.

as but 30 of the 120 acres annually under the plough, as that would correctly be at the rate $\frac{120}{4}$ arable acres, but comprehends that of a 2 course shift, *i.e.*, 120 acres ploughed, half in bare fallow.

As I understand the theory of the "free ceorls"*

* The government Domesday Indexes (Ellis) enable the postulate that the A.S. "landowners" of 1065 were considerably more numerous than the *tenants in capite* and *mesne lords* (*9,000-10,000*) of 1086; but the method of the præ-Domesday List of proprietors allows no exactitude of statement; under the heading of *Liberi Homines*, Thanes, Sokemen, *Homines*, *Fratres*, Burgesses, and Radknights, *6,000-7,000* are enumerated, and the remainder (personal names) might well furnish the balance for a total *20,000*. It may however be observed that a principle of selection, not easy to discover, has been applied to the Sokemen and *Liberi Homines* of 1065 (who account for some $\frac{3}{4}$ of the above 6,000-7,000), and as in 1086 these are practically excluded (in the 9,000-10,000 total), it is better to omit them, leaving *9,271* mediate and immediate tenants at that date, against approximately *13,000* "landowners" in 1065, and a rough equation of $\frac{A.S}{A.N} = \frac{3}{2}$.

Certain it is that many of the A.S. landowners had inconsiderable estates, as the following examples (all of the Wapentake of Claro, Yorks), collated with the Indexes in the Yorks Arch. and Top. Translation of Domesday, demonstrate; save where stated all were lords of seemingly whole Manors, presumably had no other estate enumerated, and were above the rank of the so-called *free ceorls*:

	Hidage.	Land to	1065 Value.	Place.
Claman	1 car.	$\frac{1}{2}$ plough	5s.	Arkendale
Dolphin	$\frac{1}{2}$,,	..	,,	Aldfield
Earne	2 ,,	1 plough	20s.	Neusone
Elflet, lord of $\frac{1}{4}$ Manor	$\frac{1}{2}$,,	$\frac{1}{2}$,,	2s. 6d.	Castley
Esnebern	7 bovates	$\frac{1}{2}$,,	10s.	Stollai
Ram	$\frac{12}{5}$ car.	$\frac{6}{5}$,,	16s.	Useburne
Suneman	$1\frac{1}{2}$,,	1 ,,	10s.	Grafton
Turgrim, lord of $\frac{2}{5}$ Manor	$\frac{4}{5}$,,	$\frac{3}{5}$,,	6s.	Alureton

There

they were lords as above, which hypothesis is Modern theories of Ancient Land-ownership impracticable. incompatible with the non-subjection of the majority of the rest of the population to said small owners, and hence contains in itself the elements of its own destruction; tho' of course a nation of such proprietors might exist as an aristocracy of yeomen, and a democracy of farm-labourers in proper proportions. But the postulate seems rather to be that some half of the heads of families were peasant proprietors with such relatively enormous holdings as to be quite impracticable on the given conditions; whether or not this pleasing but unreal picture has had its originals in the congested atmosphere of our own fountains of learning, or was imported already constructed from across the ocean is beyond our power to discern, but so great an oddity is there in the appearance thereof, as to deny any kinship with the open air of the fields.

The Hide appears in the Heptarchic memorandum already cited, in the laws of Ine before A.D. 694, in the endorsement of Nunna's grant (K. 1000), in A.D. 725 at the end of Wiglaf's

---

There were some *15,000-18,000 places* in the counties recorded in D. B. 1086, and possibly *Manors* somewhat corresponding, giving each of the former an average population of about 100 : in 1315-16 the *vills* fall far short of this number, but no statistical results can be drawn from these returns of 9 Ed. II., owing to deficiencies and lack of uniformity; thus, in Yorks there are about the same no. of vills, *as places in* 20 Wm. I., but in certain counties the former are less than the no. of *parishes* recorded in 1371, which in all England (save Cheshire) amounted to *8,600*, answering to an average of 300 folk, or rather less per parish, as by the Poll Tax of 1377 ; in 16 Ed. II. (Parl. Writs, vol. ii.) is a classification of vills, $\frac{1}{2}$ vills, hamlets, and parts of vills.

Places, Manors, Vills, and Parishes, 1086-1377.

grant (K. 237), in A.D. 836 in King Alfred's translation of Bede, and has not disappeared in the 15th cent. (Memoranda L.T.R. Hil. 5 Hen. V. Rot. 18) where is note of an allowance to the Sheriff for Hidage,* which is named still later in the Parliament Rolls of 20 and 23 Hen. VI., and 7-8 Ed. IV. From a period considerably before the Conquest its main importance seems for purposes of taxation, and presumably also for local rates, which latter usage appears to be maintained as long as the name persists ; allowing that in Custumals and the Hundred Rolls etc. the Hide is further used as an areal measure for 120 acres or other quantity. The artificial nature of Hidage plainly appears from the Domesday Tables, and in the Pipe Roll passing for 31 Hen. I. are notes of fines (pp. 123 and 125 printed vol.) that the Manors of Burwardescota and Etton shall from that date rate at a presumably lower hidage ; Kings Wm. I., Hen. I., and Hen. II. taxed the lands by hides (21 Hen. II. Pipe Roll—1 marc allowed for carrying the summonses of Danegeld) and Ric. I. appears to have done so in his 6th year, Somerset yielding £293 18s. 2d., Dorset £241 3s. 9d., and Worcester £99 12s., which at 2s. per Hide practically agree with the Domesday figures. In the Testa de Nevill (p. 295) in an inquisition of King John's, where ¼ of a carucate pays 10d. to Danegeld in Denham, and 6 acres in the same place 3½d. (the word here *may* refer to a rate), and carucage was taken temp. John and Hen. III., which in some cases may have been raised by the Hide

* Quittance from Hidage (as well as Danegeld) may be noted in the Foundation Charter of Battle Abbey, *21 Wm. I.*

rather than the plough,* and in 1222 (St. Paul's
Domesday, Camd. Soc.) Hides are continually
defended against both King and Sheriff, whilst the
jurors of Draitone name exactions made in common
by Hides, which supports the view that taxation

---

* W. H. Stevenson (writing in the E. H. R., vol. iv., *Carucage.*
p. 109) challenges the statement that *Carucage* was ever
levied on the plough-team itself (citing A.D. 1220) ; as the
Close Rolls for that year (4 Hen. III., 1220) contain writs
(Rot. Cl. i. 437*a* and *b*) to all the Sheriffs of England to levy
2s. on each plough, *as it was joined* on the morrow of the feast
of St. John the Baptist last past, it would seem to require
that extreme abstraction (so conspicuous a mark of the
ex cathedrâ writer), to explain the union of *Hides* or *Carucates*
on the morrow, etc. : the writ of course refers to the yoking
of oxen in the plough-teams, and not to some absolutely
meaningless junction of acre to acre at a particular date. The
above [E. H. R., vol. iv., p. 109] seems seriously enough
written, but merely shows the modern usages of the Schools,
whereby the critic can expound what he has either not
read, or is incompetent to understand : these writs (Cl.
4 Hen. III.) show that in Northants (and perhaps in all
counties) the demesnes of *all clerks* and their rustics were
exempted, and that the ploughs of their Knights and free
tenants were not to be answered by the collectors in their
rolls ; Subsidy $\frac{242}{29}$ (marked *t. Hen. III.* in the official slips,
and certainly of the time when Falkes de Breauté was in
power) is presumably the return for this county (the best
carucage known to the writer), stating the exemption of the prelates and their rustics, together with omissions of 9 other fees,
honours, etc., and responding for *2613¼* ploughs (possibly from
$\frac{2}{3}$ of the shire), as against *2422* teams in the whole county in
1086 (D. B.), at which date were some *1356* Hides. There
are other carucages in existence, but usually of little statistical
value, omitting mention of exemptions, and parts of the
counties otherwise collected ; in addition to this there would
be the usual mediæval tendency towards assessment rather *Mediæval*
than enumeration (*vide* writ as above) : in 4 Hen. III., *taxation.*
Yorks, and Lincs, pay £200 and £40 (the equivalent of
2,000 and 400 ploughs) respectively—figures which can
scarcely deceive the most credulous.

of this nature at least had not passed out of mind *t.* Hen. III., whilst rating as already shown continued much longer. Danegeld (exemption from) is named in a Charter to Fountains of 1 Ric. I. (Ex Rot. Chart. 5 Ed. II. per Inspex.) and also in another* of 11 Ric. I. (pp. 8 and 18 No. 67 Surtees Soc.), and the following from Madox's *Formulare Anglicanum* bear on the matter in hand (p. 238)—concession by Wm. I. of 8 Hides free from Geld ; (p. 176) Feoffment or Confirmation of the Manor of Bromham by Wm. II. to Battle Abbey, free from ghelds, scots, hidages, danegelds, shires, hundreds, and armies ; (p. 291) grant and confirmation to Battle Abbey by Hen. I. free from all gheld, scot, shires, hundreds, hidage, danegeld, and expedition, and (p. 293) King Stephen quitclaims from ghelds, danegelds, Justices' and Sheriffs' Aid,† "et ab omni exercituum expeditione."

Danegeld, etc.

---

* In 1251 Hen. III. (*anno* 36) granted lands in England, to Alexander, King of Scotland, free of Danegeld and Hidage (Rot. Parl., i. 115*a*).

† This Aid is named in Rot. Parl. (12 Ed. IV., vi. 64) A.D. 1472, the Commons praying discharge of it, amongst certain old payments, when not able to be levied (citing an unobserved ordinance of 5 Ric. II., that all Sheriffs should account, and be discharged by their oaths)—*Le Roy s'advisera.* The Commons state that these "grete Fermes and Sommes under divers olde names axed" (giving details), "the said Shirefes know nat wher ner howe to levye," and the preceding article (vi., 63) respecting riots in Cumberland further illustrates the matter. The management of the King's interest in the county in 1472 would thus seem to have retained much of the form apparent in the published Pipe Rolls of Hen. II., which themselves appeared to be foreshadowed in 1086 (D. B.), in which are divers evidences of

Sheriffs' Aid.

The Domesday Hides amount in number to about 67,000* in 34 counties, and approximate to same *circa* 1150 (see Tables): a comparison with the Leicestershire Survey 1124-9 is made in *Feudal England* (Round), and another can be done from Gale's Register of the Honour of Richmond for Hang, Gilling, and Halikeld Wapentakes 30 Hen. II. (1183-4), the carucates of which are almost identical with those of the Book of Winton (1086); the reference occurs on pp. 24-6, and on pp. 22-3 presumably of the same date (30 Hen. II.), are fines to the Sheriff computed at 4s. 7d. per Tenmantele, (10 men equal to 14 carucates), and it is curious to observe that taking the Domesday figures as 10,095† (Maitland) the Danegeld would be £165-£166, at the above rate, and that the actual amount named in 31 Hen. I. (Pipe Roll) is £114 0s. 4d., *plus* £51 19s. 2d. by pardons. Some further illustrations of the occasional stability of Hides are given later from the H. R. of Ed. I., also comparison of the Survey of St. Paul's Manors (1222) in Essex, Herts, Middlesex and Surrey shows practical identity with 1086, and the appended table collating the Ramsey Abbey Manors

Occasional stability of Hides.

---

fiscal administration, thus: *Beds*, 209*a* (*bis*), 209*b* (*ter*); *Cambs*, 197*a*; *Chester*, 262*b*; *Essex*, ii. 2 (*bis*), and 3; *Hants*, 50*a*; *Hereford*, 179*b*; *Norf.*, ii. 118, 119, and 276 (the royal treasury); *Salop*, 254*a*; *Surrey*, 30*b*; *Wilts*, 69*a*; *Worcester*, 172*a*.

* Prof. Maitland's Norfolk "Hidage" has been used here, though not agreeable to the evidence of D. B.

† For Yorks; but land between Tyne and Tees (not in D. B.) is accounted for in 8 Hen. II.

MANORS OF RAMSEY ABBEY IN HUNTS, BEDS, CAMBRIDGE,
NORTHANTS, AND HERTS 1086, AND TEMP. ED. II.*

Examples of continuity of Hidage.	*Hunts. Normancross Hundred.* 1086.	t. Ed. II.		*Bedfordshire.* 1086.	t. Ed II.
	Athelinton ..	10 H. 4 c.	10 H. 4 c.	Cranfield .. 10 H.	10 H. 4 c.
	Sawtre ..	7⅝ H.	7⅝ H.	Barton .. 11 H.	10 H. 2 c.
	Lodinton ..	2½ H.	2½ H.	Pekesdene .. 10 H.	10 H. 1 c.
	Weston ..	10 H. ⎫		Shitlingdon .. 10 H.	10 H. 5 V.
	Brington ..	7 H. ⎬	4 c. 15 H.		3 c.
	Bytherne ..	4 H. ⎭		G r a v e n -	
	Walton ..	not in	5 H.	hurst .. not in	1 H.
				Holewelle .. 3½ H.	3½ H.
	Hunts. Leystonestane Hundred. 1086.	t. Ed II.		Berford .. 5 H.	5 H.
				Cliston .. 1 H.	1 H.
	Giddinge ..	not in	7 H. 1 c.		
	Ellington ..	9 H.	10 H.	*Cambridgeshire.* 1086.	t. Ed. II.
	Dillington ..	6 H.	6 H.		
				Gravele .. 5 H.	5 H. 2 c.
	Hunts. Tolesland Hundred. 1086.	t. Ed. II.		Knapwell .. 5 H.	5 H.
				Elsworth .. 9 H. 1 V.	9 H. 1 V.
	Offorde ..	4 H.	4 H.	5 ac.	5 ac.
	E m i n g - forde ..	18 or 19 H.	18 H. 2 c.	Stowe .. ⎫ 2 H.	⎧ 3 H.
	E m i n g - forde alia ..	5 or 6 H.	5 H.	alia Stowe .. ⎭	⎩ 2½ H.
	Gyllinge ..	5 H.	5 H.	Broune .. 1 H.	1 H.
				Drayton .. ⅞ H.	1 H.
	Hunts. Hyrstington Hundred 1086.	t. Ed. II.		Overe .. 10¾ H.	11 H. 2 c.
				Girton .. 8⅝ H.	8⅝ H. c.
	Stukeley ..	7 H.	7 H.	Borewell .. 10¼ H.	10½ H. c.
	Ripton Ab. ..	10 H. 2 c.	10 H. 2 c.	Charteriz .. 2⅞ H.	3 H. c.
	Broughton ..	9 H.	9 H. 4 c.		
	Wistowe ..	9 H. 3 c.	9 H. 2 c.	*Northants.* 1086.	t. Ed. II.
	Haliwelle ..	9 H. 2 c.	9 H. 2 c.		
	Slepe ..	20 H. 3 c.	20 H. 3 c.	Whiston .. ⎫ 3 H.	⎰ 5 H.
	Houghton ..	7 H. 2 c.	7 H. 2 c.	Doddinton .. ⎭	⎱ 1 H.
	Wilton ..	7 H. 2 c.	7 H. 2 c.	Hisham .. not in	1½ H.
	Wardeboys ..	10 H. 3 c.	10 H. 3 c.	Bernewelle .. 6 H.	6 H.
				Hemington .. 2½ H.	3 H. 3 v.
	Herts. 1086.	t. Ed. II.			
	Therfield ..	10¼ H.	10 H. c.		

* H. = Hide or Hides, V. = Virgate or Virgates, c. = carucate or caru
cates, and the date of the Survey of the record of Ed. II. is not headed
nor noted in margin, but is in body of text (*Cart. Rams.,* Rolls Series).

t. Ed. II. and Domesday demonstrates the point still further. Records of the reign of Ed. I. frequently show the enquiry whether or not vills are " geldabiles," such contributing to the Sheriff's aid for Hidage, etc. ; thus 39 Hen. III. (Salop H. R.) a usual rate is 4d. for *motfey* and the like for streetward per rateable hïde (another point of interest in this record is the occasionally double description in terms of the fee and hide) ; also in Kirkby's Quest (13 Ed. I.) in Staincliffe, Yorks, a common rate is 3¾d. per carucate to the Wapentake fine (similar in amount to 4s. 7d. per Tenmentale of 14 car.), and in Pontebell, (same co.), no fine is due, because held by acres and not by bovates. Some vills have exemption from these local rates (the lords having regalities, or as being held in alms may quit them), and further instances can be seen from the H. R. (7 Ed. I.) in Wilbraham Parva, Swaffham, Bolebek, and Coteham co. Camb. of defence against the King and Sheriff ; of local rates (p. 337, Vol. II., Hoggeston), Hidage at 6d. per virgate ; (p. 829, Vol. II., Badigton) Hidage and Frankpledge; (p. 407, V. II.) Pontage raised by the Hide for repair of the bridge over the Cam, and at Elyngton and Gidding co. Hunts (V. II., 7 Ed. I.) the so-called Hidage of the Abbot of Ramsey, presumably to furnish the 40 days' expenses of 4 knights whilst in the King's Service.

As to the areal Hide its variations may be *Variations of Areal Hides.* particularly studied in the Ramsey Chartulary (Rolls Series) where at Shitlingdon *c.* 1240 it is computed at 4 virgates of 12 acres each (*i.e.,*

48 ac.), and at Therfield of 4 virg. of 64 ac.
(*i.e.*, 256 ac.) with in other cases 3-7 virg. per
Hide ; in the H. R. (referring of course to the
5 counties given at large) it is—I think—the
exception for Hides to be named, either for
defence, or as areal measures, nevertheless there
are indications of a varying no. of acres per Hide,*

---

* The E. H. R. (vol. v., p. 143, review by W. H. Stevenson) states that measurements are never given in terms of the
Hide and Oxgang, Ploughland and Yardland, as still frequently confused by antiquaries, which proposition postulates
that the critic is better informed than Domesday Book ; such
a statement calls to mind the reply of the unfortunate
authoress of the " New Atalantis," who had discovered some
special Facts (concerning the Whigs, *t. Anne*) which were
thought above her own Intelligence (*i.e.*, information), and
alleged in defence that her source was *Inspiration*, " because
knowing her own Innocence she could account for it in no
other Way."   Some of the following references to Domesday
demonstrate that the uniformity alleged in the E. H. R. is not
agreeable to the Record : *Cheshire* (body of county), 263*a*,
266*a*—bovates occur in a hidated shire ; (between Ribble and
Mersey), 269*b*, 270*a*—one Hide is equated to 6 Carucates,
which is amply borne out by the summary of 79 Hides
(scotting), whereas the Hides and Carucates add to about
80 H. by above equation ; and further the Hide is sometimes
valued at 16s. and the Carucate at 2s. 8d. ; *Cornwall*, 123*a* to
125*a* appears to prove the *acre* greater than the *ferling*, and
from the *Exon 'D. B.* the former seems equal to 10 fiscal
English acres, thus p. 92, Tretlant 4 ac. ; p. 206, Tretlant
(apparently same entry), 1 virgate and 1 acre ; also p. 242,
Delio, 1 virgate divided into $1\frac{1}{2}$ acres and another land,
suggesting 4 ferl. = 1 virgate = 3 acres, which is rather supported by the Testa de Neville (21 Ed. I., pp. 204-5), where
the Cornish acre equals the Cornish carucate ; *Devon*, 104*a*,
107*b*, 110*a*, the acre apparently normal, and the ferling the
fourth of a virgate ; *Glos'ter*, 162*a*, the Welsh carucates ;
Hereford, 181*a* and *b*, 182*b*, English and Welsh Hides ; *Kent*,

{ Domesday "measures." }

{ Cornish "acres." }

and Hides per virgate (at Haliwell, Hunts, a virg. of 16 ac., at Elyngton, Hunts, a Hide of 120 ac. in 5 virg., and at Gidding, Hunts, a Hide of 180 ac. in 6 virg.) and by collating the Ramsey Cartulary with itself and the H. R. it may be seen that in the same place changes occur at different times ; thus at Dillington, Hunts, in 1279 (H. R.) the virgate contains 18 ac., and about 1240 (Ramsey Cart.) $33\frac{1}{2}$ ac. These Hides have of course no connexion with the amount of land ploughable by one team p. a., and it may be observed both from the Chartulary and the H. R. that certain holdings are " out of Hide," and that the com-

---

10*a*, half a solin and 3 virgates, the virgate being the fourth of a jugum (see *Feudal England*, p. 108), and 2*a*, $400\frac{1}{2}$ acres make $2\frac{1}{2}$ solins, which with the entries of the Rochester Custumal (p. 153) of 40 acres per jugum, and the absence of further information in D. B., suggests that the solin might have contained 160 and not 120 fiscal acres ; *Leicester*, 232*b*, 3 carucates less a virgate ; 236*a*, 5 car. less 1 virg. ; and 237*a*, one Hide of 12 or 18 car. la. ; *Norfolk*, *vide* ii. 168, 205, 224, and 237, as instances of actual or computed measurements, which seem to have been not uncommon here, thus ii. 171, $\frac{1}{2}$ league and 2 perches long by 4 quarenteens and 4 feet wide (in co. Bucks 145*a*, one Hide less 5 feet occurs) ; *Northants*, 219*b*, 222*a*, 223*a* and *b*, 225*a* (*bis*), and *b* (*bis*), 226*b*, 227*b* and 228*b* afford 11 unmistakeable instances of bovates (oxgangs) added to or subtracted from Hides and Virgates ; *Notts*, 289*b*, a ferling seemingly equated to a bovate ; *Rutland*, 293*b*, 2 Hundreds each of 12 fiscal carucates ; *Salop*, 253*a*, 255*a*, Fines of Welsh land, and 260*b*, a ferling apparently of 10 acres ; *Suffolk*, *passim*, presumptive actual or computed measurements ; *Yorks*, 376*b*, 2 measurements of Pontefract castellate, and frequently the areas of manors, and the woods contained in same are given, see p. 129, and note on p. 131 for co. Leics.

Intermixture of Domesday "measures."

putation by Hides may differ as whether against
the King or the lord (Craunfield, co. Beds., p. 2,
V. II., Rolls Series); this together with the
changing no. of acres per Hide tends to indicate
a possible solution of the great variations noted,
on the supposition that the rural arrangements
are constructed to fit the fiscal ones. Tho' taxation & rates are paid by the Hide, nevertheless
individuals are liable and in defence for varying
proportions ; the acre is not the unit of assessment
and it might well be that an artificial unit such
as the Hide should contain in one place twice or
more, than the acres in another, with the further
fact of usually certain tenements being omitted
from the reckoning—as a rule (if I have observed
rightly) cottagers are not in defence, and both in
the Chartulary and H. R. for the Ramsey Manors
a tolerably close approximation of the details with
the no. of Hides stated, is to be found, rather than
exact coincidence. Further, Hides are to be sought
in ground unoccupied and presumably defended
by the lord of the Manor, thus D. B. (fo. 204b)
the 10th Hide wasted for the King's wood (Elin-
tune), which same is noted in the Ramsey Chart.
(*t.* Hen. I. and *t.* Hen. II.) as being in the wood
of Walberge ; the Abbot of Croyland's 5 Hides in
the Coatham Marshes (1086-1279 compared in the
sequel) ; and at Beolege (D. B., fo. 175a) in plain
and wood 21 Hides, said wood being 6 leagues by
3, and but 10 ploughs named : also the arable of
the lord's demesne is sometimes out of Hide, and
not rarely the hidation is given first for the
Manor, and then for its components, *i.e.*, demesne

Fiscal
Hides in
Woods,
and
Marshes.

and villenage. Could we transfret the centuries doubtless a landowner would be able to indicate the exact boundaries of his property, and likewise inform of its total Hides, and indicate exactly by whom each item of taxes and rates was paid— further it might be found that some tenants paid neither rates nor taxes, and others perhaps in proportion to their holdings in the common fields, the owner acquitting the demesne at a more or less arbitrary computation for arable, wood, and grass, by Hides, which may indicate different quantities of ground on 2 adjoining properties. Again either the whole estate may be, say, 10 Hides, or but such portions of it as are concerned in defending them ; in Yorkshire (1086) there can be small doubt that Yorkshire Manors. wood and rough pasture is within the carucate, as the dimensions of same are often given and comprised within the larger areas of the Manors— see also Kelham's *D. B. Illustrated* (p. 231) ; " took from this land 1 Hide of the aforesaid wood," and " $\frac{1}{2}$ a Hide of wood." Now tho' it might have been practicable to fix a tax by the acre (instead of the Hide) on arable and grass enclosures, to bring woods and rough pasture land into a similar computation in proportion to their area would be a hard matter, premising that the latter would have to be sought out and measured, and charged at a suitable and varying rate. The scope of the Hide appears to approach to 400 Scope of the fiscal acres in 1086, and its fiscal value then to be 120 Hide. ac. ; and possibly at that period a rough estimate —equivalent to 10,000,000 acres (made up as of arable, several meadow and pasture, some wood, mills and other sources of profit)—may have been in view. The same conception may be made of the Knight's Fee, either the whole tenement being regarded as X fees, or but certain portions of it which total X ; thus a fief of 10 fees might be made up of 7 of old feoffment and 3 on the "dominicum," or one of 15 fees, of 12 of old, 5 of new feoffment, and the "dominicum" quit, in which latter case there appears an excess of fees. Sure it is, there must ever have been a balance for the lord of the fee ; in the former case the "dominicum" if entirely subinfeuded would be more than 3 fees, tho' only liable for that number ; to take an actual case the Bp. of Durham said he ought (L. R. Rolls Series) the service of 10 knights, and sends in a certificate of about 70 ; he can name any 10 of these as his service to the King, and his entire tenement comprises either 10 or 70 fees,* the service being dischargeable from but a small portion of his estate. For taking the Bp.'s statement to be correct (and in an ordinary case I do not discover he ever paid on more), he is not bound to enfeoff a tenant who owes him 1 knight's service in $\frac{1}{10}$ of his estate—that, subject perhaps to custom, is a matter of arrangement between the Bp. and prospective tenant, and an excess of fees above service is easily comprehensible. In 19 Hen. III. (Testa de Nevill, aid to marry), when all tenants paid on both old and new feoffment (theoretically), as conceded by the common council of the realm, the said Bp. (p. 373 T. de N.) pays £200, equal, at 2 marcs per fee, to 150 fees ; but for the Gascony escuage circa 1242 (p. 412 T. de N.) his fees are

Marginal notes: Knights' Fees.

Bishop of Durham's Case, *Service,* and Retainers.

---

* As early as A.D. 1088, himself is a witness for his 100 *milites* (not necessarily all feudal tenants),—the *Durham MS.* is almost certainly from that of a writer, living *Wm. II.*: again *Caerlaverock* reports Anth. Bek had *160 men at arms* in *1300*, whilst *Ro. de Graystanes* (contemporary), states, *habuit de familiâ suâ XXVI vexillarios et communiter de suâ sectâ CXL*

noted as not unless 10, for the bishops had granted 40s. per fee to the King, on all those fees they ought him for scutage, obtaining in return for themselves a like grant on all their fees, so that 1166-1242 the Durham bishoprick seemed to contain 70 and 150 fees, the whole however being not unless 10. Now plain it should appear that an immediate tenant's estate was never likely to be completely subinfeuded, and that the lord would reserve for himself some portion—the above case is extreme, but 'tis contrary to reason to suppose any tenant would systematically subinfeud at what rate himself had been enfeoffed ; nevertheless such unreal conceptions have caused erudite statements as to measurement by Hides—so many Hides, so many Knights, etc., etc. ; presumptions unwarranted by evidence, and very little flattering the sagacity of our predecessors.

Without much violence to probability it may be conceded that records of Hidage before 1086 existed (thus in D. B., in North Lancs, Staincliffe, Ewecross, parts of Cumberland and Westmorland are named no persons, stock, nor ploughs—save in 16 vills near Preston, where unknown—but the Hidage is given), and it also may be allowed that 5-6 Domesday Hides make an average Fee (as a grant to a lay tenant *in cap.*), but that is not to say that the first feoffment (presumably before the Book of Winton was written) was made by Hidation ; certain it is that even in one county (Yorks) the subinfeudations vary greatly, thus 1205, 7 *John*, in Scawsby (Honour of Tickhill) $2\frac{1}{2}$ carucates make a fee (Final Concords) ; temp.

Average Fee.

milites, in the Scotch war—this of course must not be confounded with the *now* almost extinct *service*, and whether his retainers were *milites* or *men at arms*, any acquainted with the records of the period will not need to be informed they were probably mostly *ad vadia nostra* (*i.e.*, of *Ed. I.*).

Hen. III. (L. R. Rolls Series V. ii., p. 736)
Variations very considerable. 60 car. make a fee in Swynton, etc., and in A.D. 1300 (I. P. M. Rog. de Moubrai, as cited in Grainge's *Vale of Mowbray*) 159 car. make a fee—these are extremes, but ample confirmation of variations in practice may be found in the Testa de N., Kirkby's Quest, and Knight's fees 31 Ed. I. (see vol. 49 Surtees Soc.), and it may be remarked that the average 5-6 Hides would be far from applying on the one hand to Yorks, or on the other to Cornwall. The burden of supporting the 4, 5, or 6 Hide theory falls on its promoters, and receives no assistance from the subinfeudations of tenants *in cap.* which are quite untrammelled by any show of uniformity—the following from Domesday may be noted,

Examples.

			Service.
Fee of Wm. Perci in Yorks ...	$385\frac{1}{2}$ car.	}	30 fees
„ „ in Lincs ...	some $58\frac{1}{2}$ „		
Fee of Earl of Richmond in Yorks }	*circa* 1,172 „	{	50 fees in Yorks

and the Abbot of Ramsey had in all well over 300 Hides and Carucates, with a service of 4 Knights, but ecclesiastical fees are on a different scale to lay ones. Further if Fiefs had been distributed on the 4, 5, or 6 Hide plan, the value of a fee in Cornwall would have exceeded one in Derby more than 6 times ; a grant of course might well be *as* by Hides, premising no uniformity; some average fee there must be, but it would be conveying but scant information of the ages of 4 individuals, two 60 and two 20, to state their average age as 40. The £20 p. a. value is another rough standard of occasional correctness for the fee in its transit to extinction, (*12 Car. II.*), varied from £2-£3, but usually £5 to £8 p. a. (Book of Winton, by Pearson's values) to £200 p. a. (*Brady* who lived in the latter period), so it is to little purpose to cite average values, unless the times to which they pertain are observed, as the following may demonstrate :

WAPENTAKE OF CLARO (INCLUDING LIBERTIES OF RIPON AND KNARESBRO').

1065. 1085. From Domesday worth	31 Ed. 1.	20 Ed. III.
£ s. d. £ s. d. 169 19 6 54 6 7	$Claro$ $14\frac{1}{3} + \frac{1}{30}$ fees $Ripon$ $2\frac{1}{3} + \frac{1}{8} + \frac{1}{30}$,, $Knaresbro'$ $3\frac{1}{3} + \frac{1}{8}$,,	$14\frac{1}{2} + \frac{1}{8}$ fees $2 + \frac{1}{8} + \frac{1}{10}$ fees + 1 car. $3\frac{1}{2}$ fees + 2 bov.

Enrolled a/cs of the Exchequer.

That the subinfeudations by the chief lords were often in terms of the Hide and Carucate, appears from such records as the Testa, Kirkby's Quest, and Knight's Fees 31 Ed. I., but at no uniform rate, and clearly it would be easier to enfeoff in terms of already known Hides than in the often unknown acres ; but this is not to say that 2,000 acres, or yet 5-6 Hides, would contribute a couple of pounds to an *auxilium*, for the tax was primarily on the Fee, and only on Hides and carucates (for feudal taxation) as being members of same. For example in 1346 (Book of Aids) the Prior of Marton holds 1 carucate in Appletreewick of the lord of Skipton Castle (Yorks) of the King, whence 14 car. make 1 fee, and therefore is assessed at 2s. $10\frac{1}{2}$d. to a 40s. aid, but in the same vill at same date Hen. de Kighley holds

1 bovate ($\frac{1}{8}$ of 1 car.) of the Fee of Moubrai of the King, whence 28, etc., and therefore owes $2\frac{1}{4}$d. to the aid,—the one in double proportion to the other, and having examined each entry of 3 wapentakes (Yorks) the writer can state that in no other sense is land taxed there than as part of a fief. For defect of service (fees were frequently unable to be found) doubtless the King had a right to claim, the *Servitia* being based on the render of the 14 Hen. II. Pipe Rolls ; but the services of 1,000 Hides in military tenure would be a phrase of no meaning, and would have to be ascertained from former inquisitions or returns.

Baronial
Charters,
1166.

Reciting the explanation of the Barons' Certificates in *Feudal England*, which with a slight amendment appears warranted by the Charters, definite if disputed services were due by the immediate tenants to the King in respect of their holdings, which debt is named more or less distinctly in some half these documents. The royal enquiry had been not as to the service due, but how many Knights had been enfeoffed by 1 Dec., 1135 (the day in which Hen. I. was quick and dead), how many since, and how many (if any) were due on the "dominicum." The former are specified as fees of the old feoffment in contradistinction to those of new (Dec. 2, 1135 onwards), and the last enquiry refers to the balance between the service and the actual number of Knights enfeoffed, if such deficiency existed. The term

Domini-
cum.

"dominicum," tho' usually applied to land in the hands of the lord in 1166, is also applied to the non-infeuded portion of the fee prior to 1135 and 1166, thus Hugh de Dover (Kent) states that on his "dominium" are $2\frac{1}{2}$ Knights* of new feoffment, and Earl *Eu* (Sussex) that on his "dominium" are $6\frac{1}{2}$ Knights* whose names are, etc., and that he has no new feoffment. These certificates are the Primer of Feudal Tenures in England, but themselves contribute references to older times, which add to the scanty contemporary notices of Knight service, and it may be observed that no one in the days of Hen. II. (Certificates), John and Hen. III. (Testa de N.), or Hen. III. and Ed. I. (H. R.), seems to have been in doubt as to the early existence of the feudal system ; in elder times the question would perhaps rather have been if such tenures were in usage before the Conquest (see Spelman's Works, rebutting that opinion which had been "legally" successful t. Car. I.). Hence the full burden of a demonstration lies on those who hold that tenure by Knight Service arose after 1086 ; the author of *Feudal England* has given (notably on pp. 295, 296) several retrospective references, to which I will add a few from the H. R. of Hen. III. and Ed. I. In 3 Ed. I. (p. 42, v. ii., p. 42) Wm. I. gave to Hugh . . . and his heirs as $1\frac{1}{2}$ fees the Manor and Castle of Oakham ; (*ibid.*) Wm. I. gave to a certain predecessor of Gilbt. de Umfravill the Manor of Hamildon as 1 fee ; (*ibid.*) the Manor of Preston formerly demesne of Wm. I. given by him to a certain Earl as $1\frac{1}{2}$ fees ; (p. 166) 3 Ed. I., a note of a free socage from the time of Harold

Retrospective references of early enfeoffments.

* *Id est*, held by military tenants (whether knts. or not), in proportions equal to $2\frac{1}{2}$ and $6\frac{1}{2}$ fees.

the King [commended to the promoters of the
fraternal "ceorls"]; (p. 231) 39 Hen. III. a free
hundred of the Bp. of Salisbury's belonging to
the church from ancient *feoffment* of Offa the
King ; (p. 337) 7 Ed. I. the Abbot of St. Albans
holding of the King and adjoining Barony by
service of 6 Knights for 40 days, likewise *enfeoffed*
by Offa ; (p. 337) another socage tenure from the
time of the Conquest; (p. 637) 7 Ed. I. the Manor
of Overton Waterville given to Wm. Olifareli at
the time of the Conquest for $\frac{1}{2}$ fee, who after long
holding, committed a felony (seems to have been
held by the Sheriff D. B. 1086), whence forfeited
till King John, etc., and on same page another
Manor in same place of whose service the predecessors of the Abbot of Peterboro' were *enfeoffed*
in the time of King Edward before the Conquest,
and it is $\frac{3}{4}$ of a Fee.   Now it may justly be remarked
that these statements have little more than tradi-
tionary value, and that the service of Hen. III.
and Ed. I. is quietly assumed to have been that
of Wm. I. ; the same (I think) applies to like
passages in the Testa de N. (pp. 295-6, *Feudal
England*), which however can be surpassed (see
pp. 314-5, T. de N.) where " from the conquest "
is the usual form of the Jurors of Jerdeburg
Wap., *t.* Hen. III.   Of course in the present age,
with much less probability, a like statement* is not
unusual, but it seems scarcely critical to accept
the literal sense of records Hen. II.—Ed. I. as to
the 11th century, and to confront King Offa's
Knights' fees is somewhat of a problem : in the
T. de N. a pedigree may appear from the Con-

Their
authority.

---

* *Vide*, works on Genealogy, County and Family Histories,
etc.

quest (p. 87, Ric. Cheven* who would answer well enough to Richard the hunter in D. B.), and the evidence in it and similar records is good to prove the general belief in those days of the antiquity of enfeoffment. Roger de Moubrai's charter (1166), informs of 88 old fees, and 11¾ new, and 28 of the old had Nigel de Albigni enfeoffed "de dominio suo": this Nigel (his father), was one of those great men aggrandized by Hen. I., and the 60 fees (88 less 28) would seem to include parts of the estates of Robt. de Moubrai, and Robt. de Stuteville, escheats of Wm. II. and Hen. I. Dugdale quoting *Vitalis* states that Nigel de Albini married a second time in June 1118, and that his heir Roger de Moubrai was within his age 1138, 3 Step., (citing Ailredus Rieval.); the Pipe Roll passing for 31 Hen. I. makes it clear the said Nigel† was then deceased, hence all the 88 fees

---

* In D. B., i. 250*b*, the name Chenvin occurs as a tenant T. R. E., and 1086.

† In 1086, *a* Nigel de Albini's principal estates were in Beds—he also held in Bucks, Leic. and Warw., and had held in Berks (D. B. 59*b*); Hen. de Albeyni of Cainho would appear to have succeeded to all or parts of the above in Beds, Bucks, and Leic., whose son and heir (Dugdale) Ro. in 1166 returns under Beds a *carta* of 25 fees of his Barony. In the *Baronage of England* the above Henry is stated to have been a younger son of Nigel (of the text), and a grantor (with the Lady Cicely, his wife) *t. Hen. I. ;* this however can scarcely be correct, as Rog. de Moubrai (his presumed elder brother) is allowed by Dugdale to have been a *minor* at the Battle of the Standard [*3 Steph.*] ; errors of course are inevitable in a so vast a work, whose author's painstaking labour would truly reflect the greatest credit on any age. Rog. de Moubrai in 1166, returned as under Yorks, 88 old fees, and 11¾ new ones,
comprising

Nigel d'Aubigni and Roger de Moubrai.

4

FIVE TABLES OF KNIGHTS' FEES, 1166—1346.

	1166-8, Barons' Certificates and Pipe Roll.					1210-12 Inq., Total.	*a. 1253-4 Pipe Roll 38 Hen. III., Totals.	b. 1302 Inq., Total.	*c. 1346 Inq., Total.
	Render.	"Service."	Excess, Old.	Excess, New.	Total.				
Beds	$98\frac{3}{4}$	$109\frac{3}{4}$	$\frac{7}{12}$	..	$110\frac{1}{3}$	$113\frac{1}{2}$	$181\frac{5}{16}$	$89\frac{5}{8}$	$89\frac{1}{3}$
Berks	$137\frac{1}{4}$	$135\frac{1}{2}$	$5\frac{1}{2}$	2	$142\frac{3}{4}$	$36\frac{3}{5}$	$42\frac{5}{6}$	$111\frac{1}{8}$	$116\frac{1}{10}$
Bucks	$152\frac{11}{24}$	$155\frac{10}{24}$	12	$4\frac{1}{4}$	$172\frac{2}{4}$	$170\frac{1}{2}$	$81\frac{1}{10}$	$163\frac{1}{2}$	181
Cambs	$95\frac{1}{2}$	96	$16\frac{5}{8}$	$17\frac{7}{24}$	$130\frac{3}{8}$	249	$141\frac{3}{4}$	$164\frac{5}{8}$	$165\frac{1}{4}$
Cornwall	$215\frac{1}{3}$	$215\frac{1}{3}$	..	..	$215\frac{1}{3}$	$220\frac{1}{4}$	..	$165\frac{21}{4}$	$165\frac{3}{4}$
Cum'land	..	..	..	..	..	$3\frac{1}{2}$	$3\frac{1}{2}$	$8\frac{3}{4}$	$10\frac{1}{2}$
Derby	$68\frac{1}{2}$	60	$8\frac{1}{2}$	$10\frac{1}{3}$	$78\frac{5}{6}$	$86\frac{1}{4}$	$230\frac{17}{60}$	$79\frac{1}{2}$	79
Devon	$424\frac{1}{2}$	441	$17\frac{3}{4}$	$10\frac{1}{2}$	$469\frac{1}{4}$	$438\frac{1}{2}$	$420\frac{1}{2}$	$364\frac{1}{2}$	412
Dorset	$113\frac{1}{2}$	$114\frac{1}{2}$	$11\frac{7}{12}$	$11\frac{3}{10}$	$137\frac{1}{2}$	423	$411\frac{1}{3}$	$116\frac{19}{20}$	127
Essex	$379\frac{1}{3}$	$320\frac{1}{4}$	$59\frac{1}{12}$	$30\frac{1}{4}$	$409\frac{1}{12}$	$414\frac{5}{8}$	$679\frac{5}{12}$	$264\frac{7}{10}$	267
Gloucester	$392\frac{3}{4}$	$392\frac{3}{4}$	$47\frac{7}{8}$	$20\frac{3}{4}$	$461\frac{1}{3}$	Not found	$408\frac{7}{20}$	135	135
Hants	$137\frac{1}{4}$	$137\frac{1}{4}$	$14\frac{1}{2}$	2	$153\frac{3}{4}$	Not found	$142\frac{1}{4}$	$170\frac{2}{3}$	$170\frac{3}{4}$
Hereford	$170\frac{1}{2}$	$171\frac{1}{2}$	$6\frac{1}{4}$	$14\frac{1}{6}$	$192\frac{1}{6}$	203	$259\frac{7}{24}$	$83\frac{3}{8}$	$84\frac{1}{16}$
Herts	62	62	..	$4\frac{1}{2}$	$66\frac{1}{2}$	Incl. in Essex	See Essex	$85\frac{13}{40}$	$94\frac{1}{4}$
Hunts	35	35	$2\frac{3}{4}$	$2\frac{9}{10}$	$40\frac{2}{3}$	Incl. in Cambs	See Cambs	$43\frac{3}{8}$	$49\frac{1}{8}$
Kent	$215\frac{3}{4}$	193	$24\frac{3}{4}$	$7\frac{3}{4}$	$225\frac{1}{2}$	$224\frac{3}{4}$	155	$259\frac{9}{20}$	$266\frac{1}{3}$
Lancashire	..	..	..	..	..	91	..	..	$29\frac{3}{4}$
Leicester	33	33	..	$4\frac{1}{2}$	$37\frac{1}{2}$	$221\frac{1}{4}$	$287\frac{33}{48}$	..	100
Lincs	$351\frac{3}{5}$	$364\frac{9}{10}$	$5\frac{1}{2}$	$21\frac{3}{4}$	$438\frac{1}{2}$	$312\frac{1}{4}$	$392\frac{17}{120}$	$442\frac{4}{10}$	$428\frac{1}{3}$
Middlesex	35	35	$26\frac{1}{12}$	..	$61\frac{1}{12}$	$36\frac{1}{2}$	$1\frac{1}{2}$	$15\frac{5}{8}$	$19\frac{3}{4}$
Norfolk	$338\frac{11}{10}$	$337\frac{9}{10}$	$21\frac{1}{4}$	38	$397\frac{1}{7}$	475	$646\frac{2}{3}$	$450\frac{4}{5}$	458
Northants	126	$128\frac{1}{4}$	$3\frac{5}{8}$	$2\frac{5}{8}$	$134\frac{1}{4}$	$122\frac{1}{4}$	$124\frac{1}{8}$	..	$222\frac{1}{8}$
N'th'land	$77\frac{2}{3}$	$76\frac{2}{3}$	$2\frac{1}{2}$	$4\frac{11}{12}$	$84\frac{1}{12}$	68	$[91\frac{1}{2}]$	..	$145\frac{5}{8}$
Notts	141	$143\frac{1}{2}$	..	$4\frac{1}{5}$	$147\frac{11}{30}$	Incl. in Derby	See Derby	$163\frac{1}{6}$	$160\frac{2}{3}$
Oxon	$56\frac{5}{8}$	$56\frac{5}{8}$	..	$1\frac{1}{20}$	$58\frac{4}{5}$	Not found	$85\frac{11}{20}$	$168\frac{3}{4}$	$168\frac{1}{2}$
Rutland	..	..	..	..	..	$7\frac{1}{2}$	$1\frac{1}{2}$	$25\frac{2}{3}$	$24\frac{3}{8}$
Salop	$56\frac{2}{3}$	$54\frac{21}{40}$	..	$4\frac{5}{8}$	$59\frac{1}{2}$	$97\frac{1}{4}$	$62\frac{9}{20}$	..	$107\frac{1}{2}$
Somerset	253	$253\frac{1}{4}$	$4\frac{1}{2}$	$15\frac{1}{6}$	$273\frac{9}{12}$	Incl. in Dorset	See Dorset	$281\frac{1}{8}$	289
Staffs	126	126	..	$6\frac{2}{3}$	$132\frac{2}{3}$	Not found	128	..	Un-computed
Suffolk	$295\frac{1}{6}$	$297\frac{1}{8}$	5	$8\frac{1}{4}$	$310\frac{5}{12}$	Incl. in Norfolk	See Norfolk	$279\frac{1}{8}$	$281\frac{1}{4}$
Surrey	3	3	1	..	4	24	$9\frac{5}{8}$	$69\frac{7}{10}$	$73\frac{2}{3}$
Sussex	$251\frac{1}{2}$	248	$7\frac{10}{40}$	14	$269\frac{41}{80}$	$224\frac{3}{4}$	$276\frac{1}{2}$	$213\frac{3}{4}$	235
Warwick	$124\frac{3}{4}$	$124\frac{3}{4}$	..	$7\frac{1}{4}$	132	$156\frac{1}{2}$	See Leic.	..	87
West'land	..	..	..	..	..	..	..	..	$7\frac{3}{4}$
Wilts	$174\frac{4}{5}$	$174\frac{3}{4}$	$10\frac{1}{2}$	$14\frac{1}{10}$	$199\frac{1}{2}$	$176\frac{1}{4}$	$174\frac{3}{4}$	$207\frac{39}{40}$	227
Worcester	$62\frac{1}{2}$	$63\frac{1}{2}$	9	$7\frac{4}{5}$	$80\frac{3}{10}$	$248\frac{1}{2}$	78	$82\frac{1}{20}$	82
Yorks	515	$495\frac{9}{32}$	$79\frac{1}{2}$	$47\frac{1}{4}$	$622\frac{9}{32}$	$490\frac{3}{4}$	$441\frac{1}{10}$	$348\frac{3}{8}$	$394\frac{7}{8}$
	$5,720\frac{7}{8}$	$5,656$	$450\frac{3}{8}$	$340\frac{3}{5}$	$6,446\frac{3}{20}$	$5,334\frac{2}{3}$	c. 5,959		c. 6,000 *c

NOTES TO TABLES OF KNIGHTS' FEES.

*a This was an aid to Knight Prince Edward, granted by Aids of
the Prelates and Magnates, *scilicet de singulis scutis que de nobis* *14 Hen. II.*,
tenentur in capite xl solidos tam de veteri feofamento quam de novo and *38 Hen. III.*
(*Lanc. Lay Subs.*—J. A. C. Vincent—citing *Cl.* 37 Hen. III.), contrasted.
but with 2 or 3 exceptions new feoffment is quite omitted
in the returns, these for the more part being equivalent to the
render of 1168, that is, those fees alone for which the tenants
were wont to respond for escuage, so that this column may
be properly compared with the 1st one in the Table as regards
the total. It should be understood that both in 1168 and
1253-4 the counties have a somewhat nominal significance—
for a baron owning lands in divers shires *may* be returned
under only one of them, and hence for any co. the result is
likely to be both excessive and deficient, and the making a
transcript from the Pipe Rolls of any particular shire does not
of necessity answer to a list of its capital tenants by knt.
service. There are several omissions in 1253-4, amounting
under 11 entries to some 775 fees ; *viz.*, the co. of Cornwall
$215\frac{1}{3}$; portions of the fiefs of the Earldoms of Chester and
Richmond, 114 and $106\frac{7}{16}$; Hon. Wallingford, $100\frac{1}{4}$; Hon.
Lancaster, $72\frac{1}{3}$; the Archbp. Canterb., 60 ; fief of St. Valery,
50 less 11 ; Hon. B'stead, $22\frac{13}{20}$; and the fees late Wm. *f.*
Robert, Wm. Traci, and Rog. Buron, 29, 6, and 10. Fiefs
of less than 10 (*12 Hen. II.*) have not been traced, but it may
be assumed with probability that some new fees had been
granted since that date (*e.g.*, Hon. Knaresbro') ; Cornwall is
not found, having been granted to Earl of same in 15 Hen. III.
(Dugdale) for 5 fees, who also held the Hon. of Wallingford
(noted, but no payment nor return of fees) : 12 counties
answer in pairs, and N'land and Rutland have been supplied
from the Roll of 40 Hen. III. (aid to knt.)—counting *en bloc*
the composite entries under Honors (those under Boulogne,
and Peverels of Essex, and Notts are answered by tenants of
same, and taken as 3 entries) the tenants yield some 439 names,
which allowing for omissions may be taken as *c.* **450**, as against
300 in A.D. 1168. Neglecting the omissions, and taking the
fees of 38 Hen. III. as **5959** in 439 entries, 9 tenants hold a
full $\frac{1}{4}$ of them (1572), and 29 over $\frac{1}{2}$ (3012), but the majority
of tenements consist of small fees ($\frac{1}{15}$ to 2), leaving 204 names
for upwards of 2 (fees), but 74 of them holding more than
20 fees. The returns of 12 Hen. II. on the same basis (*render*)
yield 6339 fees (5721 + 618, as omissions here added) in 300
entries, of which 11 tenants hold $\frac{1}{4}$ (1600), 34 a half (3204),

4—2

and a minority (94) 2 fees and under (2 to $\frac{1}{4}$), leaving 206 holders of upwards of 2, of which 121 and 40 hold 15, and 50 fees and upwards respectively ; it is not thought probable that there were many (if any) single capital fees T. R. W. as will appear in the sequel. These rough analyses (correct, however, for practical purposes) of 12 Hen. II. to 38 Hen. III. show a natural increase of tenants due in the main to partition thro' heiresses ; after the Statute 18 Ed. I. (*Quia Emptores*) further increase should occur, but (if I err not) there are no existing records from which complete lists of contemporaneous holders of the Crown can be furnished.

Aid of
1302.

*b Fourteen of these entries have been already printed in *Lancs. Lay Subs.* (J. A. C. Vincent), but those in the Table (save Wilts), are from *Enrolled Exch. a/cs L. T. R. No.* 3, the reference seemingly given for the 14 (*ut sup.*) being now changed (I am informed) to *Subs. L. T. R. No.* 2, which is less complete than *Enrolled*, etc. (*ut. sup.*), but considerably more so than the list in *Lancs. Lay Subs.* ; with regard to which (p. 248 *ibid.*) Surrey is given £164 2s. 1d. (*i.e.* $82\frac{1}{20}$ fees), a reading which neither of the above originals assign it (either reads £139 8s. od.), but both refer to Worcester, which the author of above vol. refrains to mention, nor were N. R., and E. R. of co. Yorks assessed as such (p. 248, *ibid.*) but portion of the former was taken with the latter, and balance of the former separately, as the details in the *Exch. Enr. a/cs* (*ut sup.*) amply demonstrate.

Total of
Knights'
Fees,
t. Ed. III.,
by con-
temporary
Scribe.

*c Sum of all the great fees in England (save Staffs) $5,831\frac{3}{4}+\frac{1}{8}$ plus 2s. $7\frac{1}{2}$d. more in total = £11,663 17s. $7\frac{1}{2}$d. at £2 per fee ; small fees of Moreton in Somerset, Dorset, and Bucks, $60\frac{1}{4}+\frac{1}{13}=$£80 8s. $8\frac{1}{2}$d. at 2 marcs per fee ; small fees of Moreton in Devon, $61\frac{1}{12}=$£76 7s. $0\frac{1}{2}$d. at 25s. per fee : total sum, **£11,820 13***s*. **4**$\frac{1}{2}$*d.* The writer being unsatisfied with the incomplete returns in the *Book of Aids* for this *Auxilium* instructed Mr. N. J. Hone, to search for it in *Enrolled a/cs of the Exch.*, where it was found in No. 3 ; the record certainly deserves publication *verbatim et litteratim.* It must be explained (the original MS. it is believed is a triumph of addition) that the writer for reasons of expediency has used slight license with Mr. Hone's figures (who must not therefore be accused of lack of accuracy) ; thus Hereford is returned as fourscore and four fees and the sixteenth part, and the half of the forty-eighth part of a fee, whereas $84\frac{1}{16}$ fees appear in the table, and similar *slender* deviations (never $\frac{1}{4}$ fee) occur in same.

are proveably old ones. Now the Moubrai fee (Hen. II.—III.) is always rendered between 88 and 89 fees (usually 88¼ fees), and in the Inquisitions 12-14 John (pp. 469-574, L. R., v. ii.) it is curious to observe 60¼ fees (the ¼ fee held of the Archbp. of York) are given by the Yorks sheriff, and just 28 by those of Lincs, Leicester, Cambridge, Hunts, and Warwick; Dugdale (quoting ancient authors) informs of the additions of the Northern Baronies of Moubrai and Stutteville t. Hen. I., and these would presumably pass with all the Knights those lords had enfeoffed. The Patent Roll of 20 Hen. VI. cites a grant of Massamshire from Earl Alan to Rog. de Moubrai, by the same service as his father Nigel de Albini held it, to wit 1 fee, and then proceeds to give the boundaries of his grant, which method may have run parallel with subinfeudation by hides and carucates, as where 14 car. make a fee (Skipton Fee, L. R., 1166).

Few better estimates have been made than Pearson's (cited in "Feudal England," p. 293) viz. 6,400 Knights' fees of 5 Hides each, stipulating for an average, and not a uniform 5-6 Hides; as an eclectic table is of doubtful value, the following explanations of the 1166-8 tenures are given— such entries in the Red Book (Barons' Cartæ.) as are of date posterior to t. Hen. II. are omitted,

---

comprising lands (I think) in Essex, Lincs, N'ants, Leics, Notts, Warwick, and Yorks (in the 4 last named also in Pipe Roll 31 Hen. I.); Nigel (his father), and Wm. de Albini (*Pincerna*), appear to have been younger sons of Henry of Cainho (*ut sup.*), who presumably was himself the son or brother of Nigel the Domesday tenant (vide *D. B.*; *Ord. Vit.*, and *Chron. Abingdon*).

whilst *some* in a hand later than the original are retained (*e.g.* nearly all the Yorks entries by the Sheriff) as of those who had not sent Charters, with further additions from the 14 Hen. II. Pipe Roll of fees military, but not from later ones, excepting the Abbot of Malmesbury (required to complete the military church tenants) who appears neither in the returns of 1166 nor 1168. By this method some 700-800 fees are lost, thus the Earl of Richmond 64, the balance between 140 (the least probable no.) and 76 named in the L. R. 1166 returns, the Honour of Boulogne, say 113, Earl of Leicester say 121_{10}^{7}, the Honour of the Constable in Essex, say 57, part of the Earl of Chester's fees, say 118, Bernard de St. Valery, say 50, Simon Crevequer $13\frac{1}{2}$, with Peverel of Dover $8\frac{1}{2}$, and Hon. Lancaster $72\frac{1}{3}$.* The service due (including escheats) in 1166-8 there can be little doubt exceeded 6,000 fees, but by how much is difficult to estimate, as the largest tenements are those where most uncertainty prevails—to state the number as under 7,000 may be probable, but scarcely proveable. The 1st col. of the table gives the render of account in Pipe Roll 14 Hen II., with allowances for omitted returns from later Rolls (thus the whole of the Salop tenants sending charters are wanting 14 Hen. II.); the 2nd the services due where stated, and where not the "render" which method is erroneous for large tenements; the $3^{\underline{d}}$ the excess of old feoffment over service, by equating latter with "render"

Explanation of 5 column Table, t. Hen. II.

---

* The fees of Earl Hunts. and the complement of the Chester fief (both unknown to writer) are here omitted.

where unstated, the 4th the excess of new feoffment on the same plan, and the 5th the total,
probably short of the real one on the ground of
incomplete returns from the larger tenements,
where as a rule nothing is assigned to the
dominicum. The 1st and 2nd column would be
practically equal, if deductions were made from
the former of excess by tenements in the hands of
a *custos*, and certain exceptional cases (noted in
the sequel) where the render is excessive and
corrected in future returns. There are some
51 cases of fees from **10-75**, where the service
seems to be stated ; made up as under, using
O = Old, N = New, S.D = Super Dominicum

	⎧ 24	cases of	O + N + S.D.	(1 ecclesiastical)		Composition of known "Service."
51 cases	⎪ 14	,,	O + S.D.	(1 ,,)		
	⎨ 8	,,	less than O	(3 ,,)		
	⎪ 3	,,	O.			
	⎩ 2	,,	O + N	(1 ,,)		

and 76 cases of fees of Lay Tenants, of service
unknown but presumably exceeding 10, as under

42 cases of O.		4 cases O + N + S.D.	Composition of unknown "Service."
15 ,, by Sheriff		4 ,, O + N	
8 ,, of O + S.D.		3 ,, less than O	

Total, 76 cases.

Thus it plainly appears in the known cases that
O + N + S.D. is the most frequent service ; whereas
in the render of the unknown lay fees, O occurs
very commonly ; here the ecclesiastical fees are
omitted, their conditions not being applicable to
lay ones. For example the Honor of Totnes
returns 49 old, $19\frac{4}{15}$ new, and $6\frac{11}{15}$ s. d., which
amounts to 75 fees, the probable tho' unstated

Remarks on above.

service ; whereas the render is $55\frac{7}{8}$ fees, which being palpably deficient, a debit of $19\frac{1}{8}$ is entered against the tenant on the Pipe Roll (nevertheless $55\frac{7}{8}$ fees or thereabouts becomes the basis of returns of Ric. I. to Hen. III.) ; but the Earl of Glos'ter whose service is unascertainable renders $261\frac{1}{2}$ fees, whereas his charters inform of some $258\frac{1}{2}$ old, and $13\frac{1}{2}$ new in Glos'ter, besides 23 fees in Kent, which would be lightly rated at 300 (the Honor reputed to have been granted to Ro. Fitz Hamo by Wm. II.) ; also the Earl of Clare rendering 142, and debited with $7\frac{3}{4}$ new, informs by charter of a similar number of fees, making no statement either as to service or a balance on the *dominicum*, and it may be noted the Exchequer seems not to have material available for completing a defective return.

Total capital tenants (*ut de coronâ*), by Knight Service : *render* the usual basis of subsequent returns.

The total of tenants is about 300, and with some 11 exceptions (I think) the render of 14 Hen. II. (or a later render where not returned in that Roll) became the basis of assessment for Ric. I. to Hen. III. throughout England ; and in Yorkshire (and presumably for all England) for the reigns of Hen. III. and Ed. I. (as is proved by the aids to marry and Knight 29 and 38 Hen. III., and the Welsh Scutages of 42 Hen. III., 7 and 14 Ed. I. see Pipe Rolls) ; by the render is meant the *reddit compotum* only, not including the additional amount now and then debited to the tenant t. Hen. II. Of these 11 exceptional renders 5 were adjusted by 18 Hen. II. (the Irish scutage), and 4 more by 2 Ric. I.,

Exceptional Cases.	1168 R. C.	1172 R. C.	2 Ric I. R.C.	
Northumb. Bolebec Walt	$4\frac{1}{2}$			Exceptional cases.
Bertram Rog.	$6\frac{1}{2}$			
Yorks. Bulmer Bert.	$3\frac{28}{30}$	$3\frac{1}{15}$	$3\frac{1}{15}$	
Camerar: Herb; Steph. f.	$1\frac{1}{4}$	$1\frac{1}{8}$	$1\frac{1}{8}$	
Gaunt Ro. de	17	not in	$12\frac{1}{2}$	
Laci Hen.	$63\frac{3}{4}+\frac{1}{16}$	$43\frac{3}{4}$	$43\frac{3}{4}$	
Paganel Wm.	16	15	15	
Ros Everard	$8\frac{13}{32}$	not in	$6\frac{1}{12}$	
Skipton Hon.	21	,,	12	
Stutteville Wm. ..	$8\frac{1}{4}$	8	8	
Vesci Wm. de	$26\frac{19}{40}$	not in	$24\frac{1}{3}$	

and of the rest, the fee of Bolebec Walt. has avowedly a service of 5 (Charter 1166) and is so given in Swereford's extracts from the Pipe Roll of 4 John, also p. 392 Testa de N. in the inquisitions of 1212-1214, and not only is Rog. Bertram's service stated as 5 (Charter 1166) but is so returned in the above named inquest (p. 392, T. de N.).

Some 146 Charters state or practically state the service, which in 103 cases agrees with the render, and in 27 disagrees (the remainder not being found on the 14 Hen. II. Pipe Roll), but this excess is largely composed of very small fees, and this to such an extent that there are about 800 *fees* agreeing with the r. c. and the same number disagreeing; the majority of the important barons very prudently declining any information either as to their service or the debt on their " dominicum," are thus practically at their own assessment. Certainly in the reign of Hen. II. there are additional charges on new feoffment (much of which was due to the Crown), the relative payment or non-pay-

"Render" and "Service."

New feoffment.

ment of which would require to be sought out, but the attempt to enforce even the new that was owing (where not included in the render of 14 Hen. II.) seems to have been abandoned in later reigns (Ric. I.-Ed. I.). The consequence of the above probably was that there was much loss of service due, in addition to considerable difficulty in collecting the scutage on the basis of the 14 Hen. II. *render*, and doubtless numerous bad debts ; Swereford has given enough extracts from the Pipe Rolls of Ric. I. and John (pp. 70-184 V. i. L. R. Rolls Ser.) to trace the " services " of fees, and there are the Inquisitions of 1210-1212 (pp. 469-574 *ibid.*), in addition to the already named Pipe Rolls of Hen. III. and Ed. I.   Of far

Excess of old feoffment, on ecclesiastical fees, not usually paid.

more importance than the supposed increase of service from 1168, and permanent change of assessment (p. 286, " Feudal England ") was the attempt (likewise unsuccessful) of the Crown to make the church fees pay on excess of old feoffment ; in 15 Hen. III. (Brady's " Hist. Eng." V. i., App. p. 42, citing Pat. Rot. 15 H. III.) the prelates conceded to the King 40s. per fee, on those fees they were wont to answer for to military service, but were permitted to have service of all their fees for themselves at the like rate ; again 19 Hen. III. (Brady *ut supra*, pp. 43 and 44, citing Close Roll) an aid had been conceded on church and lay fees of both old and new (to marry the King's sister), the collections, etc., for which appear in the Testa de N.; and that the concession of 19 Hen. III. was exceptional is plainly brought out by Pat. 20 H. III. m. 8 (cited by Madox) to

wit, that it was from all the ecclesiastical fees, as
well those of which response is made to scutage,
as of others retained to the tenants' own use, the
grant not to be drawn into a precedent.
In 27 Hen. III. the lay tenants who did not Aid to
join the Gascony expedition fined and conceded 1235, and
scutage (voluntarily) of both old and new, but the Gascony
Bishops conceded 40s. per fee on their *service*, and 1242.
in return were allowed for themselves, to take
40s. from all their fees (Mich. Comm., 27 Hen. III.,
as cited by Madox) ; the inquisitions and collections (from the prelates) may be found in the
Testa de N. ;* where the 19 and 26 Hen. III.
items are the chief contents as regards feudal
service alone; the inquests of *John's* reign
being frequently as to the rights of the Crown
and subtractions of service (with tenure by knight
service, serjeanty, and socage often occurring
together), and no systematic returns about old and
new feoffment. The difference between the aid

* It is to be hoped, in case of a new issue of the Testa de *Testa de*
Nevill, *Minerva* will temporarily endow its editor with so *Nevill.*
much of discretion as to enable him to distinguish, say,
between an undated inquisition of the reign of John and
Hen. III. ; see the note p. 733, vol. ii., Red Book Rolls
Series, placing the extent of Nigel de Moubrai's fee (probably 15-25 Hen. III. during the heir's minority) as later
than the inquisitions of the Gascony Scutage (pp. 363 and
366, T. de N.) of *circa* 26 Hen. III. Either these inquests in
Yorks are fragmentary or incomplete returns ; the Moubrai
fee proves this, for the inquisition (p. 733 as above) is
considerably fuller than that in the Testa for this county.
With reference to the date of the Testa returns (pp. 363 and
366), both the form of the record and the names of the
tenants should have been sufficiently significant.

to marry 19 Hen. III., the Gascony escuage
26 Hen. III. and an ordinary aid (as 29 and 38
Hen. III.) and escuage (as 42 Hen. III.) was that
in the two former payment was made on all fees
or all that could be found, in the latter on those
only recognised in the *renders* of the tenants' antecessors in 14 Hen. II. ; what old and new feoffment meant 19 and 26 Hen. III. is not significant,
and was perhaps differently understood by divers

Northum-
berland In-
quisitions,
26 Hen. III.

tenants, but in the 1242 Inquisitions Northumberland (p. 381, etc., Testa de N.) old feoffments are
those made in and before Hen. II., new ones from
t. John, which is to be seen by reference to the
Inquisitions of 12-13 John (T. de N., pp. 392-3,
under heading T. de N.), which latter are abstracted
in the L. R. (pp. 562-5, v. ii. Rolls Series).
There is not the least witness of *general* inquisitions of old and new feoffment prior to 1242
(saving the case of the aid to marry 19 Hen. III.)

Evidence
of Testa de
Nevill.

where the evidence seems to have consisted partly
of charters of the magnates (referred to in the
sequel), and partly of inquiries made by the Sheriff ;
as examples the Bp. Durham (service 10) pays on
150, 19 Hen. III., is noted for 10, 26 Hen. III. ;
the Bp. Hereford pays on 18, 19 Hen. III. (service 15), and the Archbp. of York is noted for 20
(his service) 26 Hen. III.; but the monastic houses
on both occasions (in theory) pay on all their
fees ; thus 19 Hen. III. Abbotsbury (1) pays on
$3\frac{3}{4}$, Cerne (2) on 5, Pershore (2) on 5, and also in
26 Hen. III., when Ramsey (4) pays on $33\frac{1}{3}$,
Winchcombe (2) on 5, and Malmesbury (3) on $6\frac{2}{3}$,
but perhaps sometimes these were compositions.

Returning to 1166-8, there were I think nearly 500 fees newly created (1135-1166) of which

About 210 debited on the 14 Hen. II. Pipe Roll.

Due to the Crown	...	...	...	45	fees
By *custos*	...	...	...	$1\frac{1}{2}$	,,
Not due, but claimed	...	...	...	35	,,
Doubtful	...	...	...	128	,,

Extent of so called exactions of " new feoffment."

About 273 not debited on the 14 Hen. II. Pipe Roll.

Of which, no returns	...	...	...	15	fees
Included in render	...	...	...	$96\frac{1}{2}$	,,
Not due nor charged	...	...	...	78	,,
Doubtful, not charged	...	...	...	70	,,
Due, but not charged	...	...	...	$13\frac{1}{3}$	,,

so that far from annexing all new feoffment, the Exchequer did not even always demand payment when due. Some new fees are included in the render, and the majority of doubtful cases appear to be due, and after all the total demands for further payments, owing, doubtful, or otherwise, were but on a minimum of fees, *i.e.*, 210 out of some 6,000-7,000 : the following examples are of fees due, not charged.

	Service.	Old.	New.	S. D.	Paid.	Debited.
Pinkeni Gilb. ..	15	$11\frac{1}{2}$	$1\frac{1}{2}$	2	$13\frac{1}{2}$	*Nichil*
Windlesores Wm.	20	$16\frac{1}{2}$	$1\frac{5}{8}$	$1\frac{3}{8}$	$18\frac{13}{80}$	,,
Wahull Walt. ..	30	$27\frac{7}{12}$	$1\frac{1}{4}$	$1\frac{1}{2}$	27	,,
Foliot Ro. ..	15	$13\frac{3}{4}$	$3\frac{1}{4}$	—	$13\frac{3}{4}$	,,
Cormeilles Ric. ..	10	6	1	3	9	,,
Chauz Ro. ..	15	$12\frac{1}{2}$	$2\frac{1}{2}$	$\frac{1}{2}$	$12\frac{1}{2}$	,,
Fossard Wm.	$33\frac{1}{2}$	27	1	$5\frac{1}{2}$	$31\frac{1}{2}$	,,

The chief features of the 14 Hen. II. Pipe Roll seem to be the presumptive escape, of many of the

Evidence of Pipe Roll, *14 Hen. II.*

magnates, from a payment adequate to their probable service, and the attempt to tax the church on all her fees of old feoffment; few lay barons of known service of 10 fees and upwards had any excess of old; these cases are all in Essex, viz., Essex Galf. Comes, Mountfichet Wm., and Walt. *f.* Ro. (who all fall back on what their men tell them, and whose charters were perhaps indebted to the ingenuity of the same scribe), with the possible exception of Earl Ferrars; but on the other hand excess of old was quite common in church fees, which (if I have observed rightly) are somewhat as under

Summary of Church Fees, 1166.

					Total.
Service.	Archbps. and Bps.	$461\frac{1}{2}$	Monastic Houses	$294\frac{3}{5}$	$756\frac{1}{10}$
Total Fees.	" "	$743\frac{3}{4}$	" "	$343\frac{2}{5}$	$1{,}087\frac{3}{20}$

	Service.			*Excess.*	
	Old.	*New.*	*S. D.*	*Old.*	*New.*
Bps. etc.	$451\frac{1}{4}$	$3\frac{1}{2}$	$6\frac{3}{4}$	$240\frac{3}{4}$	$41\frac{1}{2}$
Mon. Houses ..	$284\frac{14}{15}$	$\frac{1}{2}$	$9\frac{1}{6}$	$45\frac{7}{15}$	$3\frac{1}{3}$
	$736\frac{11}{60}$	4	$15\frac{11}{12}$	$286\frac{13}{60}$	$44\frac{5}{6}$

Ecclesiastics as a rule " render " their services, and are debited with excess old, but not excess new, which latter just in a few cases is included in the r. c., so that of some 263 cases of excess old debited on the 14 Hen. II. Pipe Roll almost all belong to the Church; this is a less total than 286 (above) but the Archbp. of Canterbury's fee (paid by a *custos*) is included in the render, and the Abbot of Peterboro' is not charged (with his excess),—in addition slight deficiencies in the charters render exact figures (when collating with the 14 Hen. II. Pipe Roll) impracticable. Of the balance between $450\frac{3}{8}$ fees (total of $3^{\underline{d}}$ col. being excess of old) and 263 (Pipe Roll), Wm. de Romara is charged with $9\frac{1}{2}$ fees relaxed, which with the excess of render over service by certain lay tenants accounts for about 80 fees ; of the remainder most of 84 fees were probably due tho' not rendered (service unknown), and with the cases of Canterbury and Peterboro' account for the total. Thus Nigel de Luvetot (Hunts) probably owes the $12\frac{3}{4}$ fees he names in his Charter, tho' he escapes by paying on 10, hence he must be supposed to have excess of old (service unstated), so that I presume about 84 of the $450\frac{3}{8}$ excess of old were due to the Crown—taking the Church fees to have been correctly assessed by their renders. Perhaps amongst the curiosities of the Exchequer might be found a case of a Bishop or Abbot paying on a fee he did not recognise, but saving by a *custos* it has not been the writer's good fortune to discover an example thereof—thus in Pipe Roll 1 Ric. I. (1189) the Archbp. of York and Bp. of Durham still owe their contributions (of unrecognised fees) for the aid to marry the daughter of Hen. II. (1168). Pearson's table of Valets (Hist. Eng., pp. 665-9) for 21 Southern Counties estimates the home ecclesiastics as being lords of about $\frac{3}{10}$ of the land in 1086 ; and of the total fees of 1166 the Church possess $\frac{1}{6}$ to $\frac{1}{7}$, so that the presumption lies, that tho' in proportion to their service the religious had far more Knights than the lay barons, their " dominicum " was still in greater comparative excess.

In the 40,000 acres of the Liberty of Ripon,

Margin note: Unrecognised liabilities, and extensive demesnes of ecclesiastics.

the Archbp. of York had (31 Ed. I. and 20 Ed. III.) not quite 3 fees, which I suppose in the language of the Exchequer (still current) would be some 12 or 15 Hides of 160 acres each, or at most 36 carucates of 120 ac. (each); it is very evident the ecclesiastics were lightly rated, which perhaps explains their exemplary fines or promises when the King was going on an expedition. As already noted the second col. in the Table termed "Service" is erroneous, for the Render is not likely to equal same in the larger unascertained fees, as there is no reason why in these the old feoffment should be the total due, when $S = O + N + S$. D is the commoner equation. Finding therefore that in known fees with a service of 1,232 (taking the 45 lay cases from previous table of 51 known) there are some 1,070 of old, the "service" from unknown fees may be gauged roughly from the old feoffment: of the 76 cases named before, 15 are returned by the Sheriff (and hence omitted), leaving some 2,653 fees of old, which it is presumed might be answerable for a service of 3,055 fees, and the difference 402 is a supposed balance to bring the estimated service more in line with that of the known fees, enabling subject to correction the underwritten table, which is thought to be low rather than high:

Marginal note: "Liberty of Ripon."

Marginal note: Inadequacy of Col. 2, Table I.

Marginal note: Estimate of "Service," 1166.

"Service," as shown in 2nd col.	...	...	...	5,656
Deficiency (estimated)	...	...	...	402
*Omissions (see list)	...	...	...	618
		Service	...	...	6,676 fees

* *Vide* p. 54, and note pointing out what fees are still uncomputed in list of omissions (618).

Making the convenient assumption of 6,756 fees of which the Church held 756 and the lay Barons 6000, and supposing 9,000,000 acres held by the former, and 15 millions by the latter, a Knight's fee† as against the King, would then have a scope of some 12,000 acres if ecclesiastical, and 2,500 acres if lay: in addition to the above (to estimate additional fees beyond service) there would have to be added such excess of old and new feoffment as has not been calculated in the adjustment (402), which (if I have not erred) would be somewhat as under:

Estimate of acres in Church and Lay Fees.

Fees, answered by the Sheriff	745
Old feoffment	4,903
New feoffment	483
Super dominicum $(108\frac{1}{2} + 315\frac{1}{2}) =$ ...	424
Omissions (see list)	618
	———
Total	7,173 fees*

Estimate of Total Fees.

the "deficiency" (402) of the former table being found amongst the new, and s.d. in the above; whilst the omissions and Sheriffs' estimates do not permit of being further specified. Perhaps one might say the lay Barons had some 32,000 Domesday Hides plus 2,000-3,000 imaginary carucates‡ in Durham and Northumberland, which would furnish nearly 6 Hides per Fee as against the King, of a scope of 430 acres each, or somewhat approaching to 400 ac. if allowance be made for land which never was

Estimate of Hides in Lay Fees.

---

† It is not of course meant to be conveyed that an entire fee comprised nothing but military tenants; nevertheless the tenants in socage, and all the acres of land on a feudal lord's estate may from one point of view be regarded as portion of his fee, and therefore of his service; and thus in defence towards the king.

* *Vide* note, p. 54; hence total more than 7173.

‡ There is no intention to state the non-existence of carucates here, in and prior to 1086, *vide* Hist. St. Cuthbert.

hided, and "carucates" in hidated counties : these 400-430 acres might by a convenient Exchequer fiction be reckoned as 120-160 ac. of lucrable land.

Taking characteristic examples from the **1166** Certificates

		Service.	Old.	New.	S.D.	Render.	Debited.	Notes.
Charac-teristic Examples.	*Ecclesiastical Fee.*							
	Bp. Lincoln	60	102	2	—	60	42 old	
	Lay Fees (known).							
	Hamo f. Meinfelin	15	$11\frac{7}{10}$	$\cdot1\frac{9}{10}$	the balance	15	quit	
	Wahull Walt	30	$27\frac{7}{12}$	$1\frac{1}{2}$	$1\frac{1}{2}$	27	,,	
	Scalars Steph.	15	10	—	5	15	,,	
	Ro. f. Wm.	30	$26\frac{1}{2}$	1	$2\frac{1}{2}$	29	1 new	
	Beauchamp, Wm.	7	16	—	—	not found	not found	In later re-cords quit for 7; an unusual case
	Pagnel Ger-vase	50	50	$5\frac{2}{3}$	—	50	quit	
	Foliot Ro.	15	$13\frac{3}{4}$	$3\frac{1}{4}$	—	$13\frac{3}{4}$	,,	
	Lay Fees (unknown).							
	Glos'ter Earl of	—	$258\frac{1}{2}$ } $+22\frac{5}{6}$ }	$13\frac{1}{2}$	—	$261\frac{1}{2}$	quit	
	Lascy Hugh de	—	$54\frac{1}{4}$	$5\frac{1}{2}$	—	$51\frac{1}{4}$	,,	
	Reginald Earl	—		$215\frac{1}{3}$ fees		$215\frac{1}{3}$	,,	
	Hugh Earl	—	121	$35\frac{1}{2}$	—	$125\frac{1}{4}$	$37\frac{1}{2}$	
	Richmond Earl	—	—	—	—	50	quit	In Yorks by Sheriff

In a return (pp. 26-7) in Gale's Honor of Richmond purporting (see Observations) to be of Hen. II., $68\frac{1}{2}$ knights' fees are noted for Richmond-

shire (service 50) ; and altho' the Redvers fee answered (14 Hen. II. Pipe Roll) for but 89 fees, it avowedly contained over 100 (20 Hen. II. Pipe Roll); the above table shows somewhat the easy assessment of such important tenants as make indefinite returns. It may be suggested that in his charter a tenant now and then states his new feoffment within his statement as to *s. d.* ; but as *Super do-*
a whole the certificates demonstrate this term (s. d.) *minicum.*
to be used for land in the lord's hands in 1166 : Lamb. de Scoteni informs of a service of 10, and has 5 fees of old, and 5 *s. d.*, remarking that he has ¾ new, enfeoffed " ex illo dominio," and renders 10, but is debited with ¾ new, but probably his charter should be read as service 10, old 5, new ¾, and *s. d.* 5 less ¾. Again Rad. de Worcester states his service to be 1, and that he has enfeoffed $4\frac{1}{4}\frac{1}{2}$ of his few of new, the balance being *s. d.*; accordingly he renders 1, but is debited with $4\frac{1}{4}\frac{1}{2}$ new ; taking a line from all the certificates together demonstrates that usually the addition of old, new, and s. d. determines the service. The total entries are about 300, not including the tenants of the 618 fees given under omissions, but the former number contains a few double entries ; of this total 261 *Statistics of*
are lay, and 39 church fees. There are in all 125 *Fees.*
cases of fees less than 5, and 155 less than 10, leaving 145 of 10 and upwards ; of known fees from 10-75 are 51 cases, of which, I think, some 10 cases with fractional dimensions, the remaining 41 being by service 10, 15, 20, 25, 30, 35, 40, 50, 60 and 75 ; where the service is unstated (for large fees) there is little uniformity, probably pointing to a defective render, and

further, cases of subsequent addition (known service) may have disturbed round figures, as in the case of Hen. de Lacy (Yorks) whose service (if I have observed rightly) should be read as 60 less 20 plus $3\frac{3}{4}$.

The Computation of the Service of the Lay Tenants is entirely based on their own statements, which are scarcely likely to have exaggerated the debt, and it may be called to mind that in 1086 (D. B.) were some 1400 tenants in capite (Ellis), of which it seems unlikely that 300 (if so many), were capital tenants of the Crown by Knight service.

Capital tenants, 1086 and 1166.

Inquisitions *t.* John.

The returns in the Table for 1210-12, are of somewhat doubtful accuracy; the totals for 1166-8 and 1346 have been considerably laboured, but that of the former date quickly run up; the inquisitions of King John give lists of tenants of whose services the sheriff is ignorant, and are otherwise incomplete, etc., for example 200 fees may be subtracted from Worcestershire (p. 567, V. ii. L. R. Rolls Series), as Walter Beauchamp is there given 207 fees instead of the correct 7, (see T. de N. p. 43).

Later Inquisitions.

The method of raising scutage and aid (T. de N.) temp. Hen. III. from all fees has already been referred to, which is repeated in the reigns of Ed. I., Ed. II. and Ed. III. for both purposes; from whence the valuable topographical inquisitions of Kirkby's Quest and Knights' Fees (Ed. I.), the Book of Aids (Ed. III.), and of Knights' Fees 6 Hen. VI.; the Crown seemed in constant alarm lest lack of service should occur and it is not

surprising to find that England contained little
more than 6,000 fees in 1346. These I suppose
were all that the jurors could or would find, and
consisted of old and new without distinction;
whether most of the fees which had formerly been
returned as " super dominicum " were discovered is
not quite so clear. Again deductions should be
made from the total, as presumably there would be
cases similar to those of the Abbots of Fountains,
Furness, etc., who successfully (I think) disputed
their indebtedness on some of the fees they were
charged with. The aid to marry Blanche daughter
of Hen. IV. is set forth in the Enrolled A/^{cs} of the
Exch. (partial returns in the Book of Aids); thus
for W. R. Yorks (some 150 fees in 20 Ed. III.)
the collectors render account of £12 6s. 11¾d. for
11¾ fees, and the third part of a ⅓ part of a fee,
and 4 car. 7 bov. of land whence 10 etc., and
whence 8 bov. make 1 car. held immediately of
the King in W. R., of each fee 20s., and of more,
more, and of less, less etc.; and of 27s. 2d. of
£27 3s. 5d. worth of land held of the King in
socage (*sine medio*) at the rate of 20s. for £20 and
for more, etc.: this is an interesting return, as it
would appear that the lands held by others* of " les

---

* *Vide* the government volume, " Feudal Aids," in co.
Berks, where the returns cite tenor of Statute 25 Ed. III.
(20s. per Knight's fee held immediately of the Crown, for
more, etc., and 20s. for each 20 *li.* la. held of the King *sine
medio*, for more, etc.), but the editor in his introduction
(p. xxvi) renders this 20s. per Knight's fee, and the like for
20 *li.* la. held in socage. The form in the record is of
course correct, and as is not unfrequently the case with

grauntz" escaped taxation as knights' fees. Comparison should be made with similar aids of 14 Hen. II., 29 Hen. III. and 38 Hen. III. where

Change of method observed in these returns (1403).

volumes published at the common charge, discovers their editor's failure to understand his subject ; thus, in the co. of Cornwall is but $\frac{1}{2}$ fee immediately held, and no capital socage tenant of the Crown [whereas in 1346 (see p. 50) were some $165\frac{3}{4}$ Knights' fees and of course numerous socagers holding of lords of same] ; had the levy in 4 Hen. IV. been per Knight's fee, the above would have owed to respond, as they did in 31 Ed. I. and 20 Ed. III. on like occasions, being then required to be answered *de quolibet feodo militari* (Rot. Parl., i. 25), and *de singulis feodis militum* (" Feudal Aids," A.D. 1346). No reader of course should be content to take his views at second hand, when the originals can be consulted, but regarding the vast accumulations of ancient evidences printed during the 19th cent., a certain understanding of mediæval usages might justly be expected from any historical writer allowing himself to expound them. It is quite clear that in the 12th and earlier part of the 13th cent. a capital tenant was answerable as well for his fees held in demesne, as for those held of him by others : it is equally certain that in the 15th cent. the fees held by others *of* a tenant *in cap.* were not esteemed to be by him held in chief —the returns of this aid (4 Hen. IV.) for 30 counties are extant amongst the Exch. enrolments (the Book of Aids is very incomplete as to same), and *including socage* total under £1,075, whereas from *each* Knight's fee (1346), *with no socage included*, the collectors are burdened with £11,663 17s. 7$\frac{1}{2}$d. from 36 cos. (the rate £2 per fee), which would appear to demonstrate that $\frac{1}{6}$th of the total Knts' fees were then in demesne. A tax of 20s. on every 20 *li.* la. held in socage indiscriminately would of course have produced a very considerable sum, but it betrays a singular confusion of ideas to consider the immediate socagers of the Crown as answering to above : some or all capital tenants by serjeanty responded to the 4 Hen. IV., but (I think) not so from Wards, Escheats, or Honors, nor from Baronies (to the collectors at any rate). At this date the Bp. of Ely held by the latter tenure for

the barons answered the tax (in the two latter cases
on the scutage assessment, *i.e.*, the 14 Hen. II.
render); and with those of 19 Hen. III., 31 Ed. I.
and 20 Ed. III., where usually the King's collectors
gathered the aid from all the fees they could find :
the 6 Hen. VI. Inquest cited above, applies but to Returns of
6 Hen. VI.
those who had more than ¼ fee, and the returns
are extremely slender for W. R. Yorks (see Book
of Knights' Fees, and the Yorkshire Lay Subsidy
of that date), so that the land was presumably held
for the more part by tenants under the limit ;
regarding the later aids of Hen. VII. and Jac. I. No returns
of Knights'
Fees, *t.*
Hen. VII.,
and *Jac. I.*
I have not found that *any estimate by fees* was
attempted.

In the Inquisitions of 12–13 John (as abstracted
in the Red Book) I find but one note of new feoffment in the case of Gilbert Peche, whose fee might
then be in the hands of the Crown ; his father's
certificate (1166) is practically repeated, the new
being $\frac{1}{2}+\frac{1}{3}+\frac{1}{8}$ in both cases, but occasional
references to new fees occur in the records *t.* John
in the T. de N., presumably of those which had Further
evidence
from the
Testa de
Nevill.
been enfeoffed in that reign. In 19 Hen. III. the
aid to marry was paid to collectors, to the Sheriff,
and also directly into the wardrobe, or Exchequer
(see T. de N.) ; to all or many of the magnates
the King had written, instructing them to return
to the Exchequer a list of their fees as well old as

---

6 fees, and the Abb. of Glastonbury for 3 (fees), which is the
precise no. of Knts. for which they answered in the Marshals'
Rolls of 29 Hen. III., 5 and 10 Ed. I., and 4 Ed. II., though
their service (including fees held by others) in *1166* was
40 fees each.

new : eight of these charters may be found on
pp. 44, 415, and 416 of the T. de N., and
another (that of Ro. Beauchamp of Hache) is to
be seen along with the King's writ in Madox's
Form. Ang. I give an extract from the return of
the Abbot of St. Edmund's to the Exchequer, who
commences by naming the precept of the King, as
to certifying how much of the aid for the marriage
of his sister had been paid to the *Exch.* and how
much to be paid, how many fees, in what counties
and vills, and what of old and of new, and follows
" Nos concessisse domino Regi sexies viginti marcas.
Ex quibus jam solvimus ad scaccarium medietatem
scilicet sexaginta marcas alia vero medietas adhuc
restat solvenda. Feoda vero militum de veteri
feoffamento habemus quadraginta que tenemus in
capite de domino Rege etsi respondemus pro illis pro
temporis necessitate. Alia vero xij feoda habemus
de novo feoffamento que capta sunt et feoffata de
nostris propriis dominicis. Et pertinent ad nostram.
Que nulli respondent nec unquam responderent nec
respondere debent nisi soli abbati Sancti Eadmundi.
Et ipse abbas nemini respondet de illis predicta
vero feoda partim sunt in Norff' et Suff' partim
in Essex'. In quibus vero villis sint constituta vel
quid et quantum in quo loco Deus novit." Now
be it observed that the Edmondsbury service was
40, and that in 1168 there were some $52\frac{1}{2}$ old and
$\frac{1}{4}$ new fees ; hence it appears the Abbot in 1235
understood by new feoffment any surplus fees
beyond what he was wont to answer for to a
scutage, and also he seems to have compounded
at a rate equal to 60 fees ; likewise the Abbot of

Ramsey who pays 60 and 100 marcs respectively in 1235 and 1242 * equal to 30 and 33⅓ fees. The King's mandate to the Sheriff of Norfolk and Suffolk (p. 282 T. de N.) dated 6 May 20 Hen. III. mentions the charters of the magnates, and that the Sheriff shall certify of those holding 1 fee and less ; and presumably a like method might be used in other counties.

The Gascony Scutage has been dealt with in the Preface to Vol. II. (L. R. Rolls Series), notwithstanding the editor's failure to recognise the Yorkshire returns in the Testa de Nevill ; (see his note p. 733, Vol. II., *ibid.*, citing T. de N., pp. 625 and 638), and it may suffice to add that inquisitions of this date (*circa* 1242) occur in almost every county named in the T. de N., and to point out that the monastic houses had not commuted their service in the same way as the bishops. Northumberland is well given in the T. de N., as there are inquisitions *circa* 1210-12 (12-13 John) on pp. 392-3, collections for the aid to marry (pp. 394-5), and the later Gascony inquests commencing on p. 381 ; the following fines from Dugdale's Baronage (citing Pipe and Fine Rolls), may be noticed in this connection ; calling to mind that those who " had their service " abroad had scutage (for themselves) of their men, and that said escuage was 3 marcs per fee, but that most of those who fined conceded their scutage also.

---

* 1235 and 1242 are dates used with latitude for the aid to marry and the Gascony scutage ; in neither case were the debts all paid in those years.

	26 Hen. III. Fines *ne trans.*	14 Hen. II. Render.	Notes.
Fines *ne trans fretant.* Warwick Thos. Earl	{ 120 li. 120 li.	102½ fees (32 more 38 Hen. III.)	{ 1st fine lest he trans-fret 2nd fine to have his scutage
Albini Wm.	20 marcs	33 ,,	
Beauchamp Ro ..	80 m.	17 ,,	
Perci Wm.	100 m.	30 ,,	
Nevill Ro.	10 li.	3¼ ,,	Heir to the Yorks fee of Bulmer
Gaunt Gilb.	200 m.	68$\frac{17}{32}$,,	By Simon, Earl Hunts, in 1166
Stuttevill Wm. ..	15 m.		
Umfravill Gilbt. ..	100 m.		
Baiocis Jo.	100 m.	17 ,,	

Instances of the so-called "enfeoffment" prior to the Conquest have been already cited from the H. R., and I suppose few will deny that the Hide was a Saxon, and the Fee a Norman institution; but the theory that the figures of 1166–8 (say total *renders*) represent the number of Knights due *in exercitu t.* Wm. I., seems fully as improbable as the unwarranted emergence of the Fee from the Hide. The editor of the Red Book (Rolls Series) appears to think otherwise, as the following citations from his preface to Vol. II. indicate:

Supposed develop-ment of the Fee from the Hide.

p. clxi.
(1)
"the ancient system of assessment for imperial taxa-tion, which in the shape of a common assize continued to be apportioned according to the old plan of hidation—for scutage and aid . . .—down to a far later period."

p. clxi.
(2)
"the normal Knight's fee contained 4 hides — a scale which seems to have been recognised as late as the 16th century," with note, citing H. R., II. 830.

p. clxii.
"unless the actual extent of the holding should prove (upon inquisition taken) to contain an

(3)

equivalent for hidation. So when an inquisition was taken throughout the Kingdom, for the assessment of a Scutage, the Sheriffs were required to return the number of fees in each hundred, estimating their extent by the actual number of hides or proportions of a hide," citing the T. de N. and the Abbot of Ramsey's case.

p. clxiv.

(4)

"and moreover the extent of the hide or carucate is often stated in denominations of an acre both of arable and pasture land," citing Kirkby's Quest, fo. 228.

It has already been allowed that sub-infeudations were (or are returned) by Hides and Carucates, whence so many make a fee; the establishment of the feudal system did not of course extinguish hides (as units for rates and taxes) or acres as areal measures, but as less than 3 or more than 150 carucates might make a fee, and in a feudal tax contribute not by the rate of carucates but at that of fees, it is difficult to discern how this can be termed a tax on the land unit. For instance taking examples from the T. de N. which seems to be indicated in the 3rd of the above extracts, on p. 337 the Earl of Chester holds in Horsinton 2 carucates of which Walt. de Bolesby holds 1, whence 11 bovates (*i.e.*, $1\frac{3}{8}$ car.) make a fee, and lord Simon de Kyme holds the other whence 20 bovates ($2\frac{1}{2}$ car.) make etc., and on p. 249 in the Gascony inquisitions in co. Beds., Peter de Lekeburn holds 8 virgates (2 Hides) for $\frac{1}{6}$ of a fee; Walt. *f.* Alex. holds 1 virgate for $\frac{1}{15}$ of a fee (here $3\frac{3}{4}$ Hides make 1 fee), the Prior of Neuham 2 Hides for $\frac{1}{16}$ of a fee (32 Hides per fee), and further divers tenants

Remarks on same.

The *theory* refuted by numerous Records.

hold Hides and Virgates, with the rate of the tenure omitted. The return that the jurors are ignorant of the service is by no means a novelty to those acquainted with records of the kind, and should these unknown fees be made to contribute to a feudal aid, their Hides, Virgates, etc., will necessarily be brought into some proportion. Examples have already been given [20 Ed. III. and 4 Hen. IV. (see pp. 45, 69) aid to Knight and marry, Knaresbro', and W. R. Yorks] of odd carucates and bovates; in the latter, the number of carucates per fee is stated, but in the former not, nevertheless as (see p. 45, Knaresbro') $3\frac{1}{8}$ fees + 2 bovates are given against £6 5s. 10d. in a 40s. aid, it must be plain that the couple of bovates equal $\frac{1}{48}$th of a fee, equal to whence 12 etc., just as in the latter record where there are 4 car. 7 bov. over, whence 10 et., they are $\frac{39}{80}$ of a fee, as is proved by the amount received. And further anyone inspecting the inquests of knights' fees (apart from those of serjeanty and socage) in the T. de N. will find it quite exceptional for Hides or Carucates to be named alone; *i.e.*, without giving their varying value as fractions of fees; and naturally if the jurors did not know the amount of tenure they would limit their statement to the convenient hides etc. ; for under the same tenant in capite (see I. P. M. Rog. de Moubray 29 Ed. I., 1300) there might be extremely various scales of sub-infeudation, just as in the same Manor the Hide might (even at the same time) contain a different number of acres.

The following records from Hen. I. to Hen. VI. will bear out the above ;

	Reign.
List of Peterboro' Knights (Camden Soc., 1849)	Hen. I.
Barons' Certificates (Red Book Exch.)	Hen. II.
Testa de Nevill ⎫ Hundred Rolls ⎬	Hen. III.
"Liber Rubeus" ⎭	
Kirkby's Quest ⎫ Hundred Rolls ⎬	Ed. I.
Knights' Fees, 31 Ed. I. ⎭	
Book of Aids	Ed. III.
Aid to marry	Hen. IV.
Book of Knights' Fees	Hen. VI

The description of the Peterboro' Knights t. Hen. I. will be found on p. 168 in the Chronicle, and there is no stable relation between the Hide and Fee ; illustrations have already been given or reference made to the Barons' *Cartæ.* ;* H. R. Hen. III., Testa de Nevill, Book of Aids, and the aid to marry Hen. IV.'s daughter (Enrolled a/cs. Exch.), and the following will serve to show the rest are of like nature :

Liber Rubeus. Fee of Nigel de Moubrai (15-25 Hen. III.)
    In Haytone ... 15 bovates whence 12 car. make 1 fee
    In Swinton, etc. 3 car.   ,,   60   ,,   ,,
Kirkby's Quest. Honor of Richmond, Halikeld, 1284.
    Eskelby and Leeming ... ... 18 car. make 1 fee
    Uppeslunde 3   ,, $\frac{1}{3}$,,
Knights' Fees, 31 Ed. I. Staincliffe Wap., Yorks.
    Neuton and Elslack   6 car. whence 28 make 1 fee
    Cracoe, etc   ...   12   ,,   12 ,,   1 ,,

---

* See Round's "Feudal England" (p. 294) for 2-10 Hides, per fee in 1166, and for like evidence in Chartularies (p. 295).

Book of Knights' Fees, 6 Hen. VI.	Staincliffe Wap., Yorks.	
Lord de Roos holds in Thornton ...	10½ car.	by service of ¾ fee
Joan, Countess of Westmorland holds in Kettlewell	6 „	„ ⅓ „

In the 2nd extract from the Preface to the Red Book, the editor cites H. R., II., 830, where Hugh de Musgrave holds 1 Hide as ¼ fee, which is duly found as stated but it would be singular if so vast a bulk as the Hundred Rolls could not furnish such an instance; here are a few more to be found in same Vol. II.: p. 575, 2 fees equal to 6½ Hides; p. 578, 1 fee to 2 Hides; p. 580, ½ fee to 3½ Hides, also ½ fee to 3 Hides, p. 584, ⅙ fee to 9/8 Hides; p. 585, ⅙ fee to 1¼ Hides, also ⅙ fee to 2 Hides; p. 336, 1 fee to 10 Hides (see "Feudal Aids" where Doddington is given as 1 fee in 1284, 1302, and 1346), also Mursele, Ro. *f.* Nigel, ⅛ fee to 2 Hides and more, and p. 334, 1 fee to 5¾ Hides, which are given to show that the Hide was here a varying portion of the Fee, not touching on the point that in the H. R. it is often an areal measure or approximately so. This same extract notes a scale (where 4 Hides = 1 fee) recognised as late as the 16th century, which possibly refers to pp. 442-7 of No. 49 Surtees Soc., where is a computation as above, with an editorial note that same seems to have been compiled about the latter part of the 16th cent.; this scale also gives tables for 6, 7, 8, 9, 10, 11, 12, 13, 14, 15, 16, 18, 23, 24, and 28 carucates per fee, not stating which of the latter is "normal." Supposing for a moment this " normal " fee really ever did contain 4 Hides (and whether of 120 acres each as in the Preface to the Red Book or 160 each as in the L. R. itself does not much matter), as there were 6,000-7,000 fees (Hen. II. to Ed. III.), and some 67,000 Hides in say 35 counties in England in Domesday ; it is evident that the Barons and Church would hardly have possessed 28,000 of them (probably less) ; whereas few historians should think of rating them at less than ¾ of England, say 50,000 Hides.

With regard to the 3rd extract, which names the Sheriffs estimating Knight's fee by the hides they contained, the reference is seemingly to the Testa de Nevill, the returns from which have already been exemplified ; but these remarkable instructions to the sheriffs are not found therein, nor in the " Forma Inquisitionum de Scutagiis," nor in the writ to the Sheriff of Hereford (both these latter on Mich. Com. 27 Hen. III. as cited on pp. 472-3 of Madox's Exch., ed. 1711) nor I should imagine anywhere else than on p. clxii of aforesaid Preface ; and as to the extent of the hide or carucate being " given in denominations of an acre both of arable and pasture land," anyone finding same on fo. 228 of Kirkby's Quest will have better luck than I had.

The case of Ramsey Abbey is certainly exceptional ; but by Domesday Book that house had well over 300 Hides and Carucates, which in the language of the Exchequer (4 Hides = 1 Knight's Fee) would be the equivalent of over 70 Knights ; as a matter of fact the Abbot equipped as a rule 4 (see his Court Rolls for 1258 and 1294, in Selden Soc., Vol. II.), notwithstanding aforesaid inquisitions of 1242 estimating Knights' fees by hides (where he contributes as if he had $33\frac{1}{3}$ fees). The uniform manufacture of Hides into fees at a rate of the " normal four " would be apt to break down in practice ; suppose a Baron had a grant of 400 Hides for a service of 100 fees ; he might enfeoff 100 knights* on 350 Hides at 1 fee each (as presumably he would have some residence, and tenants in socage and villeinage), and hence (on the 4 Hide plan) the Sheriff would find not unless $87\frac{1}{2}$ fees instead of 100 ; the above by way of illustration, as $\frac{7}{8}$ of the land of a fief would (I think) be more than was usually sub-infeuded.

Scutagium and Auxilium.   The subject of escuage is I venture to think but partially understood, nor can the writer pretend to set it forth in a clear light: the author of " Feudal England " has shown how the Church was set to military service *t.* Wm. I.† (see also *Archæologia* 1863 and Steven's Royal Treasury, ed. 1725), and it is here assumed that the more important lay tenants in that reign also held by the divers duties pertaining to same. As may be seen from table (p. 55), there must have been (on the whole) a considerable balance on the dominicum *t.* Hen. I., and the following extracts from the remaining Pipe Roll of that reign seem to apply to commutations of military service, none

---

* 100 Knts., *i.e.*, a " service " of same, indefinite as to nos. and rank.

† Bigelow's *Plac. Ang. Norm.*, ed. 1879, an American work had long before borne witness on this head.

of which (if I have observed rightly) have been thought worthy of mention in the Government index of said vol. Some entries (p. 89) *re* the old aid of the Knights, two of them dating to the time of debtors' fathers ; (p. 132) the *gift* of the Knights of Durham Bishoprick ; (p. 153) the old aid of the Knights, of Baldwin de Redvers; (p. 154) the like of the Bp. of Exeter ; (p. 159) the old aid of the Knights ; (p. 49) the like ; and (p. 84) the old aid of the Knights of Croyland Abbey (see also Scutage Rolls, Bdle. 11, No. 9, where in 48 Hen. III. the Abbot fines in 50 marcs). Again Knight service *t*. Hen. I. is seen in the Peterbro' Chronicle (Camd. Soc. 1849) ; a systematic commutation of lay service *at so much per fee* prior to Hen. II. seems highly probable rather than fully* established ; the author of " Feudal England " (pp. 268-9) has given 2 references under the name of Escuage, the first* of which is reviewed in Vol. II. Red Book Exch. (Pref. Rolls Ser.) ; Madox has given another in his most excellent History of the Exchequer† (p. 435 ed. 1711), and yet a further one may be found in Stephen's Charter tc

---

* The payment of £60 by the Bp. Norwich (40 fees) seems to have no connection with "the Ely contribution" (*Feudal England*, p. 270), and the reference is quite indefinite: but I consider (as a matter of *opinion*), that the entry in *Pipe Roll* 31 Hen. I., refers to a reduction of the Ely "service," memory of which is preserved in the copy of the Charter, as cited, p. 268, *Feudal England*.

† *Westminster MSS.*: Mandate of H. the King to Wm. Const. of Chester that the Monks of Westminster should hold Peritona (D. B. 247b, under that Abbey), as free from escuage, etc., as the father of said Wm. first conceded same to them.

6

Fountains (1135), as to the authenticity of which no comment is here made. I would here remark that altho' *auxilium* and *scutagium* present different ideas to the modern historical critic, they can sometimes be shown to be terms synonymous ; and as unfortunately the scribes of elder times were debarred from having any conception of the precise meaning of technical terms in the 20th century, latter day students might with becoming humility endeavour to attain the exact usage of words when they were written. Thus the aid to ransom Ric. I. is a Scutage in the Pipe Rolls, and quite properly so called by Alex. de Swereford : likewise the aid to marry (of 19 Hen. III.) is called both *auxilium* and *scutagium :* the writ is printed in Brady and *Select Charters* (p. 364) and reference to the Testa de Nevill will (I think) plainly demonstrate the object of the collection, and the use of either term —indeed the writ itself mentions the aid, subsequently calling same the aforesaid escuage ; and further the Scutage of Gascony is distinctly called an aid on p. 412 of the Testa de N. ; reference to the same vol. (pp. 166, 169, 257-8, 263-6, 277, 349, and 416 with 357 for W. Patric's Charter), and collation with the writ, noting the dates and tax per fee, should put the matter beyond question.

Early evidence, of feudal obligations, defective.

I do not think, there is in the Pipe Rolls existing prior to 14 Hen. II. any sufficient material to construct even an approximately complete list of the services due by the lay tenants of the Crown ; nor can I find the Exchequer had any ample guide towards assessing the aid of 1168. Now altho' the daughter of Hen. II. was not married till

1168, and the certificates are of 1166, there can be
no particular improbability in supposing that the
marriage of the Princess Matilda might be in con-
templation prior to the former date, and also that
the Crown might think it prudent to have some
definite information from their lay tenants, which
views are by some considered as antiquated. In
1109 Hen. I. took (Hen. de Huntingdon) 3s. per
Hide to marry his daughter : if this is an exact
statement, a larger sum (presuming the demesne
Hides taxed), would be raised than from the tax
on the fee in 1168 ; and strengthens the belief
that the lay aids of Hen. I. differed considerably
from the escuages Hen. II. to Hen. III. After 1166, Military
and during the reign of Hen. II. it would appear Service.
that usually the tenant in chief either went on
the expedition, compounded by substitutes or
money to furnish them, or paid escuage : it is
difficult to see how the heading (Pipe Roll 18
Hen. II.) *De Scutagiis militum qui nec abierunt in
Hyberniam, nec milites, nec denarios illuc miserunt**
followed by lists of capital tenants either owing or
liberating into the Treasury could refer to anything
else than scutage quitted at a fixed rate per fee.
The editor of the Red Book (Rolls Ser.) seems to
think otherwise and that the assessment (Vol. II.,

---

* Perhaps the best evidence of early fines might be suggested from this heading, unless the "auxilium militum" of
31 Hen. I., or the promise of *servientes* (Pipe R. 11 Hen. II.),
or the *dona t.* Hen. II. are regarded in that light : an instance
of escuage being paid into the wardrobe at Worcester (one of
the places to which the "army of Wales" was summoned)
occurs on Cl. i. 572, 7 Hen. III.

p. clviii) of escuage might be to enable the lord to justice his men, which appears scarcely applicable above, nor has he cited any fines "lest they transit" in this reign. Information is needed as to the difference in obligation of church and lay barons, also to what countries the capital tenants owed to go, in what cases there was option of escuage; the obligations of the mesne tenants to their lords, as regards scutage and service, and in what fees the latter were bound to act at their own charges. The author of "Feudal England" has cited the case of the Edmondsbury tenants *t.* Ric. I., and the course taken by the Abbot thereanent; the following illustrate the feudal service of the House at Peterboro', who ought as by 60 fees:

How performed by Peterbro' Abbey.

3 John. The Abbot pays 120 marcs, and owes a palfrey, for army of Normandy of A² 2. (*Rot. Canc.*)

2 Hen. III. May come with 30 Knts., (Stamford), Newark (Scut. Rolls ¹⁄₁).

5 Hen. III. Has escuage of fees held of him—Biham (*Cl.* i. 475*a*).

7 Hen. III. Had 6 Knights by precept and to have ½ his scutage—Montgomery [¹⁄₃¹ Esc. Rolls].

1229. Seems to have paid esc.—Kery : *C. Pet.*

1230, 14 Hen. III. The Abbot fines in 100 marcs and pays 180 m. of scutage, for the Brittany *exercitus*; scutage 3 m. per fee, *to* our 1st passage. (*Chron. Pet.*)

1230, 15 Hen. III. Pays 180 marcs scutage (*C. P.*) *after* first passage.

1235, 19 Hen. III. The Abbot returns 63½ fees, pays on 60, and is debited for 3½. (Testa de N., p. 38.)

29 Hen. III. r. s. 60 fees performed by 1 Knt., 8 *servientes* (*Rot. Mar.*); quit by writ of 40 fees (30 Hen. III., *Pipe*); pays 60 *marcs* escuage (3 *m.* per fee, hence on 60 *less* 40 fees), army and scutage of Gannock (*Hist. Pet.*).

29 Hen. III. Pays 60 *m.* only (2 *m.* per fee), to the aid to marry (*Hist.*).

1264. The Abbot's Knts., joining the Barons, he pays 300 *m.* (and 30 *m.* queen gold), for defect of service, and transgression—after Lewes he has to fine with the Barons (*Hist.*; *vide etiam* p. 93 under 49 Hen. III., where the entry above seems to be given in a different way).

1265. After Evesham, the Abbot pays the King 500 *m.*, the Queen 50 *m.*, Prince Edw. 300 *m.*, and also to others (*Hist.*, see also note, p. 100).

1277, 5 Ed. I. The Abbot fines in 250 marcs for 5 fees, and 25 m. Queen's gold, for the first Welsh war, his tenants having declined to go except at the Abbot's costs. (*Chron. Pet.*)

1278, 6 Ed. I. The King conceded scutage at 40s. per fee, or the above war, which the Sheriff was to cause the Abbot to have. (*Chron. Pet.*)

1282, 10 Ed. I. The Abbot fines for the 2nd Welsh war, at the same rate as in 1277, and has acknowledgement of receipt of fine 10 Jan., *11 Ed. I.* (*Chron. Pet.*)

1285, 13 Ed. I. The King in Parliament concedes scutage *re* above, at 40s. per fee, and the Sheriff has a writ, 7 July, 13 Ed. I. to cause Abbot to have same. (*Chron. Pet.*)

28 Ed. I. The Abbot fines in £200, and £20 Queen gold; Scotland (*Hist.*), for rates per fee, see pp. 94-5.

31 Ed. I. Fines £100, and £10 Queen gold ; Scotland (*Hist.*).

34 Ed. I. Fines 100*m.*, and 10*m.* Queen gold (*Hist.*)

4 Ed. II. Fines £200 for 5 fees, and £20 Queen gold, and finds 100 *m.* of provender (for the army of Scotland), which he has to carry [*Sc. Rot.* $\frac{11}{9}$, and *Hist.* ; see also note p. 100].

15 Ed. II. Gives 200 *m.* of subsidy to repress Thos., Earl Lancaster's rebellion (*Hist.*).

16 Ed. II. Fines in £200, and £20 Queen gold, Scotland—no general levy of escuage (*Sc. Kot.* $\frac{11}{9}$, and *Hist.*).

1 Ed. III. Fines in £100, and £10 Queen gold, Scotland (*Hist.*).

16 Ed. II. The Abbot fines in £200 for 5 fees (for the Scotch *exercitus* presumably)—no general levy of escuage. (*Sc. Rot.* $\frac{11}{9}$.) ∞

now it will be observed that the Edwardian fines are not based on the " service," and it may also be noted the fine with escuage was under 5 *m.* per fee in 14 Hen. III., 1230, whereas it was but about £1 per fee 5 and 10 Ed. I. (by theory at least) as some 175 marcs should accrue on either occasion, as his escuage—the money received by the Crown being much the same as in 1230. The Exch. Common Roll 17 Ed. III. (cited both by Brady and Madox) gives the case of the Prior of Coventry who Prior of *t.* Ed. I., and *t.* Ed. II. fined for 2 fees (service 10); Coventry's case. both these authors observe the Prior's Plea was false, but neither of them record judgment: certain it is many capital tenants fined just in the same way as the Prior, and it is difficult to suppose any systematic deception could have taken place with the evidence then on record in the Pipe Rolls. The charter of the Prior of Coventry to the King (aid to marry 1235) is on p. 94 of the *T. de N.*, and an inquisition of his fees in Warwick and Leicester (p. 97) in 1242 follows; in 1166 he had $7\frac{5}{6}$ of old and $2\frac{1}{6}$ fees in demesne: the King's advocates either could not or would not answer the Prior's argument which appears to be entirely misapprehended by both the distinguished authors citing the case—what the Prior pleads is that he and *his tenants* paid on 10 fees to two aids to marry, and that his certificate of 1166 duly acknowledges 10 fees as by him and his tenants, but that he held by the service of 2 fees only, and challenges any recorded proof to the contrary— none produced. This probably refers to the $2\frac{1}{6}$ fees in demesne, for which the Prior fined (*i.e.*, 2 as above), or in other words his service was 10, two of which he recognised *in exercitu* (*e.g.*, a Marshal's Roll showing the Prior had sent 10 knights would have shown the Crown to be seized of the " service " of 10 fees in the Prior's sense, but seemingly was not so found), noting that the defendant used the term " service " with a different meaning than that which is attached to it in modern writings (including this chapter). Now if the lord could compel his men always to do corporal service at their or even his own costs, he would not have paid exemplary fines, and it is certain that nothing *Escuage* more than scutage could be had (and that sometimes tenants. with difficulty or not at all) from some of the mesne tenants; but I have not found that it was the more *usual* practice both to fine and concede scutage to the Crown. From the Church often something more than her service seems to have been expected, but from Hen. II. to 1 Ed. III. many lay capital tenants appear to have escaped by

paying or owing escuage. Madox in his chapter
on Escuage cites (I think) but 4 cases of actual
disseisin ; such however was common enough, and
no one acquainted with the records of John and
Hen. III. will consider amplification needful : it
may just be noted that *disseisin* was not disherison, *Disseisin.*
and often appears to have been a mere formal
process of taking possession on account of the unsatisfied claim of the Crown to the tenant's corporal service, or its pecuniary unpaid equivalent ;
the malevolence of the King being averted, and
seisin recovered when the tenant came to terms on
the matter.   In and prior to Hen. I. forfeiture
seems to have been frequent, but the attentive
reader of History must have often observed that
traitors and rebels by no means necessarily lost
their estates (even temporarily), and frequently,
having been disinherited, regained them in their
own persons (or by their heirs)—nor must it be
supposed that *disseisin** was the inevitable sequence
of failure to attend the royal summons (bearing in
mind that records do not show that half the Crown
capital tenants had usually a direct summons), *e.g.,*
P. Writs 30 Ed. I. where Jo. *f.* Reginald is directed
to proceed against the Scots, having previously *per
diversas vices* neglected to obey such summons,
and again 13 Ed. II. (*P. W.*) when the King states
that "very many of our realm" who should have
done service in the army of his *fourth* year, neither
did it, nor fined, which is to be compared with the
already cited heading in Pipe 18 Hen. II., and the
nec ierant nec miserunt of Walt. Coventry in 1213.

---

* For an early instance of, see p. 105.

That the undertenant (John-Ed. II.) was more frequently of pecuniary than personal assistance seems to be supported by evidence as known— Prof. Maitland cites the legal view of a Knt. failing to do service *t*. Hen. I. (*Chron. Abingdon*, ii., 128); the Earl of Chester's Knts. are to be compelled to render him service (presumably partly or wholly of a corporal nature) in 10 John (*Pat. Rot.*); and a tenant's superior lord is to have full *seizin* if former is unwilling to transit for him in 14 John (*Cl. Rot.*);—nevertheless it is apparent enough that of very many mesne tenants there is no further obligation to their lord than to pay escuage, however they may stand to the Crown in the matter of fealty, as if I have rightly observed, they would be a class liable for summons amongst the *iurati ad arma*.

In the Scutage Rolls (*Chanc. Misc.* $\frac{11}{18}$) in 10 Ed. III. is a mandate to the Sheriff of Yorks to cease distraint on the Luterell estates, because by the Rolls of the Marshal *t*. Ed. I. it appears that Ro. Luterell, deceased, had his service for 2 fees which he acknowledged, in 5 Ed. I. in the 1st Welsh war; hence it appears that the Scutage due in 1278 was still owing to the Crown in 1316-17,[*]

Inade-
quacy of
Scutage
entries in
Pipe Rolls,
t. Ed. I.

[*] It seems clear that the notes as to tenants in 1278 (*Pipe Roll* 7 Ed. I. *Ebor.*) are indefinite, as some had, and others had not done service in the war of 5 Ed. I., but Ric. de Malebisse who had been summoned to perform military service in person (Muster at Worcester 5 Ed. I.) does not acknowledge nor fine for same, but is noted in the 7 Ed. I. Pipe Roll, as paying 40s. scutage for 1 fee (which was held of the Hon. of Eye). Again Peter de Mauley did his service,

and further that when Scutage was assized, it might be collected either for the tenant or the King. Turning to the Pipe Roll 7 Ed. I. Yorks, the Scutage of Wales was assized at 40s. (£20 seems to have been actually paid then) whereof Ro. Luterell is noted with £25 for 12½ fees, with a reference to the last Welsh Scutage, *i.e.*, 42 Hen. III. at a similar rate : the names seem to have been copied from a former roll or rolls with alterations of Christian names (thus Ro. Luterell succeeded in 5 Ed. I., his grandfather Andrew being tenant in 42 Hen. III.), and hence in 10 Ed. III. it might well appear that the executors of the said Ro. stood charged with the Escuage of 1278. Now it may be remarked that the Luterell property ought the

Double meaning of "Service," illustrated by the Luterell case.

acknowledging 2 fees, (appearing in person with another Knight at the Muster at Rhuddlan 10 Ed. I.) : nevertheless both in the Pipe Rolls of 10 and 14 Ed. II. he is debited with £63 scutage for that particular campaign : his service being 31½ fees, as he inherited the estates of Wm. Forsard who rendered that number (Pipe Roll 14 Hen. II., *Ebor.*). Most of those capital tenants specially summoned for the 5 Ed. I. Welsh war, from Yorkshire [unlike the total for England, where about half of all specially warned neither come, send, nor fine—*Marshal's* Roll 1277] fine, or " make," or " have," but there are no writs of quittance noted on the Pipe Rolls of 5, 6, or 7 Ed. I. *re* this army ; that King however seems not to have effectively pressed the collection of escuage (see Parl. Writs *t.* Ed. II.), and as shown in the Luterell case, such was being collected in 10 Ed. III. Edward II. collected or attempted to collect the escuages of Ed. I.—most of the Yorkshire entries (Pipe Rolls 7 and 13 Ed. I.) give no further information than the number of fees each tenant had (the Welsh war of 10 Ed. I. is the last of which any regular entry of escuage is made for this county), and could be but of slight use as a guide to what was due to the Crown.

service of 12½ fees and recognised such by 2 knights in the King's army, and that said fees were those for which Ro. de Gant sent in a Charter in 1166 ; in 1168 (being one of the eleven exceptions) he *rendered*17, but paid then on 12½ only, and is not on the rolls till 2 Ric. I. when the fee is given as 12½ (see p. 77 "Red Book" Vol. I., likewise in 6 and 8 Ric. I., 1 and 13 John), also 38 Hen. III. where account is rendered by the Sheriff of £25 of 12½ fees of Andrew Luterel, of Maurice de Gaunt, in the aid to Knight Prince Edward.

The following illustrations save where otherwise stated are from Madox's "Hist. of the Exchequer":

Examples from *Madox*, etc.

18 Hen. II. Glastonbury Abbey in the hands of the King : therefore unrecognised fees paid.

7 Ric. I. Ro. de. St. John *r.c.* 15 marcs, lest he transit, and to have escuage of 1 fee.

7 Ric. I. Matilda Countess of Warwick *r.c.* 40 *m.*, lest she send Knights o'er sea, and to have escuage of 15 fees. [Scutage £1 per fee.]

8 Ric. I. Bp. Coventry *r.c.* £25 lest etc., and to have escuage of 15 fees of the Bprick and 10 of the Priory [seems an even fine].

1 John. Ro. de Turevil *r.c.* 5 m. for ½ fee which he holds in demesne, lest he *transfret* with horses and arms.

1 John. Hen. de Witefeld owes 4 m. lest etc., who holds ¼ fee in demesne.

1 John. Geoff. de Mandeville who holds in demesne 1 fee *r.c.* £5 lest etc., and to have scutage of said demesne.

3 John. Ric. Descrupes owes £5 for 3 fees, lest, etc.

12 John. Earl Clare *r.c.* 500 m. for his passage, Ireland, (and is quit of escuage, *Pipe* 13 John).

14 Hen. III. Fines and Scutages (3 marcs per fee) for the King's first passage to Brittany :
    Abbot Evesham *r.c.* £20 for passage, and for scutage of 4½ fees

Abbot Pershore *r.c.* £10 for passage, and for scutage of 2 fees.

Abbot Abbotsbury *r.c.* £5 for passage, and for scutage of 1 fee.

Abbot Westminster *r.c.* 100 marcs of fine for scutage of 15 fees.

Abbot Michelney *r.c.* 3 *m.* by the Sheriff for 1 fee.

Abbot Cerne *r.c.* £5 for passage and scutage of 1 fee ; *r.c.* £2 of scutage of 1 fee, for which he did not fine.

Bp. of Bath (20 fees) gave £120 of aid, partly pardoned.

Prior of Coventry *r.c.* 35 m. for his passage and to have escuage of his 10 fees.

Ro. de *Novo Burgo r.c.* 20 m. for his passage, saving to the King, scutage of his 15 fees.

18 Hen. III. The Bp. London *r.c.* 60 *m.* of fine to be quit of sending Knights, and to have his escuage, and should the King pardon scutage to any of the Bp's Knights, same to be allowed for in the fine [20 fees].

20 Hen. III. Re exceptional grant by ecclesiastics of an aid of 2 marcs per fee as well those usually answerable to escuage, as others retained to their own use ; not to be prejudicial on future occasions ; (refers to the aid to marry, and is from record citing it).

27 Hen. III. Receipt of 50 marcs subsidy of the Abbot of Hyde in consideration of which he will respond for escuage of 15 instead of 20 fees.

7 Ed. I. The Bp. Lincoln fines in £80 for 5 fees (service 60) which he recognised for 1st Welsh war.*

7 Ed. I. Order to levy scutage of 40s. per fee from capital tenants, etc., *re* above.

27 Ed. I. 2 cases of quittance of escuage of capital tenants for army of 5 Ed. I. who respectively "had," and fined for service : (*Lancs. Lay Sub.*).

31 Ed. I. (Brady Vol. I. Hist. p. 120) Hen. de Perci who was in the Scotch expedition of 31 Ed. I., to have £2 per fee scutage.

31 Ed. I. (Brady, *ibid.*) Hen. de Lacy to have £2 from each

---

* *Hist. Exch.*, p. 460, *ed.* 1711 ; *cf.* Peterboro' Abbey, 5 Ed. I., already cited, p. 84.

of his fees, as he was in the King's service nego-
tiating in France, during the *exercitus* of 31 Ed. I.

34 Ed. I. Similar order to last, *re* Scotch expedition.

9 Ed. II. 4 cases of distraint of escuage on mesne tenants
for armies of 28, 31, and 34 Ed. I. ; mandate that
same should cease, unless at aforesaid time the lord
of said mesnes was within age, and in the King's
hands.

9-12 Ed. II. Two cases showing that in this reign the
tenant of an honour was bound to give scutage, but
not to do corporal service.

10 Ed. II. Debts of Scotch expeditions of 28, 31, and 34
Ed. I. to be collected at the rate of £2 per fee as
scutage, and enquiry as to capital tenants, escheats,
honors, perquisites, wards, and vacant ecclesiastical
holdings—reference to above in a mandate to the
Commissioners.

15 Ed. II. Summons for an expedition against the Scots, in
which ecclesiastics, widows, and other women are
to be allowed to *fine* at £40 per *fee*.

20 Ed. III. (Brady, Vol. I. App. pp. 86-8) Expenses of
the army of this year, showing its composition,
wages, etc., (a Knight 2s. per day).

Payment
of Scutage.
Now it seems clear that it was easier to pay
Escuage than to fine, and certain tenants appear to
have escaped by the former plan : why some should
stand as quit paying or owing scutage is difficult
to discern, further than on such general grounds as
expediency, negligence, favoritism, relative strength
of the Crown, abilities of tenants, etc., bearing in
mind that wards, escheats, perquisites, honors, and
vacant bishopricks explain the matter in many (but
certainly not all) cases. The following references
are mainly from original matter at the Record
Office, dealing with the final period (up to
1 Ed. III.) beyond which I do not find any notice
of a general levy of scutage in England ; **as**

Madox's Hist. Exch. and Parl. Writs (the only works assaying satisfactory illustration), do not bring the History of Escuage quite to a close :

29 Hen. III. Aid granted 1242, £1 per fee, to marry the King's daughter noted for Yorks in the Pipe Roll, on basis of render of 1168. {Examples from *MSS.*, mostly unprinted.}

38 Hen III. Aid to knight Prince Edward, noted on Pipe Roll, at £2 per fee, generally on same basis as above though theoretically on "old" and "new" feoffment.

42 Hen. III. Escuage for Welsh war, at 40s. per fee, noted for Yorks on Pipe Roll, same basis as above, *i.e.*, *render* of 1168.

49 Hen. III. Chanc. Misc. *Bdle 11, No. 9.* Fines for services due to the King in his army *anno* 48 ; totalling £1,302 10s. ; (*c.* 68 entries) thus :

Abbot Glastonbury	...	60 marcs.
„ Abingdon ...	...	60 „
„ Hyde	...	50 „
„ Croyland ...	...	50 „
Thos. Kyn'	...	40 „
Chapter of Lincoln	...	40 „
Bp. Salisbury	...	50 „
Bp. Durham	...	100 „
Abb. Peterbro' (as well for service as of his gift)	...	300 „

5 Ed. I. (Chanc. Misc. $\frac{11}{18}$) Order to Sheriff of Yorks in 10 Ed. III., to release distraint on Luterell estates for scutage of 5 Ed. I., as Ro. Luterell dec<u>d</u> then had his service for 2 fees.

7 Ed. I. Scutage of Wales assissed at 40s. per fee with reference to 42 Hen. III. ; a list of most of the Yorkshire capital tenants, some of whom fined, *had* or *did* service, but nothing to indicate this on the roll, the names being proper to 7 Ed. I., and not to 42 Hen. III. ; £20 paid ; the fees on basis of 1168.

10 Ed. I. ($\frac{11}{9}$ *Sc. Rot.*) Fines for army of Wales ; *c.* 90 entries.

14 Ed. I. Another list, presumably of the second Welsh war, on same basis as *7 Ed. I.* ; both Yorks *Pipe Rolls*.

28 Ed. I. ($\frac{11}{9}$ *Sc. Rot.*)   Fines for army of Scotland, at 40 li. per fee—total £1,975 6s. 8d. in *c.* 15 entries.

28, 31, 34 Ed. I. Lay Subs., $\frac{141}{1}$. Collection of escuage (Middlesex) at the rate of 40s. per fee for the armies summoned for Carlisle (28 Ed. I.), Berwick-on-Tweed (31 Ed. I.) and Carlisle (34 Ed. I.), seemingly paid by undertenants.

28 and 34 Ed. I. King's writ in 4 Ed. III. to the Sheriff of Westmorland that the executors of Marmaduke Twenge deceased (who was with the lord Edward grandfather of the now King in the Scotch expeditions) should have scutage, at 40s. per fee, both for 28 and 34 Ed. I.

31 Ed. I. ($\frac{11}{9}$ *Sc. Rot.*)   Fines for Berwick army at 20 *li.* per fee—total £1,777 1s. 8d. in *c.* 32 entries—thus Archbp. of York (service 20), £100 for 5 fees.

34 Ed. I. ($\frac{11}{9}$ *Sc. Rot.*)   Fines for Carlisle army at 20 marcs per fee—total £1,881 0s. 0$\frac{1}{2}$d. or more, in *c.* 69 entries.

34 Ed. I. (*Chanc. Misc.* $\frac{11}{18}$) Writ in 5 Ed. III., that whereas Wm. la Zouche fined for his service in Scotland 34 Ed. I., said Wm. to have scutage at the rate of 40s. per fee.

34 Ed. I. (Yorks *Pipe Roll*) The Archbp. York fines in 100 marcs for 5 fees which he recognises : notes of presumed debts of Welsh scutage.

35 Ed. I., 1 Ed. II. Like entries as to Welsh scutage on Yorks *Pipe Roll.*

4 Ed. II. (*Chanc. Misc.* $\frac{11}{18}$) Writ of 2 Ed. III. to the Sheriff of Surrey and Sussex to the effect that, whereas our father (Ed. II.) by divers writs, commanded that our beloved Abbot of Hyde, who had his service in Scotland (4 Ed. II.), etc., should have escuage at the rate of 2 marcs per fee, and that as said Abbot has informed us that same has not been levied, etc.—to cause said Abbot to have, etc.

4 Ed. II. (*ibid.*) Writ in 4 Ed. III. to the Sheriff of Lancs that executors of Marm. de Twenge deceased, should have escuage.

4 Ed. II. (*ibid.*) Writ in 5 Ed. III. to Sheriff of Somerset to cause Wm. la Zouche to have escuage *re* 4 Ed. II.

4 Ed. II (*Subs.* $\frac{91}{5}$) Derby ; collectors' accounts of escuage, presumably from undertenants, at the rate of 2 marcs per fee.

4 Ed. II. (*Sc. Rot.* $\frac{11}{9}$) 9 entries of fines at £40 *per* fee for army of Scotland.

6 Ed. II. (*ibid.*) Fines for respite from service ; *c.* 52 entries.

6-7 Ed. II. (*Chanc. Misc. Bdle.* 11, *No.* 9) Fines thus : Jollan de Nevill 40s. for respite of service due from 1 fee till the Nativity of St. John the Baptist : Aucher *f*. Hen. recognises the service of ½ fee, and makes fine (*see* '*P. W.*).

7 Ed. II. ($\frac{11}{9}$ *Sc. Rot.*) Fines for army of Berwick, at 20 marcs per fee ; *c.* 40 entries.

8-11 Ed. II. (*Chanc. Misc. Bdle* 11, *No.* 15) Roger de Mortimer, who was with the King, etc., to have his scutage.

10 Ed. II. (Yorks *Pipe Roll*) Notes of presumed debts of 2 Welsh scutages of Ed. I. ; Geoff. Luterell pays £25 for 12½ fees, for the 2$\underline{^{nd}}$ scutage, for his father deceased ; it is interesting to note that Ro. Luterel acknowledged 2 fees in 5 Ed. I., and did his service ; in 10 Ed. I. he was summoned, and clearly seems not to have appeared nor fined (there are many writs *t.* Ed. II. stating that as tenant had fined he is not to be distrained for scutage, *or* to have his escuage), his son paying the scutage on 12½ (not 2) fees, 35 years later.

13 Ed. II. ($\frac{11}{9}$ *Sc. Rot.*) 5 fines for army of York at £20 *per* fee.

14 Ed. II. (Yorks *Pipe Roll*) Entries of presumed debts of escuage for the 2 Welsh wars of the last reign, on basis of 1168.

16 Ed. II. ($\frac{11}{9}$ *Sc Rot.*) £580 fines for army of Newcastle at £40 *per* fee :

			£
Bp. Bath and Wells ...	...		80
,, Chichester	...	...	100
,, Winchester	...	...	200
Abbot Peterbro'	...	...	200

1, 2, 3 Ed. III. No entries as to escuage found on Yorks *Pipe Roll*.

1 Ed. III. (*Chanc. Misc.* $\frac{11}{18}$) Writ of 11 Ed. III. to Sheriff of Somerset to cause Abbot of Glastonbury to have his scutage for fine made for service in Scotland 1 Ed. III.

1 Ed. III. (*Subs.* $\frac{202}{38}$) Account of collectors of the E.R. Yorks (in or after 13 Ed. III.) as to escuage of 1 Ed. III., showing that nothing had been levied, the King having stopped levying till further demand.

1 Ed. III. ($\frac{11}{9}$ *Sc. Rot.*) £778 fines for army of Newcastle, at £20 per fee ; in *c.* 26 entries.

12 Ed. III. (*Jones' Index*, citing *Hil.* 12 Ed. III. *Mem.*) Jo. *f.* Ro. de Ros to be attached for view of account of scutage.

12 Ed. III. L.T.R. Mem. Commission to collect scutage of 1 Ed. III.

12 Ed. III. Fœdera. To defer collection of above scutage till further orders (1338).

20 Ed. III. (Chanc. Misc. Bdle 11. No. 19) Fines thus : Ric. de Goldesbrough *miles*, for 5 marcs for expenses of 1 hobelar ; Humph. de Bassingbourn *miles* 26 m. for expenses of 2 men at arms and 1 hobelar —but no note of fees, being assessed on value p. a. of land or rents, commencing at £5 (one archer).

9 Ric. II. Parl. Roll. Petition (granted) that no escuage shall be challengeable on account of the King's 1st expedition to Scotland.

1372. (Fœdera). The Irish Exch. Barons not to exact scutage from persons whose possessions are held by the rebels.

There is no evidence of any general levy of escuage (*ut credo*), in England, after *t.* Ed. III., but there is not infrequent mention of it in the Rolls of Parliament, and some evidence of its existence as a rent charge*—however scutage was not abolished in 1641, when the House of Com-

its extinc-
tion in the
17th
century.

---

* *Inter alia :* Wm. Angevyn held $\frac{1}{2}$ the Manor of Hebden of the Abbot of Fountains by homage, fealty, scutage, and a rent of 8s. p. a.—I.P.M. 15 Hen. VII.

mons were to take it into consideration, possibly
in alarm lest it might be utilised to meet the
exigencies of their unfortunate monarch, who is
reported to have been benefited to the extent of
£100,000, or £173,537 9s. 6d., by the compositions
for Knighthood of the 40 librate holders.*

The popular idea of the *servitium debitum* is Popular
clearly stated by J. A. C. Vincent (*Lancs. Lay* theory of
Subs., p. 116), in his expansion of a writ of *exercitu.*
military summons, to wit, *in the proportion of one
Knight to each fee*, whereas the mandate requires
habeant ibi pro se servicium suum nobis debitum ;—
the simplicity of a theory asking credence for the
muster of the whole Knight Service of the
kingdom to a particular place on a given day
one very much admires at. Like views appear
to be expressed in *Feudal England* (pp. 270-1,
J. H. Round), and p. 292 where that author Unanimity
labours hard to equate a scutage of 2 *marcs* per there-
fee with the service of a Knight for 40 days ; in anent.
the excellent work of the Bishop of Oxford (*Const.
Hist.* i. 589) ;† and also in *The Scutage and*

---

* Archæologia, 1863.
† It would of course be impossible for any author to
fathom every detail in so vast and laborious a work as that
under note ; at the same time a levy of one-third of the
milites by *tenure*, would be (I think), as large a proportion as
ever recorded ; the chronicler himself styles it *maximam
expeditionem, ita ut duo milites de tota Anglia tertium pararent
ad opprimendum Galenses* (*Chron. Norm.* p. 993, *Duchesne*),
and it must be remembered that King John, when raising the
country to resist invasion, ordered *quod novem milites per totam* Quotas of
Angliam invenient decimum militem, and in 4 northern counties service.
a portion of this quota ($\frac{1}{10}$) was to be retained to guard their

Knight Service in England (p. 108, J. F. Baldwin), which is perhaps the best modern work on the feudal system of this country.

Certain it is the Abbots of Evesham, Ramsey, and St. Albans, and the Bishop of Durham did all, and sometimes more (the two latter) than the same service for which they responded to escuage—but what evidence remains (by no means inconsiderable), demonstrates that most of the ecclesiastics and laymen did very much less. At the siege of Calais (when conditions had entirely changed), there were perhaps at most* *1,063* English Earls, Bannerets, and Knights, with some *3,000* esquires (in feudal language *c.* 2,500 fees), all at wages [*vide MS. Harl.* 3,968, which is fuller than the *Heralds' Coll.* copy printed in *Creci and Calais*]; and a professional writer [the Hon. Gen.

own parts (*Pat. Rot.* 6 John). The same author (Ro. de Monte, *ut sup. Chron. Norm.*) gives the interesting reference (*vide* Duchesne, 995), cited in *Feudal England* (p. 280) whose author suggests the chronicler is at fault, as the escuage represented but a minority of the fees : the available records do not demonstrate that at this period the Exchequer were seized of any evidences which would enable its Barons to form a competent conception of the number of fees held by the lay Crown tenants ; it would seem probable that many records perished *t.* Stephen, as when ancient evidences are called for of a general nature, the Crown instructs its officers to produce Domesday Book, and the Barons' Certificates, so that apparently these were all the records to hand.

* This estimate of course includes all the English *men at arms* present whether Crown tenants or not : some of them presumably had no landed property whatsoever—cf. *chescun Esquier nient possessionez des terres, rent, ne chateaux, q'est en service ou ad este armez* [2 Ric. II.].

Army of Calais, A.D. 1346.

Wrottesley], states this to have been the most complete expedition despatched from England till the 19th century.

In 14 Hen. II. and 38 Hen. III. are some 11 and 9 cases of services of upwards of 100 fees (to escuage), and yet one thinks the authors of the accepted theory of all the feudal *milites** doing service together in the same army would be particularly distressed to *prove* an actual service in the army of *20* fees even in *5* cases, or of *40*, *50*, or *100* fees in any single case whatsoever: *40* may have been a possible number, as the Earl of Salisbury allows such to be his debt *in exercitu* in 1166 (fees to scutage 56⅘ and 55¼, 18 Hen. II. and 38 Hen. III.)—but the Baronial Charters themselves often furnish undeniable witness that the services are of divers natures. There is fairly ample evidence as to the armies of John and Hen. III., and no lack of same *t*. Ed. I.–II., and in no case† (*ut videtur mihi*) anything approaching 20 *milites* by any baron; nor is it likely that (in the earlier period) all the feudal *milites* could have been entirely withdrawn from the Castles, especially on the Welsh and Scotch borders, thus

Supposed "services," of more than 100 Knights.

Popular theory of Knight Service improbable per se, and lacking support of Records.

---

* *Milites*—a difficult term, Wm. I. to Hen. II., and scarcely quite equivalent to the same *t*. Hen. III. to Ed. I.; in 38 Hen. III. the Bannerets and Bachelors by *tenure* might total 1,000, or *possibly* 1,500;—*t*. Ed. I. there is evidence of a considerable force, including the *vadlets*, *servientes*, or *esquires*, but by far the more part of same *ad vadia nostra*.

† Earl Richard (89 fees *et amplius*) led 20 *milites* and 40 *servientes* (probably archers on foot for the more part) in the army of Wales, (*Pipe Roll*, 11 Hen. II.).

depriving the land of its natural leaders, and tending to place the much decried (C. Oman, M.A., *Art of War*, and Prize College Essay) abilities of our mediæval *capitanei*, more nearly on a level with those of their modern critics.

Now true it is that the wages* of a *miles* for

---

*　The siege of Kenilworth is said to have lasted from June 25 to Dec. 13, 1266 (*Const. Hist.*, ii. 96), and the Abbot of Peterboro' (as other prelates), was summoned for his service (at this period the equivalent of 5 Knts.); the expedition seems to have cost him £124-5 (*Hist. Pet.*), but no definite dates occur save 3 weeks after Aug. 24, and 15 days after Nov. 1—amongst the items are 17 horses *deprædati de pretio* £40, and 10 *loricæ cum toto apparatu de pretio* £15. Later at Shrewsbury are entries of the expenses of brother Wm. Paris, *cum toto servitio*, for 6 weeks, £14 18s. od., and in purchase and repairs of arms £6 14s. od.; in 4 *Ed. II.* the King wrote to the Abbot (*vide Hist.*) for his service for Scotland (suppose 5 *milites*) whereupon he sent him Wm. de la Zouche (*miles*), with horses and arms, at a cost exceeding 60 *marcs*, but *nihil placuit regi*, so the Abbey fines for 5 fees in £200, etc. (see p. 85).　The cost of a hired Knt. would to some extent be regulated by the fines to the Crown, to knowledge of which the contracting parties could be no strangers—thus in 1284, the Abbot of St. Augustine's (scutage service, 15) arranged with Wm. de Cobeham (*miles*), to quit them of all military service due to the Crown (*sc.* 1 Knt. *in exercitu*, see *Rot. Mar.* 10 Ed. I., and *Chron. W. Thorn*), for £20.　As the fines for this army (Wales) were 50 m. per fee (queen gold 5 m.), it is evident the Abbey saved £16 13s. 4d. by the above pact, but it should be noted that the liabilities (ransom, loss or injury to horses, etc.) of the service would probably fall on Wm. de Cobeham.　The wages of a *miles* at this period were 2s. a day, and apparently rather a mere average equivalent for housing, and provender, in time of war for himself, his *vadlets*, and horses—the King's household and hired Knts. being at the

Expenses of military service.

Bargains with hired Knights ; actual case in 1284, between tenant and *miles*.

40 days at 8d. per day, would be met by an escuage of 2 *m.* per fee, upon which it may be observed, (*a*), that the duration of service *t.* Hen II. (*ut videtur mihi*), is not clearly proven ; (*b*), that 8d. might perhaps on the average defray the daily cost of a *miles*, 2-3 horses, and an attendant or attendants ; (*c*), that it would seem to leave no surplus for casualties—*e.g.* loss of horses, and expenses to and from the place of muster ; and (*d*) that 2 *m.* is the highest scutage, and 8d. the lowest wage *t.* Hen. II., 1 *m.* and 1s. (wage) being also recorded. Further the conventions between Hen. I. and Robt. Earl of Flanders (1101-3) demonstrate that not only did the King agree to pay journeys to and fro, find board and food (*ut credo*, the equivalent of the customary wages), but also to defray all losses, as was customary with the *milites* of his own household : in addition the Earl was to have an annual retainer of 400 *marcs*, for *1,000* milites in England (in case of need), for an undefined period, each *miles* to bring 3 horses.* The editor of the *Red Book Exch. (L. R.* vol. ii.) rates the expenses of Knight Service at 3^{ce} the escuage, but *ut supra*, no proof

Margin notes: Wages of a Knight, *t. Hen. II.* Flemish Conventions, *t. Hen. I.*

Crown's risk as to losses, and in some cases (at any rate), wearing the royal livery, but it seems clear that the liabilities to losses from service *by tenure* would be taken by the tenants themselves.

* *Fœdera ; 500 milites* in 1101, and *1,000* in 1103 ; see also *Pipe* 31 Hen. I., where is some *slight* evidence for supposing the wage of a Knight in a Castle to be 4d. a day (p. 137 *ut sup.*), and *vide Chron Pet.* App. (p. 175) where Vivian (*t.* Hen. I.) ought to be a *miles in exercitu cum ij equis, et suis armis, et abbas inveniet ei alia necessaria.*

(under correction) of time has yet been advanced as to the earlier period in England ; Prof. Maitland remarking this has given the useful reference to a *certain* term (*Rot. Cl.* 14 John, p. 117*b*),

Term of Service. but at the same time it is to be allowed that 40 days is not infrequently named in connexion with small serjeanties and the *iurati ad arma*, and clearly for Knight Service in Normandy *t.* Hen. I., (Bp. Bayeux' fees). Nevertheless it seems almost demonstrable that in 1211 (12 John) certain feudal tenants served far beyond that period ; the royal army being at Pembroke, 16 June ; Waterford, 20 June ; Dublin, 24 August ; and Fishguard (Wales) 2 days later : in this expedition

Prestations. the 1st general prest to feudal tenants was made at Pembroke, 16 June, and the last notable ones at Dublin, 21 August, to some 332 *milites*, and to *c.* 116 more next day : altho' many of these advances (to *milites*) are indefinite, some, up to the close of the period, are stated to be on their demesne (or that of their lord),—in the case of Flemish Knights, on their fees. It may be remarked that Earl David (Hunts) had an advance (prest) as late as Aug. 24, and that in 14 Hen. III. (Bain's *Scotch Cal.* citing *L. T. R. Mem.*) his successor Earl John accounts for and is pardoned £80 of the prest of Ireland *t.* John—the former

Army of Ireland, 1211. Earl had 10 *milites* in the Irish army, likewise the Earls of Hereford and Essex (the Justiciar), but this is the highest number there recorded :* in

---

* It should be scarcely necessary to observe these Earls had more than 10 fees each—prests occur in the Pipe Roll 31 Hen. I. as being accounted for at the Exch., and it is

the reigns of Ed. I. and II. it is certain that
40 days is the accredited term, and appears to 40 days.
have been in 50 Hen. III. (*Pat. Rot.*) when
5 northern Barons are acquitted of further service
on that ground.

The Inquisitions of Normandy (1177-1189) Normandy
perhaps show a service to the King of *c. 652* fees tions.
from a total of *c. 1,830* fees [the record gives 581
from *c.* 1500,] some of the royal service being in
castleguard—in either case about a third of the
total, the balance presumably serving *in nummis*,
and guarding the baronial castles, which in a
certain sense are those of the King and Duke
[Hen. II.]: the earlier return of the Bishop of
Bayeux is similar, 40 knights doing service
40 days (to Hen. I.), for 120 fees.[*]

The massed capital (*c.* 1400) and undertenants
(7,871, *Ellis*), in D. B. yield **9,271** *in toto;* of
these most of the immediate and many of the
mediate ones can in no sense be regarded as holding by Knight Service : the number of *milites* Milites in
(Ellis) is **137**, but this is a most delusive return ; Domesday.

---

clear that some had been made to English *milites* for the army
of Normandy, 2 *John* (*Rot. Canc.* 3 John).

[*] The whole service due to the Duke is here stated as
774 *milites* [*Feudal England*, p. 292, citing date as 1171, and
Liber Rubeus, vol. ii., p. 647, under date *c.* 1133, noting that
the total (774) is *not* in the original], but this seems to have
been an error of the transcriber, produced perhaps by adding
the service (*c.* 652) of *t.* Hen. II. (including the Bayeux fees)
to the latter total (120) *t.* Hen. I. : it may be noted that the
Bishop had 120 fees at either date *ad servitium suum*, and is
returned as owing 40 *milites* to the Duke *t.* Hen. I., and
20 *t.* Hen. II.

as "Knights" occur also amongst the capital and undertenants : there are certainly upwards of **700** (it is impracticable to distinguish duplicates) men, to whom D. B., directly or indirectly applies this term (and many more of course of the class, not specified otherwise than by the baptismal or gentilitial names), but some of these are in no sense of the term "Knights," as obviously the *dominæ* do not militate, nor presumably does Wennenc, the priest [D. B., i., 18*a*, *bis vel amplius*], included (I think), amongst Earl Eu's *milites*.

The term therefore in its collective usage may include mere tenants by military service, who cannot be "Knights"; the same application is often to be remarked in the Baronial certificates (including *dominæ*, *monachi*, etc.), of 1166, which yield some 4,000 names, $\frac{2}{5}$ of which hold less than 1 fee ; some of these are entered more than once, and on the other hand the returns are neither definite nor complete: Simon de Beauchamp's charter names 85 tenants on $36\frac{3}{5}$ old fees, and if read (by the letter), *Auxilium,* informs of an aid on the fee *t.* Hen. I. (*i.e.*, scutage *t.* Hen. I. in nature, if not in name),—that all his tenants were *milites t.* Hen. I. or *t.* Hen. II. is improbable.

The Assize of Arms* (1181) *ut videtur mihi*, affects for the more part tenants by Knight Service;

---

* It is presumed that few tenants other than military, and townsmen, would *t.* Hen. II. be assessed at 10 *marcates* of land or goods ; the exceptions perhaps would be tenants in fee farm, retainers attached to important households, and perhaps a few tenants by socage on the ecclesiastical estates, allowing always for considerable intermixture of tenure.   The Assize *t.* John, names tenants of $\frac{1}{2}$ fee, [some of them perhaps equestrian *servientes*] ; most of the Yorkshire subsidy men

(*a*), 1 fee or more ; (*b*), 16 *marcates* of land or goods—say ½ fee ; (*c*), 10 *marcates* of land or goods—say ⅓ fee ; (*d*), all burgesses and *tota communa liberorum hominum* allowing (*d*) to include those holding other than by Knight Service, and in exceptional cases (*b*) and (*c*), and supposing the above classes to furnish the cavalry and heavy armed infantry *t*. Hen. II., and that the *villani* were not to be permitted to have the furniture of freemen.

The author of *The Art of War* lays much stress on the absence of bows and arrows, which is little to the purpose, as the assize *t*. John (*vide Rot. Cl.* 14 Hen. III., *p*. 1, m. 6^{d}) is quite definite on that point—in addition, these weapons are named in the Laws of Hen. I., and it is incredible to hold that the community of chroniclers of divers ages had entered into a pact for a systematic deception of the moderns on that head, and *vide* also *Pipe Rolls t*. Hen. II. as to archers and arrows.

Ordericus Vitalis mentions *feudum militis* as quite early in the 11th cent., thus, *Præfatus* *Decanus ex discipulis Fulberti Carnotensis Epis-* *copi fuit, et ex paterna hereditate feudum militis possedit* with reference to Dean Fulc, whom he terms *silicernius t*. Mainerius (1066-1089), and further (as to military ecclesiastics) continues, *Deinde Presbyteri de stirpe Dacorum litteris tenuiter edocti parrochias tenebant, et arma ferentes laicalem feudum militari famulatu defendebant* — whether or not the Dean of Evreux was classed as a *miles*

[25 Ed. I., No. 16, Yorks *Rec. Ser.*], are rated at less than 20s. of goods, but it is allowed that mediæval assessments are of a *formal* nature.

is left indefinite ; but certain it seems the feudal tenure of Normandy, as portrayed by that author, was the antecessor of that introduced into England.

Milites of Peterboro', *t. Hen. I.* Just as some of the *milites* of D. B. and 1166 are demonstrably and presumably not " Knights," so also in the return of the *milites* of the Abbot of Peterboro' (*Chron. Pet. t.* Hen. I.) occur *sochemanni et serviunt cum militibus*, but it would be hard to credit their appearance as " Knights " *habentes equos*, et *loricas*, et *cassides*, et *clypeos*, et *lanceas*, *in exercitu*, tho' they might very well serve *in nummis*.

Service of Evesham Abbey, *in exercitu.* Without falling back on the writ described as *startling* in *Feudal England* (p. 303) ; the writ, p. 304, *ibid.*, and also in Ellis' *Introd. to D. B.*, vol. ii. (p. 447, ed. 1833) in which the Abbot of Evesham is ordered to lead 5 *milites* [in his charter $4\frac{1}{2}$, and $\frac{1}{2}$ fee new ; returns $4\frac{1}{2}$ fees for scutage (aid) 14 Hen. II., and 38 Hen. III., and recognizes the service of as many *in exercitu*, 5 Ed. I., and 4 Ed. II.], there is no refusing* the conclusion

---

The predecessor of Ranulf Flambard *disseised* for defect of service, *etc.* * The statement that Ranulf Flambard (Bp. Durham), devised feudal service, can obtain but little beyond our halls of learning, for his predecessor temporarily lost that Bprick (1088), in that, after *oral* summons he withdrew himself, and his *milites*, in the King's necessity, *etc.*: this was Bp. Wm. *sancti Carilefi* [the American *Plac. Ang. Norm.*, ed. 1879, cites the case, giving reference, but not identifying the prelate, but *vide* Simeon of Durham], whom Lanfranc proposed to treat after the manner of Bp. Odo *t.* Wm. I.   Indeed strictly contemporary evidence (*Hist. Eccl. Dun.*, written there) renders it clear that Bp. Walcher's neglect in restraining his *milites* led to his death in 1080 : it may be suggested that A.S. history would yield a more suitable range for the *Ymagines Historiarum* of the romantic school, as furnishing for *speculative genius* a scope both ample and comparatively secure.

that certain capital tenants enfeoffed *milites t.*
Wm. I., and hence themselves had been infeuded
for their homage and service.

This is of course not to say that Wm. I. had
generally enfeoffed his military tenants by the
service of bringing all their *milites* to his armies in
England and Normandy, for, the office of holding
the former by maintaining his castles, and those of
his barons seems to have been a more essential
one ; and, that the *servitia debita* were divers [tho' Diversity
uniform as far as regards escuage and aid—saving of *Services*
due.
the small fees of Moreton], is plainly to be discovered both from the Norman Inquisitions [*t.*
Hen. I. and Hen. II.], and the English Baronial
Charters [*t.* Hen. II. reflecting Hen. I.]. Exactly
what pacts (if definitely expressed) were made with
the Conqueror's Barons can be but a matter of
speculation,—but there is no particular improbability in supposing that a tax on the fee then
existed, and that the " Knights " *in exercitu* were
supported by the contributions of their compeers,
and others, who did not militate. That the vague
service *in exercitu* due to the Crown was on a
more ample scale *t.* Wm. I. to Hen. II. than
Hen. II. to Ed. II. is highly probable (tho' no
particular information is available till Hen. I.),
but it should be borne in mind that the majority
of lay tenants of 1166 (or by their ancestors), had
been feft *post* Wm. I.—owing to the forfeitures of
the earlier barons.

Thus the fief of Moreton* escheated at the com-

---

* This fief would have been " good cheap " at a *service* of
500, according to the measure of the A.D. 1166-8 entries, and
the above *very incomplete* analysis shows *c.* 350 fees, hence 350

Partial
analysis of
Moreton
Escheat.

mencement of the reign of Hen. I., and from it
arose *very numerous* capital tenants, to all appearance, *ut de corona ;* thus, Earl Reginald in Cornwall (*c.* $215\frac{1}{3}$ fees), succeeding Wm. *f.* Richard,
whose father may have been the Earl's undertenant
in *D. B. ;* Ric. de Aquila. (35) ; Galf. Martell
($7\frac{1}{2}$); Bern. Pullein (1) ; Wm. *f.* John de Harper-
tree ; Wm. *f.* John ; Ric. *f.* Wm. ; Nich. *f.* Harding ; Ric. del Estre ; Walt. Brito (15) ; Ro.

---

or 500 or more *milites* led by the Earl of Moreton to the
musters of Wm. I.—the nos. almost alike improbable.   It may
be observed that the *services* (to scutage), *t.* Hen. II., were
approximately in total on an equality with the infeudations—
the current theory therefore involves all the "Knights" (say
6,000-7,000) being present *in exercitu :* yet the *Roman de Rou*
(lines 11,253-9, and *Feudal England,* p. 260), makes Wm. *f.*
Osbern (certainly not with the approbation of his compeers),
offer to *double* the *chevaliers* for the expedition to England
(1066),—that the barons could easily have so done is not

Evidence
of the
*Roman de
Rou.*

improbable, as *by* the Norman Inq., *t.* Hen. II., the figures
of which by no means reach *Wace's* [he names 20, 30, and
100 *chevaliers* to become 40, 60, and 200].   The *Roman de Rou*
[lines 11,364—5] cites Duke Wm. as setting his baronage an
excellent example of evading feudal obligations to his lord,

> *Petit sert mais meins servira*
> *Quant plus ara meins vos fera*

to be compared with the *tam parvam fortitudinem hominum
secum adducet quam minorem poterit ita tamen ne inde feodum suum
erga Regem Franciæ forisfaciat* of the Dukes of Flanders in
the already cited conventions of 1101, 1103, and 1163, and
the ten (1103), and twenty (1163) *milites* to the assistance of
the French Kings as *service,* whilst to the English ones, *1,000*
and *500* "Knights" can be furnished (for cash down).   What
is recorded of the Conqueror's *lay* Baronage either in England
or Normandy very little suggests they would rigidly conform
to any *fixed* and *definite* military obligations *in exercitu,*—the
diminution of the army service of Bp. Bayeux from *40*
(*t.* Hen. I.), to *20* (*t.* Hen. II.), has already been remarked.

Beauchamp (17); Hen. Lupel (18) ; Wm. Fossard ($31\frac{1}{2}$), presumbably the successor of Nigel Fossard,* Earl Moreton's Yorkshire undertenant ; and many others, including the Honor of Berkhamstead retained in the hands of the Crown ($22\frac{3}{5}$ fees),—it seems clear enough that all these *servitia debita* are of *t.* Hen. I., and have no very direct connection with the number of *milites* Earl Robert led to the Conqueror's musters, tho' perhaps in some relation to the "Knights" that had been enfeoffed, and the pecuniary assistance they could render.

The charters of Earl Hugh and Wm. de Albenia (*Pincerna*) are good evidence to demonstrate early lay systematic enfeoffments on an ample scale, by the unit of Knight Service ; for Roger Bigot departed this life in 1107 (*Vitalis*), or 1108 (*Hoveden*),† Early subinfeudations of lay tenants.

---

* The Fossard fief in the Baronial Charters (1166) is entered under Suffolk, but is essentially a Yorkshire one, and so answered in the Pipe Rolls : a few of the tenants named were capital tenants (apart from the fees of Moreton), thus Nich. *f.* Harding, whose fief of Meriet had been held since the acquest of England [*T. de N. ;* also in D. B.], but very few of any minor capital tenants of 1166 can be traced to D. B. : of these Rog. de Berkeley is one, but part of his holding had been at fee farm, part under his reeveship, and but a minority by possible Knight Service. The fief of Belet [1210-1212 ; vol. ii. *L. R.* p. 545] is clearly that of D. B. [i. 84*a*], and is rated as 1 fee in 1166 [*debet servitium j militis*], but the Wm. Belot of 1086 [*ut sup.*], is returned amongst the *servientes regis*—I do not suppose that one in 100 of the numerous thanes and *servientes* of the King (1086) could be traced as capital Crown tenants 1166, by knt. service. Fees held since the Acquest of England.

† *Vide* also Florence of Worcester, from whose Chronicle it descends to *Rog. de Hoveden.*

Duke
Richard's
military
service.

before which he had feft to the extent of 115 fees
[*vide* his son's charter 1166]—likewise before the
death of said Roger, his son in law (the said Wm.),
had of the gift of Hen. I., 15 and 10 fees *already*
subinfeuded [*vide* his son's charter 1166]; in
addition *Florence* of Worcester (1086) uses the
expresssion, *quot feudatos milites*, referring to *D. B.*,
and tho' that valuable record is no Feodary, it
gives the information the chronicler records, tho'
not in so ample a manner, as would occur in a
specific return of Knight Service.

Subin-
feudation,
t. Wm. I.

The Exon. *D. B.;* the *I. C. C.*, and *I. E.* (ed.
Hamilton), in conjunction with D. B. set early
feudal tenure in a clearer aspect : in the latter
[*I. E.*, presumably *t.* Wm. I., and almost certainly
11th cent.], amongst the list of ploughs (p. 168,
ed. Hamilton, and in all 3 of his originals), occurs
the following [hitherto unnoticed, *ut credo*], with
reference to the vill of Teusham,*—*Hoc tenet
iohannes in feudo de abbate pro duobus militibus.*

Duke
Richard's
Military
Service.

Another reference to military service occurs in
Will. Gemet., of the early 11th century [*accipiens
munere comitatum ut inde exhiberet ei militiæ statuta*,
compare, *in statuto servitio Milicie* in the Charter
of Hen. I., *Lib. El. III.*], which (former) is cited
more fully in *The Scutage and Knight Service of
England.†*

---

* *Vide* D. B., i. 191*a* and 201*b*, where the lordship of the
vill is divided between the Abbot of Ely and John *f.* Waleran,
perhaps the same tenant as in I. E., *ut sup.*

† The reference to *Wm. de Jumièges* was made known to
writer by this work (J. F. Baldwin, *Univ. Chicago Press, 1897*),
which is well deserving the attention of all—interested in the

Feudal System—either in America or England : there are (and it can scarcely be otherwise with a vol. written so far from original sources) many demonstrable errors, and also a rather too conspicuous tendency to combine the opinions of English writers (named). But the subject has been well laboured from printed works, and the author, having a clear conception of his own views, is intelligible enough to the reader : a certain well known *historical* method, is to attempt to consign to oblivion, all *intrusive* works, at the same time quietly making use of their references (occasion arising), as suitable *novelties*. There is another citation of *servitium militum* (*t. Wm. I.*, p. ix., *ut sup.*), and should his occasions permit, it is to be hoped, this writer will continue his investigations in English History, for readers both of his own, and this country.

It is not, of course, to be inferred that the *mere* fact of residence on a Western continent confers a particular im- munity on historical writers, for I would not suppose that, even the most ingenious of our own artificers of History could hope to surpass, and scarcely to equal, *Ancient Britain in the light of modern Archæological Discoveries.* This *magnum opus* states that "albeit the true character of the false Saxon chronicles have (*sic*) been frequently exposed, they still con- tinue to colour our popular histories, and to injuriously affect our national policy" (p. ix) ; that its design is "to restore to the pages of British history those circumstances of which forgery and imposture have deprived it, and which archæology has found safely preserved in the pure bosom of the earth " (p. x) ; that the *A. S.* chronicles are "patched forgeries of the eleventh or twelfth centuries, probably done in Rome, and wholly unworthy of credit" (p. 74) ; that "ancient trash piled . . . accepted by the modern world as the groundwork for a history of Britain and the construction of its national policy" (p. 74) ; that "so far as books go, the Sacred College of Rome had the entire making of European history . . . until the invention of printing put an end to its monopoly" (p. 180) ; that Beda's information concerning the Anglo- Saxons "was hopelessly wrong and defective" (p. 73), and terminates by bringing "to book" "the theory" of Beda (p. 181).

Now be it observed that a certain grandeur, and magnificence of language (well enough adapted to exploit the discoveries of Professors of the Arts of Graphology, Phrenology, Palmistry, etc.), is in itself no proof *absolute* of their author's lack of more real attainments ; such is apt, in the mind of certain readers, to raise a curiosity as to the fulfilment of expectations suggested by a platform of premises so great. Now it is at once allowed that even from the most pretentious, and least solid of books, some useful information may issue, but whatever success "circumstances" "safely preserved in the pure bosom of the earth," might or might not have in refuting "the false Saxon chronicles," such are (in *Ancient Britain, etc.*) neither exposed, nor digested in a manner calculated to afford (at least to the *tenuiter edocti*) any proof of their existence (as on p. x) ; that is, the author does not favour his readers with that special access to their* repository which himself must be presumed to have.

The ancestors of the English brought with them "the polytheism of the Mongolian steppes" (p. 53), and the Romans found in Britain, "the Buddhic polytheism of the Goths" (p. 54), whose "bitter hatred of hierarchical government" was not "an Aryan sentiment, nor a Teutonic, nor a German one," but "purely and distinctly Gothic" (p. 190), so that the hitherto illiterate reader, now rather persuaded of the error of believing his predecessors were of the *Indo-European* race (as he might have imagined), is amply compensated by the possible reward of Chinese *originals :* as the Gothic sentiment (*ut. sup.*) is anti-Teutonic, he will naturally be distressed to understand why he, or any other Scandinavian or English descendant of the Goths, should now be speaking a language essentially Germanic—here the author might well come to his aid in revealing one of those secrets of the "pure bosom, etc." (p. x) to which he alone has so easy an access.

Formation of *A. S.* Chronicles.   The *A. S.* chronicles doubtless took their present form *t. Alfred* (*9th cent.*), and are in hands of the 9th to the 12th cent. (the last terminates in 1154, but most of the writing would seem to antedate 1066, the French form of letters of

---

* *Sc.* the interred, and now disinterred, "circumstances," a notional meaning, and exact particulars, of which are so difficult to attain.

the 11th cent. being notably different from those of Saxon England), being compiled from Beda, and presumably embodying divers local memoranda : the existence of such for *Northumbria*, 732-801, can easily be demonstrated by drawing out the provincial entries from the *Northern Annals* (praised for *Symeon* of *Durham*), and by comparison with the National *Chronicle*, the consistent and more complete notices in the former (or rather its *original*, or *originals*), evidently having furnished the more slender items in the latter. It is not easy to see why the "Sacred College" (p. 180) should have wrought essentially heathen pedigrees for the *A. S.* kings in the *Chronicle;* it is still less easy to understand why the statements of contemporary historians are *usually** confirmed by *records*, nor how the works of Matth. Paris and divers others containing matter extremely hostile to Pontifical authority could escape the censorship of said College—it, it may be repeated, is difficult, but not impossible of explanation to one having a source of authority—"the pure bosom, etc." (p. x)—unhappily denied to ordinary mankind. The Annals of Northumbria.

Chroniclers.

As to English events in Britain prior to the time of Beda, it may be remarked that learning reached the North from Ireland *c.* 565, a few years after the reputed landing of the 1st King of *Northumbria*, prior to which, let it be supposed, *Runic* letters would not be unknown in England : a chronology of the authentic *Kings* of his province, is appended to a copy of Bede (the writing praised for the 8th cent.), and traditional predecessors of the royal houses might well be handed down in the verse of *Scalds* (even, if not in writing), their authenticity of course not being alleged. Introduction of Learning in the North. Royal Genealogies.

In the vol. under note the *Suevi* appear as a *Slavic* tribe (p. 138), a Gothic or semi-Gothic one (p. 193), where also, as of the "Sacæ or Goths of the Euxine and Baltic, the *Gothones* of Tacitus," so that it would appear that Goths and Sclavs were all one ; without, however, attempting to determine whether the author's authority on the ethnology of the *Suevi* derives from *inspiration*, or *exhumation*, it may be stated that Gothic and Germanic are often used (*not* in *Ancient Britain, etc.*) as terms interchangeable, but perhaps the most convenient *modus* is to include Scandinavians, Angles, Saxons and *Deutschen* under the term *Germani* (the *Germania* of Tacitus is of course not the present German Empire, and *Gothic* and *Germanic*.

---

* No particular accuracy for dates, nor correctness in matters statistical, is here suggested.

Beda counts as *Germani* Angles, Saxons, Frisians, Danes, etc.),
and to consider the Anglo-Saxons akin more particularly to
the Norse [leaving open the question of whether or not
Angulus was part of 5th century Scandinavia*], rather than to
the inhabitants of the Empire to which *Charlemagne* succeeded. To class Norse, Angles and Saxons as *Goths* of
Mongolia, and the *Deutschen* as Germans and presumably
(p. 190) *Aryans,* has certainly the advantage of novelty, and
needs but some trifling explanation [as that *Confucius* had,
with considerable foresight, instructed the Gothic races (prior
to their emigrations), in the speech of Germany], to become
impregnable ; doubtless, by an oversight (not altogether
irremediable) the learned author has omitted to supply from his
often named, and particular repository, this necessary explanation (for a dull reader), as to language.

Goths,
Gutæ,
Gothones,
and
Gothini.

Dani,
Suethans,
and
Suethidi,
not neces-
sarily
Gothic.

Angli and
Suevi ;
their loca-
tion.

*Regnar
Lodbrog* in
English
History,
A.D. 870 ;
his speech
under-
stood.
Deficiency
of the
Collection
of the *Mon.
Hist. Brit.,*
as to early
evidences
of the
English
races.

* How to apply and limit the term Scandinavia, 5th cent., is beyond
the power of the writer to discern, but it may be observed that the
earlier writers make no mention of *Goths* in it, unless indeed the *Gutæ*
(see p. *109j,* and for further illustration) of *Ptolemy* are held to be such :
at the same time that author (whose *Geography,* praised for A.D. 120,
seems sometimes to antedate *Tacitus*) locates the *Guthones* (within the
Venedi) in *Sarmatia,*—apparently the *Gothones* of the *Germania,* who
live more under the constraint of monarchy than the other Germanic
gentes. The *Gothini* of *Tacitus,* who pay tribute, and work the iron
mines, were not far from the Danube ; now certain it is that *Jornandes*
(c. 552) derives the notable *Goths* (who overran much of S. Europe
from the 3rd to the 5th century) of the Danube, from *Scanzia,* in which
he locates the *Suethans, Suethidi,* and *Dani* (who also originate in it),
whereas the classifications of its inhabitants by later writers, render it
particularly doubtful that any *Goths* had more than mere settlement in
certain parts of *Scandinavia.* Both King *Alfred* and *Beda* consider
the *Danes* as Germanic, and derive the *Angii* from the *Schleswic*
district, whereas *Ptolemy* and *Tacitus* agree in esteeming the latter, as
of the *Suevi* (*cf.* p. *109j*) a *gens* noted by Cæsar, and occupying about
the Elbe, *t. Strabo* (c. A.D. 30), and at the time (c. A.D. 100), of the
two above-named writers, the former of whom (*Ptolemy*), does not locate
the *Angli* on the actual coast (the *Saxones,* for one, on the neck of the
Cymbric Chersonese cut them off), as does the latter (or near it,—the
island, etc., *Germania,* 40) : besides the evidence for esteeming the
Scandinavians to be also, to a great extent of the *Suevi* (see p. 109*j*),
the St. Alban's Chronicler (praised for Rog. Wendover, and Matth.
Paris), using some unknown *Passio* of St. Edmund, names the likeness
of the Danish to the Anglian speech, in the converse of *Regnar Lodbrog,*
with the King and Martyr (*in anno* 870). The *Mon. Hist. Brit.* (a
work laborious enough) concerns itself, at some length, with notices of
the early inhabitants of Britain, but although produced at the common
charge of the English is singularly deficient as to their *originals,* a line
of investigation which might have been esteemed just as pertinent, as
a collection relating to Roman subjects ; this (some illustration of the
Germanic races who settled in England as *Angles, Danes, Norse,* and
Saxons), the present writer hopes to essay (occasion permitting) as an
introduction to *A History of Northumbria.*

A NOTE ON THE AGRICULTURE IN TACITUS' ACCOUNT OF *GERMANIA*.

Tacitus' (born *c.* A.D. 40 to 56) wrote his account of *Germania, c.* A.D. 98; dismissing the question as to the exact value of this author's information, and gathering *data* from the whole of his short work, it may be observed that although some of the *gentes* noticed are under more or less despotic rule (25, 43-5),* many exist as communities enjoying and appreciating a considerable degree of liberty (11, 37, *cf.* 45), under *reges* (7, 11, 43-4), or *principes* (11, 15, 22). The Germanic† tribes appear to have dwelt in villages (*vici*, 16), their ranks being composed of *nobiles* (7, 25, 44), *ingenui* (20, 25, 38, 44), *liberti* (25, 44), and *servi* [24, 25, 32 (*familia*), 38, 44, 45] : a difference between the warriors and actual cultivators of the soil is apparent (14, 15, and *perhaps* 26), the *principes* [who maintain a retinue (*comites*, 13, 14), averse to the labour of husbandry (14)], receiving a voluntary tribute of cattle and grains (*armenta* and *fruges* 15), suppose for consumption. The distinction is by no means so clearly marked as to enable the statement that *warriors* and *cultivators* are terms inconvertible; but the bravest of the former class are depicted as leaving the care of the fields (*agri,* 15, *cf.* 26) to the women, aged, and infirm of their households; these (latter) are presumably *ingenui* rather than *servi.*‡ The *plebes* (11) include the *ingenui,* and perhaps the *liberti;* the *reges* and *principes* appear to be of the *nobiles* (7, 11, 13) ; and the *duces* (7) not necessarily above the rank of the *ingenui:* no

---

* The bracketed nos. refer to the divisions of *Tacitus'* text.

† *Tacitus* does not consider all the tribes he names as Germanic ; of those he names as such, no comment as to origin is here made.

‡ At any rate in section 15.

permanent property in land exists (26), but in its products
(26), and in *servi*, household goods, farm stock, armour and
horses (5, 12, 18, 32). That the latter (12, 18, 32) were
used in Husbandry is not made apparent ; oxen (*boves*, 18) ;
herds (*armenta*, 5, 15, 21); flocks* (*pecora*, 12, 21, 25),
and of course cows† [tho' *indirectly* (23)] are named : the
food of the *gentes* includes fresh meat (23), cheese or an
approach to it (23), and grain stuffs (15, 16),—the common
drink is beer or its *antecessor* (23), and those tribes nearest
the Rhine buy *vinum* (23). Of crops, *Tacitus* distinctly
mentions wheat (*frumentum*, 23, 25, 45), barley (*hordeum*,
23), and, I think, unclosed meadow (*pratum*, 26), noting
an appreciation of the winter, spring, and summer seasons
(26) : as horses are used in warfare, cattle for consumption,
oxen for the plough (*iuncti boves*, 18), cows for breeding and
milk (23), the Roman writer scarcely needed to inform the
readers of his day that *oats* and *hay* were known to the
Germani, perhaps also *rye*. In the commentary on *Tacitus*,
in the excellent *Const. Hist.* (i. 18), wheat is cited as the
only corn crop, a statement having of intrinsic probability
little enough ; reference to sections 2 (*asperam cœlo*) ;
5 (*satis ferax*) ; 15 (*frugum*) ; 16 (*receptaculum frugibus*) ;
23 (*ex hordeo aut frumento*) ; 26 (*seges*) ; 26 (*hiems et ver*) ;
and 45 (*frumenta ceterosque fructus*) will demonstrate it to
be opposed to the witness of the Roman writer, whose
work should always be used to test the interpretations of his
exponents. The *servi* are pourtrayed rather as *coloni* (25)
than domestics, paying their lords a tribute in wheat, live
stock, or raiment, their position being somewhat akin to
that of our *villani* (12th to 14th cent.), though the lord of a
Manor would not usually have been able to kill, or strike
his *villein* with impunity (25) : the land occupied by the
servus would presumably be regarded as the property (for
the time) of the *dominus*,—as a kind of rent is paid therefrom, the slave in a certain sense worked for his lord, even
supposing he never cultivated the fields more particularly

---

* *Pecora*, not necessarily flocks, but (21) *armentorum ac pecorum*
seems to require some meaning other than herds.

† *Lac concretum ;* even, if not the produce of cows, *boves* and *armenta*
compel their existence.

set apart for the household of the *dominus*. There are no mediæval Manors, no theories of the *mark*, nor of the *120 acre* system ; there is nothing (*ut uidetur mihi*) to be adduced in demonstration of 2 or 3 course shifts, nor (*ut credo*) is there any decided negative of rotations ; there is ample testimony (4, 14, 15-17, 22, 26, 45) of a general aversion to labour, wastefulness of Agriculture, and abundance of land (*agri*). Section 26 particularly relates to Husbandry ; in it I understand *Tacitus* to remark that the arable, meadow, and grass fields of the Germans are occupied (or put to profit) by all, in their respective villages to an extent regulated by the number of actual cultivators (*agri pro numero cultorum ab universis in vicis occupantur*), supposing that *all* signifies each free household, and that a husbandman, free or the contrary, is indicated by *cultor*, rather than an inhabitant, and that should *in vices* be the true reading,* the sense turns on *alternate* periods of labour for individuals : the conclusion of the sentence (*quos mox inter se secundum dignationem partiuntur*)—which fields they (the heads of each free household) soon (suppose in April or May) divide amongst themselves according to their dignity (*sc.* a lord with many *servi* would naturally need a share much more ample than an *ingenuus* with a few, or a *libertus* with none). *Facilitatem partiendi camporum spatia præstant* follows, indicating that the abundance of land renders partition easy, there being therefore ample sustenance for each individual : this is succeeded by the lines *Arva per annos mutant et superest ager*, which (*ut videtur mihi*) implies that the Germans change their arable lands (or some of them) yearly (by ploughing land out of grass), and (nevertheless) land in grass is left in plenty (owing to the already mentioned abundance) : the section closes with further notice of the supineness of the husbandmen, and the amplitude of the soil (*amplitudine soli*), and a remark that the arable is only taxed with grain crops (*sola terræ seges imperatur*), indicating that beans, peas, *etc.*, were not cultivated. The entire Chapter comprises less than twelve lines, including a thrice-repeated statement as to excess of land beyond the immediate requirements of the population : in spite of this particular assistance from *Tacitus*, the Roman writer has of

---

* *Cf. Cæsar* (*c.* B.C. 50), in his a/c of the *Suevi :* a possible reading would be—frequent changes of pasture, by reason of its superfluity.

late been credited with statements, whose inconsistencies could scarcely have failed to impress the well informed readers of his own day. In one version the word *mutant* is supposed to refer to a rotation, and *ager* is rendered *fallow*** (I know not on what authority); it is clear therefore *arva* is either equivalent to all the ploughed land, or such of it as is sown, so that *Tacitus* is constrained to say that (*a*) the entire arable is in rotation, and (*b*) a fallow is left, the (*b*) statement being contained in (*a*), as the mere fact of a *shift* denotes a *fallow, or else* that the land under crop (or some of it) is changed to a *fallow*, and a *fallow* is left, which reading is alike elegant and cogent with the other.† In another *lectio* (A. J. Church, M.A., Latin text, 1898, notes) the word *mutant* is attributed to a change of occupancy; but certain it is that the mere usure of a piece of ploughed land by either *princeps*, *dux*, or *ingenuus* in turns has nothing whatever to do with the relative abundancy of the fields other than arable (here *agri*), the above version leaving the rest of the sentence connected by *et* in suspense "betwixt earth, air, and seas," and void of meaning, whereas the ploughing of *ley* land reduces the *ager*, for the simple reason that land left from the plough would not be particularly profitable *ager* for some time to come; further, the alternate occupation of arable presupposes a rotation, and how mere difference of owners year after year on the *arva* could affect the *ager* is a mystery that no one (*tenuiter edoctus*) can hope to explain. It has been stated (*supra*) that *Tacitus* does not absolutely negative rotations, but if *arva per annos mutant* requires the rendering that *all* the arable is changed *p.a.*, the ploughed

---

* If it is held that the change implies rotations which include *fallow*, and hence a diminution of the grass land (*ager*), this would mark a contrast between a nation using no, or not so much bare *fallow*, and one accustomed to some, or more of it, and hence relative extravagance of Husbandry: at the same time the latter would *not* change their arable (as with 2 fields in a 2 course shift *both* would be *arva*), but merely its cultivation; further the *literal* rendering of the words *arva per annos mutant* (an actual change of fields), is full of meaning, whereas ideas *read in*, to support theories (*e.g.*, they change their fields amongst themselves, *or* change the crops in their fields, *or* change their arable from crop to fallow) are rebutted as well by the context, as the inconsistencies they involve.

† *Arva* seems to denote the entire arable (whatever was "ered"), rather than *only* that portion sown; and a possible, but improbable, reading might be formed by limiting *arva* to seeded arable, and by supposing the Romans made little use of bare *fallows*—rendering *ager* as land not under the plough.

fallow of a 2 or 3 course *shift* is of course impossible ; the Roman writer perhaps did not intend a remark so entirely definite, tho' it must be allowed he pourtrays the husbandmen as very little patient of labor, further than the necessities of the times render expedient. The absence of landownership is well explained in *Tacitus*, and it seems perspicuous enough that a division of the earth's products could be more suitably arranged towards hay time and harvest : it does not seem to follow that the partition, when made, was necessarily in proportion to the number of the actual tillers of the soil in autumn and winter from each free household, as the warlike occasions of the *gentes* would disturb such an arrangement, and the *princeps* and his *comites* (who seem to foreshadow the *feudal system*) might be generally allotted a return out of proportion to the contributions to the labor of husbandry made from their households, in addition to the voluntary tribute already cited. To bring into the sketch the mediæval system of agriculture as to rotations and ownership, the text of *Tacitus* scarcely permits ; any sort of settled property in the *arable* nullifies the word *mox*, as the writer would scarcely expect the critics of his day to believe in divisions of property whose descent, tho' not successive, was *already* defined by alternation. These tribes include the *Angli* (40), who *may* have been the ancestors of the race of the same name, who afterwards settled in England ; those of *Tacitus* belonged to the *Suevi*, and appear to have been one of the freer communities : English and Scandinavian traditions unite in representing the later *Angli* as deriving from what in *historic* times was Denmark, rather than Germany, but both countries are of course included in *Germania* (1st cent.). The exact ancestors of the modern Scandinavians*

Angli and *Suevi.*

* *Pomponius Mela* (*c. 45*) names the island [always so till the 6th century, at least, and of unknown magnitude] of *Scandinavia*, as *yet* held by the *Teutoni : Pliny*, the naturalist (*c. 79*), says part of it, containing 500 *pagi*, was held by the *Hillevioni*, noting also the islands of *Scandia, Dumna, Bergos* and *Nerigo*, from which (latter) the voyage to *Thule* is wont to be made : *Solinus Polyhistor* (*c. 80*) mentions *Scandinavia*, as the largest of the islands of *Germania : Tacitus* (*c. 98*) places the *Suiones* [this term recurs in *Eginhard* (*c. 820*) as applicable to Swedes and Norwegians, and in *Adam of Bremen* (*c. 1077*), who

Early notices of Scandinavia.

Scandi-
navian
English.

(*t.* Tacitus) I have never seen satisfactorily determined ; but certain it is that a very considerable proporti n of the inhabitants of England (*t.* 1086) were of Norse (chiefly Danish) origin, as is witnessed by *D. B.*, the old records of *Northumbria* (which should be read with the *A.S. Chron.*), and other notices of the *Danelaga*, in addition to such evidences as nomenclature ; and tho' the Normans were a compound race, speaking a foreign language, it is scarcely to be supposed it was other than the *Northman* element which enabled them to acquire England at that period.

The *Angli* and *Suiones* of *Suevia ; Dani,* Dacians, and *Gutæ.*

Brittia and the *Varni* in the 6th cent.

Traditional kinship of Angles, Danes, Jutes, Northmen, Saxons, and *Suevi.*

seems to confine it to the former] with a fleet, certainly in the mainland of Sweden, and probably in some of the Danish isles ; beyond the *Suiones* are the *Sitones* (presumably a Finnish tribe, N. of Upsala, and near the ancient city of *Sictona*), and here *Suevia* ends [this writer, be it observed, classes both *Angli* and *Suiones* as *Suevi*, and calls the Baltic, the *Suevian* Sea] ; *Ptolemy* (*120 or before*) places the *Dauciones* and *Gutæ* in the island of *Scandia* [whether Danes and Jutes, or not, the *Dani* are frequently termed Dacians, thus, *Gerald de Barri, 12th cent.*, notes the corruption of the Northern speech by the frequent invasions of Dacians, and Norwegians, and *Wm. f. Alan,* 1166, owes one knt. in Norfolk at *Carlesli*, against the Dacians, there being no immediate connexion with a nation on the Danube in either case] : *Jornandes* (*6th cent.*) locates the *Suethans* and *Dani* in *Scanzia* (*quasi officina gentium*) island : *Procopius* (*6th cent.*), seems to place the Danes about Denmark, near the *Varni* (extending to the N. Ocean, and separated from the Franks by the Rhine) ; calls *Scandinavia*, the island of *Thule*, which he has only visited by the converse of those coming therefrom—this is that author who mentions *Brittia*, as inhabited by Angles, Frisians and Britons, an expedition by sea of the former, led by their king's sister against the *Varni* (*supra*) ; and as well notices of British legations, lack of cavalry and horsemanship, navy, marriage (*cf. Tacitus*), as various poetical legends : *Beda* (*c. 730*) gives the Danes as one of the nations from whom Angles and Saxons derive ; and *Wm. Malmesburien.* (*t. 1135*) makes a traditional ancestor of the *A. S.* kings, first a foundling in the *Scanzia* of *Jornandes*, and afterwards a ruler in *Slaswic* (Haithaby), which may be a compilation from *Ethelward* (writing 975-1011), who states that *Old Anglia* was situated between the Saxons and Jutes (*Gioti*), with a capital town *Slesuuic* (*Saxonice*), or *Haithaby* (*Danice*), that Hengist's ancestor was *Uuothen*, whom the Danes, *Northmanni* and *Suevi*, worship to this day, citing *Lucan* (1st cent.) as to the latter, *fundit ab extremo flavos aquilone Suevos*, which corroborates *Tacitus ;* and in another passage makes Scef (the son of Scyld), Cerdic's 19th ancestor, land on the island of *Scani* and become king, whereas in the *Beowulf*, Scyld Scéfing, is the foundling, and then king of the gár-Denum (spear-bearing Danes).

CHAPTER III

AGRICULTURAL STATISTICS

" This is an Age wherein to commend or extol an Ingenious
Art or Science might be deemed a Needless Labour, especially
in a Country so highly improved in everything ; but that we
find the more Noble, Advantagious, Useful, or Necessary,
any Art, Science, or Profession is, the stronger Arguments
are framed against it ; and more particularly against the
Rustick Art and its infinite Preheminances and Oblectations,
by the vainer and more pedant sort of persons, despising the
worth or value of what they are ignorant of, who judge it
below their honour or reputation to take any notice of so
mean a profession ; that esteem the Country no other than a
place for Beasts as Cities for Men."—Worlidge's *Proemium* to
Systema Agriculturæ, ed. 1681.

THE fiscal Hide of Domesday contained (or 120 Fiscal
often did) 120 fiscal acres, and the normal Acres.
areal Hide 120 actual ones, which perhaps
accounts for the statement that a like quantity was
tilled by each plough *per ann.*—which is opposed
to the common experience and knowledge of any
English farmer of arable, and would predicate
weather suitable for constant aration ; whereas
30 weeks in the year is perhaps a high estimate of
the period during which land can be worked, and
40-60 acres may be roughly taken as the present
land of one plough. The work on Husbandry
derived from the MS. of Sir Walter de Henley
(and printed by the R.H.S.) presumes a 3 or

2 course shift, of which respectively $\frac{1}{3}$ or $\frac{1}{2}$ in bare fallow ; for the former take 180 ac., for the latter crops 160 ac. (in each case *statute*), plough once for and twice for fallow ;† allow 8 weeks for holy days (presumably including the 3-4 weeks noted in Custumals at the Nativity, Easter, and Pentecost, and the time occupied by the ploughmen on their own holdings, etc.), leaving 44 weeks for unbroken aration, thus

Scheme of
Perpetual
Aration.

THREE COURSE SHIFT.

	Days
180 acres (120 ac. in crop, 60 ac. in fallow) at $\frac{7}{8}$ ac. per day	$205\frac{5}{7}$
*60 acres (2nd fallowing) at 1 ac. per day	60
	$265\frac{5}{7}$
Add for Sundays	$44\frac{2}{7}$
Total	310

TWO COURSE SHIFT.

	Days
160 acres (80 in crop, 80 in fallow) at $\frac{7}{8}$ ac. per day	$182\frac{6}{7}$
80 acres (2nd fallowing) at 1 ac. per day	80
	$262\frac{6}{7}$

With Sundays, *Total c. ut sup.*

in either case, the total working out as above, viz., nearly exactly 44 weeks.

The above has been construed to mean that for a continuous period of 44 weeks the ploughmen

Welsh
evidence,
t. Hen. II.

† *Gerald de Barri* (*t.* Hen. II.) remarks the neglect of husbandry of the Welsh, stating they *only* plough *once each* for wheat and oats in winter and spring, and *twice* in summer— the husbandman leaving his oxen on occasion of war, whereas the theoretical ploughmen (*ut sup.*) are depicted as having little existence other than as members of their teams.

* In Canon Taylor's learned paper on "The Ploughland and the Plough," the accomplished writer seems to imagine that (in a 3 Course Shift) either fallow land was unploughed, or that each team ploughed 240 acres.

not only *could*, but also *did*, plough all day and every day (saving the 7th), no matter the weather, storms, snow, frost, floods, hay time, harvest, etc. ; now if the author means to make this assertion he must be postulating that he conceived his day and generation equally as credulous, as some of the writers on agriculture in the 19th century. The 60,000 knights and fees of King William (apparently still in repute, see " Social England ") and the 45,000 parish churches supposed to exist in 1371, are errors one can understand, but why such exceeding mystery as to an art daily in operation before our eyes, should appear in the productions of scholars who honor (?) Agriculture with their notice, is not easily conceivable.

Returning to Walter de Henley it may be suggested that he intended to convey that if the above evidently unreal programme took place, then would the amount tilled by each plough in the year be such a quantity of land, as is termed a carucate : in addition the author is supposed to have flourished in the first $\frac{1}{2}$ of the 13th century, and is describing cultivation of demesne land, which it must have been known, was to a considerable extent tilled by the tenantry—this he says nothing about.

Before proceeding to discuss ancient evidences, a contrast of the agriculture of 1086, 1696, and 1897 may not be out of place ; the crops of 1086 were *Wheat, Barley, Oats, Rye, Beans, Peas, and perhaps Vetches ; of 1696 in ordinary rotation, the same including Vetches ; for 1897 add such

Agriculture 1086, 1696, and 1897 contrasted.

---

* D. B. Wheat 11*a*, 32*a*, 176*b*, Oats 214*a*, Rye 257*b*.

ENGLAND AND WALES (KING) 1696.

	1696, Acres.	1897, Acres.
Arable at 5s. 1od. per acre ...	10,000,000	
Flax, Woad, etc., at 5s. 1od. per acre	1,000,000	12,505,049
Pasture and meadow at 9s. per acre	10,000,000	15,122,121
Woods, coppices at 5s. per acre	3,000,000	
Forests, parks, commons at 3s. 6d. per acre	3,000,000	1,847,351
Heaths, moors, etc., at 1s. per acre	10,000,000	3,363,281
Houses, gardens, orchards, etc.	1,000,000	
Rivers, lakes, meres at 2s. per acre	500,000	4,480,181
Roads, ways, waste land ...	500,000	
Average value, 6s. 2d. per acre	39,000,000	37,317,983

ENGLAND AND WALES, 1897 (excluding tidal water and foreshore).

	England in acres.	Wales in acres.
Arable	11,602,191	902,858
Pasture	13,191,789	1,930,332
Mountain, heath, etc. ...	2,208,844	1,154,437
Orchards	218,261	3,707
Woods and plantations ...	1,665,741	181,610
In inland waters, *say* ...	180,000	
Towns, houses, waste grounds, *say*	3,477,258	600,955
	32,544,084	4,773,899

TEAMLANDS AND CROPS (21 COUNTIES),
A.D. 1086-1897.

Counties.	1086, Team-lands.	1086, 120 Acre Theory; Arable Acres.	1897, Grain Crops, Acres.	1897, Vetches, Acres.	1897, Fallow, Acres.	1897, Total of Crops grown 1086, Acres.	1897, Total Arable, Acres.
Devon ...	7,972	956,640	243,165	3,581	7,675	245,421	588,639
Lincs ...	5,043	605,160	560,195	9,014	25,692	594,901	1,018,886
Somerset ...	4,858	582,960	98,692	3,960	3,348	106,000	209,618
Wilts ...	3,457	414,840	149,449	16,591	7,676	173,716	318,719
Northants ...	2,931	351,720	127,234	3,918	10,502	141,654	213,605
Hants ...	2,847	341,640	192,286	17,159	15,898	225,343	443,759
Oxon ...	2,639	316,680	124,096	6,836	5,477	136,409	221,424
Cornwall ...	2,377	285,240	124,504	518	5,105	130,127	366,178
Dorset ...	2,303	276,360	83,184	5,260	3,671	92,115	187,108
Warwick ...	2,276	273,120	93,927	2,263	6,587	102,777	168,511
Bucks ...	2,244	269,280	94,439	4,371	8,564	107,374	165,001
Berks ...	2,087	250,440	106,049	6,946	9,403	122,398	202,558
Herts ...	1,716	205,920	124,894	3,937	14,007	142,838	218,115
Cambs ...	1,676	201,020	221,693	4,687	15,341	241,721	372,765
Beds ...	1,557	186,840	89,425	3,255	11,700	104,380	152,574
Staffs ...	1,398	167,760	84,088	1,841	1,765	87,694	173,744
Notts ...	1,255	150,600	121,300	2,492	9,780	133,572	241,092
Surrey ...	1,172	140,640	57,681	3,521	8,546	59,748	131,041
Hunts ...	1,120	134,400	73,863	2,225	9,275	85,363	123,531
Derby ...	762	91,440	47,974	1,303	2,570	51,847	97,602
Middlesex ...	664	79,680	10,606	1,245	1,374	13,225	32,955
Total ...	52,354	6,282,480				3,098,623	5,650,425

N B.—In above 21 counties the teams in 1086 are 43,932, *i.e.*, 83 per cent. of the teamlands; the arable 1897 being 90 per cent. of that in 1086 by 120 acre theory, as above.

ARABLE OF ENGLAND, 1897 (11,602,191 acres).

	Acres.
Grain and pulse crops (all grown 1086)	5,780,782
Vetches	186,604
Bare fallow	369,254

Acres.
6,336,640

Green crops (excluding vetches), mostly the food of stock, 1897, almost or entirely uncultivated 1086 2,263,879

Clover, sainfoin and rotation grasses, in arable rotation, partly for hay and partly fed off—entirely the food of stock 2,885,863

Flax, hops, small fruit 115,809

Total 11,602,191

crops as Potatoes, Cabbage, Rape, Mangolds, Turnips, Clover, Sainfoin, and Grasses in arable rotation, so that the present Agriculture is far more remote from that of 1696, than the latter from 1086, and for aught I can discover there was little of food importation T. R. W. I. or T. R. W. III.   For 1086, take the population of England at 1,800,000 (Ellis' count × by more than 6), and for 1696, 5½ millions (incl. Wales) from King's estimate from the Hearth Tax (also reckoned at 7 millions ; the houses were 1,300,000 at the Revolution, which shows King's cast to have been low) ; the Lancaster Herald (King) allowed 10 million acres in 1696 in ordinary rotation, the same amount in pasture and meadow, allotting to heaths, moors, woods, and forests more than 3$^{\underline{ce}}$ their now extent, and less than 3$^{\underline{ce}}$ the present amount of land in towns—a reference to the 1897 Agricultural Returns shows 11½ million acres arable, and 13 millions in pasture and meadow in England.   King gives a total produce of 90,000,000 bushels, of which 17 millions for seed ; he estimates 3,200,000 acres barley land, of which one-third (say 1 million) fallow, so 'tis plain he is thinking of a 3 course shift, which allows from 6,666,666 acres under crop, some 73 million bushels for use for 5½ million folk ; this amounts to 13 bush. per head, and between 13 and 14 bush. per sown acre yield, (of which about 3 bush. for seed), so that deducting from the sown acres some 1,166,666 acres for seed, there would be about 1 acre per head,—in other words some 5½ millions (of the 10,000,000 arable) actually feeding the same no. of folk as found.   King's estimate of yield is 13-14 bush. p. ac. (no items save barley at 15 bush.) all round ; in **1333-5** from 8 estates of

Merton College (over 1,000 acres for 3 years
in different parts of England) Wheat yielded 10,
Barley 16, Dredge 14, Rye 11, Oats 10, Peas 11,
and Beans 10 bush., or an average of 10-12 bush. ;
these results have been wrought out from Prof.
Rogers' Tables (*Hist. Agr.*) presumably derived
from the actual Bailiffs' A/cs. At this period
(1333-5) varying amounts were sown, but from
the figures it would appear that about 1 quarter
(8 bush.) might be stated as the all round yield
(after deduction for seed) ; against about 10 bush.
in 1696. There seems to be no evidence of yield
per acre T. R. W. ; and no reason to suppose the
agriculture of the 11th century (1086) much more
futile than that of 1333-5—hence the statement of
a supposed yield of 6 bush.* p. ac. (of which 2 b.
for seed) can be supported by nothing unless its
author's wish to prove the existence of a fanciful
ploughland at any cost (p. 438 *D. B. and Beyond*).

Now no assertion is made as to the correctness
of King's figures, but let it be remembered he was
a notable statistician living at the period of the
Revolution ; that an estimate of $4\frac{1}{4}$ people per
house is less than medium, and that his method or
calculating the fallow of the barley area, would
suggest that rather more than $\frac{2}{3}$ of the land in tillage
was sown.

In 1086, in 30 counties of England there were

---

* *D. B. and Beyond*, p. 438, says this hypothesis is taken
from Walt. de Henley : what that writer actually says is that
a yield of 6 bush. p. ac. means a loss of $1\frac{1}{2}$d. p. ac., in addition to the land being rent free (suppose 4d. to 6d. p. ac.) : in
the same vol. cited by Prof. Maitland, the anonymous and
coeval writer on Husbandry gives the returns from wheat as
5 times the seed sown, *i.e.*, 10-12 bush. p. ac., from 2 or $2\frac{2}{5}$
bush. seed, which yield is similar to the actual figures of the
Bailiffs' a/cs, *ut sup.*

Average yield of Wheat per acre: neither evidence, nor proba- bility in placing it at 6 bushels.

Agricultural *data*, 1086.

70,606 ploughs (8 oxen), with an average of 3·56 folk as recorded per team; in 34 counties (including, however, most of Lancs. and parts of Cumberland and Westmorland) the recorded population was 283,242; assuming 300,000 as the total for the 40 modern counties, and ploughs in proportion then would there have been a total of 84,000 teams; for a moment, allow 120 acres of tillage per plough, then would there have been *over* 10,000,000 acres arable in 1086, keeping alive some 1,800,000 folk as against a lesser amount (10,000,000 ac.) for more than 3^{ce} that number (*i.e.* 5,500,000 people) in 1696.

Consumption of Beer.

Of the 2,200,000 acres sown to barley (yield 15 bush. per ac.), King estimates to malt $\frac{2}{3}$ of the yield, *i.e.*, $21\frac{1}{2}$ million bush. (of 33,000,000), to return a total of 12,400,000 barrels of beer (weak and strong), which allows rather under $1\frac{3}{4}$ pints per day per head of population, which amount (about 78 barrels) would be produced from $\frac{1}{4}$ of that acre, per head, found by taking the statistics of 1696: a result differing largely from Prof. Maitland's $\frac{1}{2}$ gallon per day for every man, woman, and child, amounting to some $2\frac{1}{2}$ gallons per recorded man, which princely munificence might well cause the modern labourer to envy his antecessor in the days of King William. Again, take the 21 counties* whose teamlands are set forth on p. 401 (*D. B. and Beyond*), and multiply them by 120, with a result of 6,282,480 ac. arable, against 5,650,425 in the present decade, of which latter but 3,098,623 are in the crops of 1086 (the balance mainly being food for stock): and were one to apply 180 acres (Canon Taylor in "Domesday Studies"), arithmetic would be set at defiance

---

* *Vide*, p. 114.

in some of the shires, whose total area would be unable to furnish the acres required—which result would also sometimes occur if the actual teams (in place of the teamlands) were taken.

How much of the acre per head as thus found from King's tables would be subtracted for stock, there is no material to determine, but Fitzherbert writing t. Hen. VIII. (probably a Derbyshire squire and farmer) does not, if I remember rightly, allow any very considerable proportion of corn for the working oxen. King's estimate for the consumption of Bread, Bread Corn, Cakes, Biscuit, Pastry, Pudding, and all things made of meal and flour is 15s. 8d. per head* p. a., and 'tis clear he calculates practically all the Wheat and Rye, and part of the Barley, Oats, Beans, and Peas under this item, presumably the produce (by his mode of estimation) of $\frac{9}{20}$ acre, as roughly by King's figures 14 bush. p. acre (rather less) was the yield from some $\frac{2}{3}$ of 10,000,000 acres under the plough in 1696, and as in 1333-5, some 11 bush. p. acre (rather more) are found in practice; then should there be, by these figures, some $8\frac{1}{2}$ million sown acres in 1086 for an assumed population of $5\frac{1}{2}$ millions (as in 1696); but as the population in 1086 cannot be shown to have exceeded $\frac{1}{3}$ that amount (*i.e.*, about 1,800,000), then would 2,830,000 sown acres have sufficed, and therefore it is hard to imagine a total exceeding 6,000,000 arable acres, which allows for much of the plough-land being under a 2 course shift,† and some of it

Consumption of Bread-Stuffs, etc.

Population of 1696 treble that of 1086.

* In the *anon.* Husbandry (*c. t.* Hen. III.) farm servants have an allowance of 1 qr. of corn per 12 weeks.

† There is a great deal about 2 and 3 course shifts in Yorkshire (with reference to *gheld* rate) in Canon Taylor's "Ploughland and the Plough," the furrows of which systems

in a rotation partly grass,* but counted as arable, which presumably would occur in other counties than Cornwall.   Hence some 70 acres per plough would follow, and but three score or less might be calculated if the land in grass (in rotation, and estimated as arable) were excluded ; and this amount (60 acres) seems to have been Agarde's estimate of a ploughland in Q. Elizabeth's days.†

The well-known Poll Tax Returns 1377, 1379, and 1381 bear on the matter ;‡ the population at

are yet to be discovered by the zealous antiquary, and the rotations identified ; these arguments (which seem to have little support from D. B.) appear to arise from certain entries (even better represented in Lincs.), where the jurors roughly *Terra dupliciter ad arandum.* estimate the teamlands as in proportion to the *gheld* rates; thus 364*a*, 2¾ bovates for *gheld*, land to 2$\stackrel{\text{ce}}{}$ as many oxen ; 364*b*, 13⅝ bovates for *gheld, terra dupliciter ad arandum ;* compare 352*a*, 2½ bovates for *gheld*, land to 5 oxen, which is similar to the last named, but that it would have seemed singular to write, land to 27⅔ oxen ; see also 350*a*, 351*a* (*ter*), 351*b* and 352*a* (*bis*) ; for cases *where the teamland equates* the *gheld* 343*b*, 344*b* (*bis*), 348*b* (*bis*), 350*b*, 351*a* (*quinquies*), 351*b*, 353*a*, 358*a*, 362*b* ; where *the Teamland is half* the *gheld* 349*b* ; and other simple proportions occur in this county.

Meadow, 1086.
* Not of course meaning "rotation grasses" ; see note, p. 22 ; also as illustrating meadow, etc., vide *D. B.* 2*b* ; as much meadow as pertains to 10 ac. of land ; 38*b* ; 46s. of herbage ; 134*b* ; land to ½ pl. ; meadow to ½ pl., and 10s. over, a mill of 3s. and 200 eels, the whole worth 20s. ; 142*b*, Meadow 6s. and 4s. of hay ; 143*b*, Mea. to 3 pls., and 20s. over ; 143*b*, Pasture to stock, and hay to farm of Archbp. for 8 days ; 156*a*, of hay 10s. ; 183*a*, Of mea. 5s., besides pasture to oxen ; and 376*b* ; the men of N. detain 16s. of the customs of the pastures.

† A Ploughland, which is about Three Score Acres ; p. 10 App. Reg. Hon. de Richmond.

‡ For 1377, refer to "Archæologia," vol. vii., which gives a more extended return than that published in Powell's

this period seems to have been 2½ millions or more, and the following figures taken from the detailed returns of Claro Wapentake (Yorks) in 1379 suggest omissions:

Per 1,000 of Popu- lation, Claro, 1379.			19th cent. Model 1,000 England.
358 ...	...	Men wed ...	... 273·3
358 ...	...	Women wed ...	... 273·3
284 ...	...	Over 16, unwed	... 453·4
1,000			1,000

the inference being that many over 16 years of age were not taxed as they should have been ; and further, so far as the imperfect returns at the Record Office (of 1377 for Claro) allow comparison, there were in 1379 found to be actually more folk living over 16 than in 1377 over 14, which would seem to point to a not altogether extinct desire on the part of taxpayers to escape payment, rather than to any particular catastrophe in that district. The total of 1377 furnished £22,607 2s. 8d. by 1,356,428 groats from 37 counties from all over 14 years of age, excluding Mendicants, and the Clergy (about 30,000 ; see Clerical Subsidy 51 Ed. III.) ; by allowing for Monmouth, Chester, and Durham, the total population over 14 might be 1,500,000. But as what was true of Claro might be applicable to all England (a recorded excess in 1379 of those over 16, over those over 14 in 1377), it may be reasonable to estimate the 1,500,000 as over 16 and not over 14. On the assumption that there would be 37%

"Rising in East Anglia," which should also be consulted for 1381, and separate clerical subsidies are to be found in both vols.

of the total population under 16, then would there have been *2,380,000* persons in all England ; but presuming 35% of the total population wed (and noting that in Claro of 1,000 recorded, 716 are found as married), then would there be approximately 1,074,000 wed folk of 1½ millions as above, which being $\frac{7}{20}$ (taking 35% of whole community as married) of the total, would bring the population in 1377 to *3,069,000*, so that the true total should lie between these estimates, say some 2,700,000, called 2½ millions. Unless the chroniclers are to be regarded as mere relaters of fables, there must have been enormous mortality in

The Black Death.

1348-9 (the Black Death); given at ⅓ to more than ½ the population, so that in the 1st half of the 14th century the English population might very well be estimated at 4 millions. As the postulators of the 120 acre theory are burdened with an arable of over 10,000,000 acres in 1086 for some 1,800,000 people, it easily follows that 20,000,000 (on the same theory) would not be an excessive amount for 4,000,000 folk temp. Ed. III. prior to 1348-9, and (still on that theory) some 30,000,000 of arable, *what time* the Saxon estimate* of 242,700 Hides was made ; after this, it would be but little astonishing to hear that the whole country at one time consisted of a vast ploughed field, and that traces of terrace cultivation had been discovered on Scawfell Pike itself.

Ploughs and Population 1086.

Prof. Maitland has counted *70,606* ploughs in 30 of the recorded counties of D. B., which answers to an estimate of *84,130* for the 40 modern shires of England by as follows :—

---

* *Vide*, p. 28.

32,544,084 total acres of which 3,759,671 in 5 counties (Cumberland, Durham, Monmouth, Northumberland, and Westmorland,) not in D. B., assuming Lancashire as returned ; total recorded population *283,242* (Ellis), expanded to *300,000* for the missing shires, giving 5,586 ploughs for their supposed " recorded folk." Of the 4 counties Prof. Maitland does not give Yorkshire has some 2,959, Rutland 239 teams, and I have assumed 940 for Cheshire, and 3,800 for Suffolk, which with the 5,586 (above) and 70,606 adds to *84,130*. The population for Lincs, Norfolk, and Suffolk seems quite untrust- Fallacy of worthy (see note, p. 12), and to estimate the figures in some number of oxen possessed by the average *villein*, counties. it is therefore necessary to omit them, and take statistics from the 31 remaining counties of D. B. : empirically divide the population into 4 classes, *A*, villans, sokemen, *liberi homines*, coliberts, and *censarii ; B*, bordars, cottars, and coscez ; *C, Homines*, radknights, Frenchmen, *milites*, thanes, and drenghs ; *D*, the balance, including lords, mesne lords, burgesses, priests, swineherds, Welsh-men, reeves, etc. ; and assume Class *A* at 3 per plough, *B* at 8, *C* at 1, *D* at no teams save the demesne ones of mediate and immediate lords. This is of course incorrect, as many of the bur-gesses, priests, etc., had ploughs, but one assump-tion to a certain extent balances another, and the erudite supporters of the villeins should allow this mode of computation rather increases (unduly perhaps) their *status :* taking the recorded popu-lation of the 34 counties, Class *A* consists of some

145,009 folk, *B* of *89,443*, *C* of *2,360*, and *D* of the balance needful to total *283,242* ; as explained in the note on p. 12, Lincs, Norfolk, and Suffolk would mar the calculation, (and unduly depreciate the *villani*), so it is necessary to subtract their totals, leaving *100,667* in Class *A*, *69,182* in *B*, *2,027* in *C*, and a total recorded number of *210,359* in these 31 counties.

The demesne ploughs are about $\frac{3}{10}$ of the total (see p. 145), and as there are some *65,179* teams in these counties, the lords thus have *19,554*, and the ploughs not in demesne would be *45,625*, *i.e.*, *33,556* in Class *A*, *8,648* in *B*, and *2,027* in *C*, leaving a balance of *1,393* which would not cover the omissions, as for burgesses, etc.   In other words, suppose *1,000* acres arable in aforesaid 31 counties, thus

Scheme of *1,000* acres arable 1086.	Acres*	Ploughs.	Servi.	Class A,*i.e*, Villans, etc.	Class B, *i.e.*, Bordars, etc.	Class C.
Demesne	400	$4\frac{3}{4}$	$4\frac{1}{2}$			
Tenantry	510	$8\frac{1}{3}$		25 at 20— 21 acres each		
,,	50	$2\frac{1}{8}$			17 at some 3 acres each	
,,	40	$\frac{1}{2}$				$\frac{1}{2}$
Totals	1,000	*c.* 16	$4\frac{1}{2}$	25	17	$\frac{1}{2}$

leaving *47* recorded folk as against 16 ploughs,

* For very precise information as to the modern statute acre, *vide* tables at end of *Chron. W. Thorn* (St. Augustine's), where over 50 variations are given, all conforming to present measures ; the above history terminates A.D. 1397.

which is agreeable to the addition of Classes
A, *B*, *C*, together with the *23,252* Servi (of 31
shires) ; viz., *195,128* for *65,179* teams, the remaining *15,231* (of *210,359* total recorded) not
being necessary to the example, but of course
supported by above ploughs, and bringing up the
number of people (as found) to the correct figure.
This estimate presents the classes in due proportion to each other, and assumes each villan plough
will average about half an acre per week, on the
lord's land for 10 months, *tilling* some 15-16 acres
p. a., as by Walter de Henley's scanty aration.

Prof. Maitland (p. 430 *D. B. and Beyond*)
seems to create and then admire at the difficulties
of the Norfolk and Suffolk " *Hidages*," with little
success in solving them ; he rightly observes " that
there are upon an average about 2 teams to every
carucate is apparent on page after page of the
record," and therefore concludes these carucates
are not teamlands, falling back on the supposition
that they may be units of assessment. There
should be little room to suppose they are either
Hides or *Teamlands* (as Prof. Maitland under-
stands a ploughland, *i.e.*, 120 acres),—to demonstrate the former the Hundred of Thingo is ample,
occurring on fos. 286, 289, 349, 356-8, 381, 391,
401, 425, and 435 of D. B. ii., where the vills are
assessed to *gheld* in no proportions whatsoever to
the number of carucates they contain, as the following approximate list [given in the order in which
the vills occur on p. 100, *Feudal England* (Round)]
demonstrates: $7\frac{1}{4}$ carucates, 7d. ; 1 car. 6d. ; $5\frac{1}{4}$
c. 6d. ; $6\frac{1}{2}$ c. 20d. ; 5 c. 7d. ; $2\frac{3}{4}$ c. 7d. ; $3\frac{1}{4}$ c.
$6\frac{1}{2}$d. ; $3\frac{3}{4}$ c. 1cd. ; 3 c. 1od. ; 3. c. $7\frac{1}{2}$d. ; $6\frac{1}{2}$ c.

Norfolk Carucates not Teamlands, nor "Hides" ad gheldum, but mainly areal estimates of arable land.

6½d. ; 4 c. 7d. ; 2½ c. 7d. ; 3½ c. 7d. ; 1 c. 6d. ;
6½ c. 2od. ; 4¼ c. 13½d. ; 4½ c. 6½d. ; 6 c. 2od. ;
and 5 c. 6od. Prof. Maitland, with needless
candour, states that to a knowledge of Agriculture, he does not attain—but founds his historic
theories on conceptions (or rather misconceptions,)
of that necessary Art, his admissions notwithstanding ; the Abbot of Ely plainly informs (p. 122
I. E. in Hamilton's *I. C. C.*) that (*c.* 1086) he
has *83* (67 + 16) carucates of land *plus* 33 acres,
land to *191* ploughs, of which 122½ there, in
Norfolk ; and *109* (69 + 40) car. of land *plus* 42
(32 + 10) acres in *Suffolk*, where land to *248*
ploughs, and 219½ there, which is good evidence
that the teamlands are better than twice the
number of carucates. That these carucates are
not the usual *fiscal* Hides has just been shown ;
besides the assessment to danegeld, etc., is given
in quite an unusual form in these counties ; as a
rule the carucates of Norfolk and Suffolk seem to
be the amount of land that might be under the
plough, together with *perhaps* the appurtenances
(several meadow and pasture), of a teamland, each
carucate computed at 120 acres ; the idea that
this amount of land is the work of one plough
is unknown to experience, and however practicable
it may appear to any *ex cathedrâ* theorist, he is
here confronted by the fact that such a calculation
is refuted on "page after page" of his record, and
by the singular appearance of the statistical conse-
quences of such a surmise. If the carucates of the
Ely Manors in either Norfolk or Suffolk are
divided by the Teamlands, the quotient in both

Proof of
above
statement.

cases lies between *52* and *53* acres—a result which any agriculturist would allow to be reasonable ; working from these figures, and estimating for the excess of population as recorded in these counties (*vide* note p. 12), the difficulties named on p. 430, *D. B. and Beyond* disappear, and the ratio of Teamlands to Population appears as it should : see also D. B. ii., 169, where the estate of 18 sokemen (always 2 ploughs) is delivered for *a land ;* and ii., 171, where 1 Manor delivered for 5 carucates seems to consist of 2 car. *plus* odd acres adding to 362.

Passing to the evidence of Domesday Book and later records, in 1086 (D. B.) it sometimes happens that a rough approximation of the area of a Manor or district is given in leugæ, each of which have been taken to represent $1\frac{1}{2}$ statute miles. Thus a Manor one leuga in length by as much in width (by this computation) would contain 1,440 modern acres ; no exactness of dimensions can be expected, and of course the reality of rectangular blocks of lands is not postulated. Sometimes one imagines that greatest length and breadth is alluded to ; at other times an average, and in most cases the figures seem a rough estimate (the above remarks follow after testing Yorkshire examples by Jeffery's 1770 1″ maps) ; now 3 of the Ripon "*mile*" crosses (Sharow, Bishopton, and Littlethorpe) are about or within 1,760 yards of the Minster (D. B., fo. 303*b*, about the church one leuga), and in the Manor of Hackness (D. B., fo. 323*a*), a modern mile would seem an excessive quantity. A very telling example is given on fo. 303*b*, as to the berewicks of Ripon (6 leugæ in length by as many

Leugæ.

Ripon "mile" crosses.

in breadth); here it may be stated with absolute certainty that the leuga was nothing approaching $1\frac{1}{2}$ miles; for the whole liberty of Ripon would not comprise 51,840 acres, and the portion of it included in the Domesday berewicks would well answer to a leuga of a modern mile or a trifle less;* at the same time by taking the greatest length and the greatest breadth a leuga of $1\frac{1}{2}$ miles would be found. An example like this on the large scale enables a statement of some certainty that here the leuga was either the modern mile, or else that (if $1\frac{1}{2}$ miles) the greatest and not average length and breadth was taken; and is of far greater worth than rash calculations from assumed perches of 18 to 20 feet, which by the way might reasonably be expected to be derived from the

* Ripon and its Berewicks as given correspond to about half the Liberty of Ripon, the whole of which is considerably less than the area comprised in 6 leuga long × 6 l. broad, taking 1 leuga as $1\frac{1}{2}$ miles linear measure; by the area of the modern townships with additions the leuga works out just under 1 statute mile; a like explanation may then be reasonably postulated for such entries as would give enormous ploughlands of up to 360 acres on a rectangular block calculation. For the berewicks of Ripon do extend 9 miles by 9 miles (6 leuga × 6 l.), but that is their greatest length and breadth, from which nothing can be asserted, and as demonstrated the actual area was but about $\frac{2}{5}$ of such as would be found by multiplying the greatest linear measures; in addition to this it may be held a ploughland contained in itself both pasture (not common of pa.) and meadow of the tenantry, at least for the plough oxen, of which numerous instances may be noted in the Yorkshire I. P. M.'s. (Yks. Record Series), and the Hundred Rolls (vol. ii.); also sometimes houses were on the "ploughland."

extremities of the " mesurabill " man (Ancient Scotch Laws), and therefore very well short of 12 inches. It may be noted that the marks (some yet in existence) representing the Banleuca of Ripon are locally known as mile crosses, nevertheless on what authority I know not, the Yorkshire Arch. and Top. Soc. have produced a modern ancient map of the county, with a scale rating the leuga at 1½ miles, which I venture to think will not be found applicable for areal measurement: however the following examples are wrought from that calculation, estimating a leuga in length by as much in width, as equivalent to a rectangular block of 1,440 acres. It will be observed that a piece of ground of the shape of a right-angled triangle by this computation would contain nothing unless 720 acres, and the nearer the approach to an **L** shape, the lesser the extent ; in many of the cases (below*) the impossible assumption that the whole Manor was under the plough has been made, for it is not always stated how much of its extent was in wood, meadow, and common of pasture ; where given, it is deducted from the total manorial area as shown. For example in Little Smeaton the Manor is given at 1 leuga long by ½ as much wide, and unspecified underwood contained therein ; this cannot be deducted and it is calculated as a rectangular block of land entirely tillage of 720 acres, and 13 teamlands of 55 acres each, or less per actual plough (14 pls.). In the 2nd entry (Berg, *i.e.*, Barugh) no ploughs are

Yorkshire Manors.

---

* See table, p. 129.

named by reason that the Manor was waste; omitting this the total amounts to less than 5,115 acres, containing 103 teamlands and $121\frac{1}{2}$ ploughs, on an estimate from rectangular blocks raised from

Examples therefrom.

*AVERAGE PER TEAMLAND, 1086 (D. B.), ASSUMING THE SQUARE LEUGA EQUAL TO 1,440 ACRES, AND RECTANGULAR AREAS.

	Orig. fo.	Extent in leugæ.	Acres.	Plough-lands.	Acres per plough-land.	Notes.
Dewsbury	299*b*	$\frac{1}{3} \times \frac{1}{3}$	160	2	80	4 ploughs there.
Barugh, etc.	303*a*	$\frac{1}{2} \times \frac{1}{4}$	180—7	3	58	7 acres meadow *plus* unspecified waste.
Welleton, etc.	304*b*	$1 - \frac{5}{12}$	840	20	42	21 pls. there.
Bulmer	306*a*	$\frac{1}{2} - \frac{7}{72}$	580—20	8	70	10 pls.; meadow 20 acres.
Farlington	306*a*	$\frac{1}{6} - \frac{1}{36}$	200—12	4	47	2 pls.; meadow 12 acres.
Fleetham	310*b*	$1 \times \frac{1}{2}$	720	15	48	$9\frac{1}{2}$ pls.
Scruton	310*b*	$\frac{1}{2} \times \frac{1}{2}$	360	10	36	5 pls.
Burton	312*a*	$\frac{1}{2} \times \frac{1}{2}$	356 - (?)	8	less than $44\frac{1}{2}$	14 pls.; unspecified underwood.
Sutton Hongrave	312*b*	$\frac{5}{12} \times \frac{1}{3}$	200	3	67	4 pls.
Middleton Quernhowe	312*b*	$\frac{5}{12} \times \frac{1}{4}$	150	3	50	3 pls.
Foston	313*a*	$\frac{1}{4} - \frac{1}{16}$	270	4	$67\frac{1}{2}$	6 pls.
Smeaton Little	316*a*	$1 \times \frac{1}{2}$	720—(?)	13	55	14 pls.; unspecified underwood.
Tanshelf	316*b*	$\frac{3}{4} - \frac{1}{2}$	360—3	9	40	22 pls.; 3 acres meadow.
Tadcaster	321*b*	$\frac{5}{12} \times \frac{5}{12}$	250—16	4	59	7 pls.; 16 acres meadow.

linear measurements of the leuga ($1\frac{1}{2}$ miles), which does not greatly flatter the 120 acre theory. Again on fo. 165*a* D. B. is a clear instance of a teamland of 64 acres ; here is 1 Hide which when ploughed 1 team to 64 acres in Domesday. contains not unless than 64 acres, and there is one plough ; truly a small Hide (for their average areal scope is 300 acres and more), but nothing to show it is a small ploughland, as it is worked not by 2, 4, or 6 oxen, but by one plough.*

Very similar results follow from an examination of the lands held by the tenantry of the Bishop of Ely, for which reference should be made to the Ely Manors. Inquisitio Eliensis as well as D. B. ; thus under *Cambridge* to each plough of the tenants are in Wittleseia *32 acres*, Doddintona *60*, Litelport *35*, Stoneteneia *30*, Stratham, *50*, Wilbertona *52*, Lyndona *80 or 58*, Heilla *40*, Wisbeach *56*, Ely *42½*, Dunham *45*, Winteworda *48*, Wickham *68*, Sutton *50*, and Wicheforda *45*, and in *Herts*, Haddam *28*, Hatfield *58*, and Chilleshelle *40*, but here a difficulty arises, for the areas ascribed to the tenantry may be rather rateable than real, and also each villein plough will owe to till some of the land of the lord. Now certainly Seebohm,

---

* It is interesting to note how this passage has been twisted, for in the Rev. Bawdwen's translation he renders it that there are 64 acres when the land is not ploughed ; the point seems to be that when you plough the land, you roughly know its measure ; but perhaps the most singular misapprehension of any writer on D. B. occurs on p. 71 of Morgan's "England under the Normans," where, referring to 63*a*, *ipse quoque transportavit hallam et alias domos et pecuniam in alio manerio* the writer suggests this would not be difficult, as the buildings were constructed of wooden boards, etc.

and more cautiously Prof. Maitland, accept such entries as areal extents, and thereby attach considerable holdings to the villeinage of Middlesex (the average villan here holds 1 virgate, cases of 1 villan with 2 Hides at Hanwell and W. Bedfont) ; now a test case can be found in the Manor of Heruluestune (Harlesden Green, fo. 127*b*, and but once noted in D. B.), belonging to St. Paul's, where are 4 Teamlands, 2 ploughs in demesne, and ½ plough held by 22 villeins, of whom 12 hold virgates and 10 half virgates. The total in villeinage (assuming each virgate $= 30$ acres) amounts to 510 acres, against which set 4 oxen, or if the land were fully stocked 2 ploughs, and whether or not 510 acres could be tilled either by 4 oxen, or a couple of ploughs must be left to the sober judgment of any in the least acquainted with practical agriculture. To them it must be clear either that the acres here are rateable, or that they consisted largely of pasture (not improbable owing to proximity to London), or that the virgate in this Manor actually contained but a small number of acres.

Middlesex Villeins, and their holdings, 1086.

Concerning the appended[*] tables, the virgate has been taken as 30 acres arable (save Alwoltuna, where 25 ac., see Rot. Hund., vol. ii., p. 638), though ancient evidences do not establish it to have been entirely in tillage ; and it may be seen that in 1086 there were 109½ teamlands, 104 teams, and 348 recorded folk, against 139 teams and 434 pop. (recorded) in 1125-8, and at the

Peterboro' Villeins, and their teams, 1125-8.

---

[*] See tables, pp. 132, 133, and note that *Estona* has 12 fiscal carucates in 1086, and 3 hides *ad in Waram*, 1125 ; co. Leics. being rated both by Hides and Carucates : see note, p. 39.

latter date the ploughs of the sokemen have been added in brackets—the average acres per villein plough (including work on demesne) being 64.

Now it would seem to be an extremely obvious rule that as folk increase more food is required, and consequently more land tilled and ploughs used, but this simple fact would appear to have escaped the attention of philosophers : an argument based on the theory that because in certain Manors in 1222 a mixture of tenants holding by rent and villein services cultivate X acres, their predecessors in 1086 also arated the said X acres, and that therefore the acreage per plough in 1086 may be discovered by dividing the X acres of 1222

(margin note: Population varies as Ploughs.)

---

*1125-28, LIBER NIGER DE MON. SANCT. PETRI DE BURGO.

	County.	Villeins.	Virgates.	Ploughs.	Acres.	Villeins' work on Demesne in Acres.	Total work of Villein Ploughs.	Acres per Villein Plough.	Ploughs in Demesne, **1125**.	Arable Acres in Demesne, **1321**.
Kettering ...	N'ants	40	40	22	1,200	314	1,434	65	4	300
Tingwell ...	,,	33	2 ½	12	795	34	820	68	2	110
Oundle ...	,,	25	20	9	600	144	708	78	3	205
Pilesgete ...	,,	8	5	2	150	16	162	81	1 +(8)	
Colingham	Notts	20+50	6+10	14	480	90	548	39	2	208
Cotingham	N'ants	17	15	6	450	45	484	80	2	153
Estona ...	Leics	21	21	12	630	50	667	55	2	102
Wermintona	N'ants	49	34½	16	1,035	117	1,123	70	4+(6)	210
Turlebi ...	Lincs	8	4	2 at least	120	12	129	65	1	55½
Alwoltuna	Hunts	29	18	7	450	9	459	66	2	
Totals ...				102	5,910		6,524	64 aver-age.	23+(14)	

N.B.—The 6,524 acres is obtained by adding ¾ of the work on demesne to the tenants' acres, as the demesne is counted as but one ploughing—according to Sir Walter de Henley, in a 3-course shift each acre had ⅔ ploughings : the demesne arable of 1321, is of course but an indication of same in 1125, liable to increase or diminution—in 1321 are 460 ac. ar. at *le Bigginge* under Oundle, 260 being *frisca*.

* DOMESDAY, 1086, CONTRASTED WITH L.N.P.

Place.		Hidage.	Teamlands.	Ploughs.	Value.	Population.	DETAILS OF POPULATION.			
							Villans.	Bord. and Cott.	Servi.	
Kettering	1086	10	16	1+10	11 li.	34	31	—	—	1 ancilla, 2 mills
,,	1125	10	—	4+22	26 li.	52	40	8	—	2 herds, 1 freeman, 1 miller
Tingwell	1086	5½	8	2+ 7	7 li.	37	24	11	—	2 mills
,,	1125	4½	—	2+12	15 li.	43	33	4	—	4 herds, 2 millers
Oundle	1086	6	9	3+ 9	11 li.	37	23	10	3	1 mill
,,	1125	4	—	3+ 9	11 li.+	43	25	10	—	2 freemen, 6 herds
Pilesgete	1086	6	6	1+11	4 li.	39	9	2	1	26 sokemen, 1 mill
,,	1125	3	—	1+(8)+2	14 li.	57	8	1	—	44 sokemen, 2 herds, 1 mill
Cotingham	1086	7	14	2+10	3 li.	44	29	10	4	1 mill
,,	1125	5¼	—	2+ 6	12 li.	30	17	7	—	1 mill, 5 freemen
Estona	1086	12c.	16	2+ 8	5 li.	27	10	5	—	12 sokemen
,,	1125	3	—	2+12	12 li.	34	21	—	—	1 *homo*, 2 mills, 11 sokemen
Wermintona	1086	7½	16	4+ 8	11 li.	36	32	—	3	1 mill
,,	1125	8	—	4+(6)+16	10 li.+	60	49	—	—	1 mill, 8 sokemen, 1 clk, 1 freeman
Alwoltuna	1086	5	9	2+ 7	7 li.	22	20	—	—	2 mills
,,	1125	5	—	2+ 7	4 li.+	36	29	6	—	1 renter
Colingham	1086	4 1/16	14	2+14	9 li.	67	8	20	—	37 sokemen, 2 mills
,,	1125	4 1/16	—	2+14	20 li.	70	20	—	—	50 sokemen
Turlebi	1086	1½	1½	1	1 li.	5/9	1	4	—	
,,	1125	1¾	—	1+2	3 li.		8	—	--	1 priest

Collation of some Peterboro' Manors, 1125-8, with Domesday.

Eccentric views of philosophers.

by the ploughs in Domesday may at first sight appear plausible, but if one finds the recorded population in 1086 Y and in 1222 2Y, or 2Y *plus*, one can be of no other opinion than that their ingenious author has not mastered the above plain idea as to increase of population, etc. Such an illustration is set forth in a table on p. 288, *English Historical Review*, 1897 (composed by

F. Baring), and the patient reader is gravely informed " he can thus arrive at the exact acreage of holdings 1086," that is, like a modern Charon, by *transfretting* the villans and their ploughs of 1086 on to the acres (by no means all in villeinage) of 1222. Just to exhibit this happy method of enlivening the " bald details " of Domesday, take the cases of Runewell and Cadendone (Domesday St. Paul's, 1222), as cited by our author on p. 288 (E. H. R., 1897); one is told of 240 acres in 1222 (best part of them set to a rent by the way) described as 8 tenants' virgates, and of 8 villans and 8 bordars with $2\frac{1}{2}$ ploughs here (Runewell) 1086, and invited to believe that therefore the D. B. villans each had 30 acres, working 120 acres per plough. On referring to the Camden Society's vol. (D. B., St. Paul's) the jurors of Runewell state the Hide was formerly computed at 80 acres, but now (1222) it is 120, and that on account of the poverty of some of the villein tenants their holdings had been taken into the demesne ; on adding up the occupants of the Manor 1222 one finds 34-38 tenants (not eight as our author suggests, supported by nothing unless his endeavour to tie a virgate to each D. B. villan at all hazards) against 16 in 1086. Turning to Cadendon, by some process of adding up divers sorts of holdings in 1222 what are styled $24\frac{1}{2}$ " tenants virgates " of 28 acres each (686 ac.) are discovered for 22 D. B. villans (1086)* who had 6 ploughs, hence 112 acres

Examination of their methods.

---

* The writer seems to have been unaware there is further notice of this Manor of St. Paul's on fo. 211*a*, hence his

per team ; but referring to the records the population noted in 1086 is 29 against over 100 (not $24\frac{1}{2}$), of which some are probably named twice over, so that one certainly cannot credit that where the population had doubled (and more) in 1222, there had been no increase of ploughs over the number given in Domesday.

After such glaring examples of our author's manipulations, it must be left to the judgment of the candid reader whether or not this mode of work is an abuse or use of Records, but if instructive comparisons are to be made, it is important that none of the essential particulars be omitted. From the following the reader may form his own inferences, and by referring to the originals make any additions of matter bearing on the point ; not wishing, however, to emulate the pea and thimble tactics of a certain school, nothing has been suppressed in the first instance, with a view to prejudice the case.

Utility of the philosophic treatment.

The Manor of Alwalton is illustrated 1086 (D. B.), 1125-8 (L. N. P., Camden Soc.) and 1278-9 (Rot. Hund., vol. ii.) ; by turning to the tables above,* it may be seen that in 1086 are recorded 9 teamlands, 9 ploughs (7 in villeinage) and 22 folk (bordars and servi perhaps omitted) ; in 1125-8, 9 ploughs and 36 people, and in 1278-9 (H. R. no ploughs given) are $5\frac{1}{2}$ Hides and $1\frac{1}{2}$ Virgates of land, the virgate 25 acres, at 5 to the Hide ; of which the details account for

Manor of Alwalton, 11th, 12th, and 13th centuries.

figures are incomplete—nevertheless are used here as they serve well enough to illustrate his statistical methods.

* See pp. 132, 133.

726 acres, *i.e.*, 5½ Hides, 1½ Virgates plus one acre, as under :

```
200   acres arable in demesne
450    „    land by 18 villans of 25  acres each
 62½   „     „   „   5   „    „  12½  „     „
 13½   „     „   „   34 cottars
726   acres
```

In addition 2 free tenants hold 28½ acres, and belonging to the demesne ½ acre of court and garden, 1 ac. of several pasture with 8 of meadow, and of course (tho' unnamed) presumably some considerable amount of common of pasture, and wood, which if extra manorial the tenants had access to ; the writer is of opinion that several pasture and meadow is included in the villein holdings (the plough oxen would require hay), but has made no deduction on that ground. There are 59 tenants, but 4 are 2ᶜᵉ named, and 5 widows in cottages, and as the extent seems a full one, I do not think the record population should be put higher than 50 ; the 18 virgates (450 ac.) seem to appear as the same amount in 1125-8, held then by 7 full and 22 semi-villani, and the 62½ acres of 1278-9 might well have been assarted for the support of increasing population since 1125-8, in which there is no mention of them. But I cannot find that one has right in saying that the 756 acres (keeping some 50 recorded folk) in 1278-9 were in cultivation therefore in 1125-8, (keeping 36 people), and that therefore 9 ploughs worked 746 acres then and in 1086 ; even if after the most *ingenuous* manner of the *English Historical*

10—2

Review, you suppose population may increase or double without a corresponding cultivation, the calculation would work out at nothing unless 83 acres per team.

Attention is also called to the following interesting references from D. B. and the Hundred Rolls (Vol. 2, well indexed):

HISTON.

D.B. Cambridgeshire; Lands of Bp. Lincoln, fo. 190 *a and b.*

	Hides.	Teamlands.	Teams.	Villans.	Bord.	Cott.	Servi.	Total Pop.
Manor of Histon 1086, and 1278.	$8 + 8\frac{3}{4}$	$3 + 10$	$2 + 9$	18	18	4	4	44
	$9\frac{3}{4}$	$2 + 4$	$1 + 2$	10	19	—	—	29
	$26\frac{1}{2}$	$5 + 14$	$3 + 11$	28	37	4	4	73

1279. *Hundred Rolls. Vol. II.* (*pp.* 411-13); *rough Summary.*

The Abbot of Eynsham holds $15\frac{1}{2}$ Hides of the Bp. of London.

		Pop.	Acres.
Demesne	$201\frac{7}{8}$ acres arable, 10 ac. mea. ...	—	$211\frac{7}{8}$
Liberi	$46\frac{1}{2}$ ac. by 7 men	7	$46\frac{1}{2}$
Villani, etc.	$\begin{cases} 612 \text{ ac. (12 each) by 51 men ...} \\ 83\frac{3}{8} \text{ ac. by 14 men ... ...} \end{cases}$	51 / 14	612 / $83\frac{3}{8}$
Crofters	no land named	35	—
		107	$953\frac{3}{4}$

Philip de Coleville holds 11 Hides of the Bp. of Lincoln.

		Pop.	
Demesne	1 Hide 10 ac. mea.	—	1 Hide 10 acres.
Liberi	69 ac. by 10 men ...	10	69 „
Villani	300 „ 30 „ (10 each)	30	300 „
Cottars	20 ac. by 28 men ...	28	20 „
*Military tenant subinfeuded ...		20	$160\frac{1}{4}$ „
		88	1 Hide $559\frac{1}{4}$ acres.

* Items of this holding on p. 138.

Details of above 160¼ ac. ⎧ Demesne : 40 ac. (? 1 ac. yard) 40-1 ⎫
⎪ 1 ac. by 1 free tenant ... 1 ⎬ 159¼
⎨ 110 ac. by 11 villani ... ... 110 ⎭ or 160¼ ac.
⎩ 8¼ ac. by 7 cottars 8¼

The Hidage at both periods totals 26½, but whereas 73 folk are on record 1086 ; 195 are noted in 1278, and the Inquisition then finds by detail 1 Hide and 1513 ac. of land,—so that there is presumably a balance of land in common of pasture, waste, etc., which inference the D. B. entry (fo. 190*a*) seems to confirm, for in demesne there were 2 Teams, 3 Teamlands, and 8 Hides ; supposing the Hide (not recorded in acres) in 1278 contained 120 acres, then would there have been 1633 (less, as some described as meadow) acres arable, and yet in 1086, with less than half the recorded population, there were 19 Teamlands and 14 Teams.

The Hundred Rolls often set forth the total Hundred Rolls. Hides* and proceed to give them in detail approximately agreeing at the rate of 120 acres per Hide (or some other stated no. of acres), but in the above the fiscal Hidage of D. B. is given as a heading ; and lest the view that such Hides might be answered from land not all arable be thought fanciful, I append the following† :

---

* In some cases, however, the Hides of the Hundred Rolls do not seem to correspond with the cultivated area of the Manors described.

† Assumptions that the *fiscal Hide* is of necessity rated on arable alone, merely discovers their authors' lack of acquaintance with Domesday, and that such are of a certain class or historic writers, the brightness of whose genius enables them to expound that record without having read it ; but though

Manor of
Coatham,
1086, and
1297.

D. B. 1086.   Cambridgeshire, Coatham, Abbot Croyland (fo. 192*a*) ; 6 + 5 Hides ; 2 + 6 Teamlands ; 1 + 6 Teams ; 12 Villans, 8 Bordars, 1 Servus, that is 21 recorded folk, also meadow to 8 plough teams, and pasture for the vill stock, and a marsh rated at 500 eels.

Here again are 6 Hides set against 2 demesne teamlands giving rise to suspicion that the marsh

Genius of
the
Romantic
School.

our fountains of learning inspire their votaries with something of the " divine afflatus," those subtle qualifications may, by the simple, easily be mistaken, for the mere manipulations of the *prestidigitateur ;* and at any rate the dull path of History is too confined a sphere for talents so impatient of necessary bounds and limits, and better adapted to the more sympathetic regions of Romance, for which their *alma mater* has so adequately equipped them.   There are of course genuine students of History, even within the precincts of learning, and one in especial, who *has* shed a particular lustre on a School which stood greatly in need of it, of whom every Yorkshire and English scholar may well be proud, and whose works may justly rank with those of Brady, Dodsworth, Dugdale, Madox, and Rymer.   By way of illustra-

Fiscal
Hides do
not always
denote
Arable
land.

tion of Hides other than arable in D. B. ; for *wood* see 180*b*, 205*a*, 212*a*, 216*a*, 228*a*, and 244*a* ; for *castles*, 62*b*, 248*b* ; for *pasture*, 49*b* (defends for $\frac{5H}{4}$, the King claims $\frac{H}{2}$ as pa. for his oxen), 65*a*, 96*a*, and 104*a* ; for *gardens*, 298*a* ; as *in the forest*, 32*a*, and 263*b* ; as in *meadow*, 7*a* (1 jugum at farm, nothing there but 2 ac. mea., worth 10s.), 28*b* ($\frac{H}{2}$ and scots for it, but only 10 ac. mea. worth 5s.)*;* and 377*b* (Warnode of 10 ac. mea.) ; as *between wood and plain*, 164*a* and 175*b* (numbered for 15 H. between wood and plain) ; the *County of Yorks* generally, where the areas and values of whole Manors, and the woods in them, are often separately computed, the latter as part of the former ; *also see the I.P.M.* of Elizabeth Moubrai, where the Manor of Kirkby Malesart contains no arable land, but 2 carucates, the herbage of which, etc., 38 Ed. III.

was both rateably and really within the Hide, which inference is established beyond any reasonable doubt as in 1279 (p. 409, vol. ii., H. R.) " they say that the abbot and convent of Croyland hold and defend in the vill of Coteham 11 Hides as in lands, meadows, pastures, and marshes," and " they hold in demesne of the said 11 Hides, 2 Hides arable, and 5 Hides in meadows, pastures, and marshes* pertaining to the said vill," and in tenants 3½ Hides arable.

Now ½ Hide is unaccounted for, and it may be that the tenants held it as in meadow, pasture, and marsh, or rated against a couple of windmills: of the 3½ Hides arable, 9 free tenants hold 59 acres *plus* (the 2nd best by rent being undescribed as to acres), 44 villeins have 335 acres, and 5 men pay house rent, so possibly the omitted acreage was 26, the amount necessary to bring up the total to 420 acres (3½ normal Hides). If the 5½ Hides of arable are taken at 660 acres, it may be observed there were 8 Teamlands and 7 Ploughs in 1086 with a recorded population of 21, which now

---

* In 1086, *arable land* was perhaps worth 2d. (1d. to 3d.) per acre; see D. B., 165a (64 ac. ar. worth 16s., formerly 20s.); 197b (10 ac. land, 8d.), ii. 3, 118, 260, and 341 ; also ii. 275 (120 ac. land, and 5 ac. mea. worth 30s.) ; ii. 94 (80 ac. ar. and 200 ac. marsh worth 20s.) ; as to *meadow*, 7a (2 ac. worth 10s.) ; 28b (10 ac., 5s.), and see note, p. 139; *wood*, 228a, worth 10s. ; 244a, worth 3li. Perhaps land, as per team would be worth 16s. (or less), if the Northern counties were included, but not more than 10s. of this should be set against each plough (8 oxen), leaving the balance against meadow, pasture, woods, and other sources of profit, as jurisdictions, mills, fisheries, etc.

(1278-9) has increased to 58 : according to the statistics from D. B. (Ploughs to Recorded Pop.) there would be 16 Teams in the Manor at the later date.

Now these are not isolated instances, as the following if worked out would show : Wodestone, co. Hunts, Abbot of Thorney ; Fletton, co. Hunts, Abbot of Peterboro' ; Newton, co. Hunts, Abbot of Thorney ; Drayton, St. Paul's, Middlesex ; referring to D. B. and the Rot. Hund., and in the last case to St. Paul's Domesday (Camden Soc.).*

Other Manorial Examples.

It often occurs that the Hundred Rolls estimate the arable demesne in carucates (as where it was out of the Hide), and this may be 120 acres ; indeed Seebohm has given an instance of one of 200 acres, (Eng. Vill. Comm.) but on turning to the record (p. 328 H. R.) it runs " 1 carucate of land which contains 10 score acres of land, meadow, and pasture," and I believe the following are all the entries in co. Beds.

160 acres.	120 ac.	100 ac.	80 ac.	60 ac.	Total	Average.
½ car.	5¼ c.	6 c.	8 c.	5 c.	25 car. ⎫	91½ acres
80 ac.	660 ac.	600 ac.	640 ac.	300 ac.	2280 ac. ⎭	per carucate.

Bedford-shire Carucates.

Thus it will be seen the carucate was a variable quantity, hitherto ingeniously explained by the

---

* The Hundred Rolls are useful for 5 counties only, and of these Church Lands are most suitable for comparison, owing to the great changes in ownership and partition of lands since 1086, in addition summing up the items in 1278-9 is a troublesome process, and likely to be interrupted by gaps : it is of course open for any one to demonstrate the 120 acre theory by the same method, if they have luck enough to find the least confirmation of it by a just comparison.

relative lightness or heaviness of the soil ; this I believe has little to do with the matter, as fewer or more oxen and horses would be used, instances of which can be seen generally in the fields nowadays, and occur so numerously in custumals, etc., as to need no specification. In a certain sense the ploughland was 120 acres, that is examples are taken from the demesne not from the land in villeinage, and as the Bedford table shows the greatest no. of acres hit that amount (660 acres in 120 acre lots), but this is nothing to the point, for the variability of the carucate alone should indicate its meaning (missed by at least every modern writer), *i.e.*, that these demesne ploughlands were such varying amount of land as one plough of the lord tilled with the assistance of his tenants ; for proof of which the following may be taken, all from the Ramsey Cartulary (Rolls Series), 1251 contrasted with Rot. Hund. 1279, and other records, being the only* returns which I have been able to discover, where the aid of the villein teams is estimated in ploughs per annum, and all here set down :

Proof that demesne Carucates were not tilled by One Team.

Inquisitions 1251-2 *Ramsey Cartulary.*			1279 *Hundred Rolls.*
	Demesne.	Assistance.	
St. Ives ...	3 ploughs	equal to 3 ploughs	3 carucates in dem.
Halliwell ...	2 ,,	,, 1 pl. *plus*	2 ,, ,,
Wardeboys ...	4 ,,	,, 2 ploughs	3 ,, ,,
Ripton Abbas	5 ,,	,, 2 ,,	5 ,, ,,
Broughton ...	4 ,,	,, 2½ ,,	4 ,, ,,
Upwode ...	7 ,,	,, 3 ,,	not found.
Wistowe ...	4 ,,	,, 2 pl. *plus*	4 carucates in dem.
	29 pls.	say 16 pls.	

* *Rot. Norm.* 6 John ; the precations *alone* worth 1 plough (that is *per an.*) in Ashby de la Zouche, co. Leic.

Ramsey
Manors.

Except Upwode all these places may be found in the Hundred Rolls under Hunts, and in all of the 6 cases there is complete agreement, save in Wardeboys, where there were 4 demesne ploughs in 1251 against 3 carucates in 1279: the total assistance to 29 demesne ploughs in seven Manors is 16 ploughs (as by villeins), the $\frac{1}{2}$ plough being made up of two cases of *et amplius;* now the average demesne carucate in Beds has been shown to be 91$\frac{1}{5}$ acres, which as above would leave about 60 for the plough of the lord, and the rest (31$\frac{1}{5}$) for that of the tenant.   On p. 629 (Rot. Hund., vol. ii.) under Westone the Abbot (Ramsey) holds

Assistance
from
ploughs
of the
Customary
tenants.

in demesne 8 carucates of land *together with the assistance of his customary tenants* which said demesne contains 548 acres, which can mean nothing unless that his own ploughs together with the assistance of his tenants equal 8 ploughs and suffice for 548 acres, or else that there were in demesne 8 ploughs in addition to assistance from the villeinage.   The Manor of Weston (as cited above 1279) contained the hamlets of Brington and Bitherne in which were 4 demesne teams 1086 (D. B.), and as many as 7 temp. Hen. I. (Ramsey Cart.) and unfortunately there are no further records of the ploughs there till 1279.

Of the 7 Hunts Manors in the table, all (save Broughton perhaps) were out of Hide in 1086, at *St. Ives*, 3 demesne ploughs, 1086, at *Haliwell* 2, and 2 temp. Hen. II., at *Warboys* 3 and 3 temp. Hen. II., at *Ripton Abbas* 2, at *Upwode* 2 and 4 temp. Hen. II., at *Broughton* 4 and 4 temp. Hen. II. and at *Wistowe* 2, and 3 temp. Hen. II.

In 1232 (*ex Rot. Mai. Archiep. Gray.   In dorso*

No. 64) the Archbishop of York leased to the Lease of Hexham demesne, 1232. Prior and Convent of Hexham the demesnes there for a term of 15 years, to be returned in the same condition as received as to crops and fallow ; the total being 179½ acres of arable land in 9 fields or portions of fields (all specified), of which 78 acres in Oats, 51½ in Wheat, and 50 in bare fallow (*terra warrecanda*), together with the precations of ploughs and harrows of the tenantry, and with pasture for 16 oxen, and ploughbote for the draught of 2 ploughs—so that here were 90 acres per demesne plough, part of which 90 acres the villeinage would cultivate.

Again in 1292 (Malmesbury Reg. Rolls Series) Lease of *le Blakelound* 1292. a lease was made by the Abbot to the cook 20 Ed. I. April of *le Blakelound* consisting of 105 acres sown (fallow not named) to wit 62 of wheat, 11 barley, beans, and vetches, and 32 of oats, together with 10s. of pasture, 10s. of customary works, 16 oxen, 2 horses, ploughs (*caruc'*), and 2 harrows, etc.*

Further, in 47 Hen. III. (I.P.M. Yorks Record Series), in the I.P.M. of Baldwin de Insula, there are at his Manor of Harewood 279 acres arable in Manor of Harewood, 47 Hen. III. demesne worked by 3 teams, nevertheless immediately follow the plough services of the tenantry on those acres equal at least to tilling 130 of them once over, so that tho' he may have 3 ploughlands of 93 acres each, and 3 ploughs in demesne, this is nothing to the purpose in the matter of actual work of one plough. Also in the same vols.

---

* The deed cited in the Malmesbury Reg. just before this one makes clear that *caruc'* means ploughs here—and not a plough—presumably two.

in another inquisition 'tis noted that each sokeman must bring to the work of the lord at the rate of one plough for every 4 bovates held in socage. Not that a carucate of land in demesne always means the amount of land which corresponds to the number of ploughs the lord holds, for in the *Reg. Roff.* on cross-examination the bailiffs of the Manors state the number of dominical teams, and also that they have not as many carucates of land, because there are not in those Manors the number of acres which by custom of the district would make corresponding carucates, and further it must be remembered that this word is sometimes used for fiscal (not areal) units, as in the carucated counties in Domesday, and in Kirkby's Quest, the Books of Knights' Fees, and of Aids for Yorkshire, also sometimes in I.P.M.s.

Rochester *Carucates.*

A.D. 1086, NINE COUNTIES TABLE FROM D. B.

Proportion of teams in demesne, 1086.

	Teams.	Lords'.	Tenants'.	Percentage of latter.	Villeins,* etc per Plough.
Bucks ...	2056¾	689¼	1367½	66½	2·1
Dorset ...	1826	752½	1073½	58¾	2·5
Glos'ter(T.)	3909	1058½	2850½	72	1·37
Herts ...	1369½	475	894½	65	2·0
Kent ...	3141⅜	697¾	2443⅝	77¾	2·7
Middlesex	546	152	394	72	3·0
Oxon ...	2461	818½	1642½	66¾	2·2
Rutland ...	238⅝	43⅝	195	82	3·75
Yorks ...	2958⅞	782⅜	2176½	73½	2·33

* The result arrived at by dividing the number of villeins in the county by the *tenants'* ploughs, as the latter are owned by as well *villani* as others, the quotients of course are usually far too low.

Seebohm appears to have made a nice approximation to cultivated England in 1086 at 5 million acres for the recorded counties, which if I understand the *Village Community* rightly is as under :

108,407 villans with	2,250,000 acres and ploughs.	
23,000 sokemen with	500,000 ,, ,,	
12,000 liberi homines with	500,000 ,, ,,	
In demesne	1,500,000 ,, ,,	
89,000 bordars and cottars	250,000 ,, and no ploughs.	
	5,000,000 acres.	

Estimate of England, 1086, in the Village Community.

counting ½ as many ploughs of 4 oxen as villans, and at that rate, the normal villan holding 30 acres and having 2 oxen (p. 85), altho' he allows his average villan of D. B. with 21 acres the same (?) number, but more or less on a scheme of 8 oxen to 120 acres. This infallibly breaks down in detail when tested, for as evidenced by the figures for 9 counties, the lord had at least ¼ of the total ploughs in demesne, and in the recorded counties were some 78,000 ploughs (see pp. 121-2) ; supposing therefore Seebohm's method, which I gather to be that the demesne ploughs were of 8 oxen, and the tenants' ploughs of 4,* then would there be 12,500 large ploughs of the lords for 1,500,000 acres, and

In some respects unreliable.

---

* The following examples do not necessarily, but may sometimes illustrate actual husbandry in 1086 : D. B. — *one ox* in plough, 211*a* ; *two oxen*, 22*a*, 264*b*, 307*b*, ii. 184 ; *two and a half oxen*, twice, but in the same place, see 358*a* ; *three oxen*, 49*b*, 110*b* ; *four oxen*, 366*a* (only time found, but half a plough *passim*) ; *five oxen*, 14*a*, 235*a*, 278*b*, 293*b* ; *six*

Oxen per team the standard of Domesday.

58,333 small ploughs for the 3,500,000 comple-
mental acres ; that is, 70,833 (*i.e.*, 41,666⅔ only
by the method of *D. B.*) teams for 5,000,000
acres arable, and more particularly 37,500 four-ox
ploughs for 2,250,000 acres held by villeins, at
the rate of about 3 villeins per 4 oxen, which is
not agreeable to what he has written about the
gebur and normal villein being stocked with a
couple of oxen.

There seem to be several sources of error, for
the 9 counties table demonstrates the lords' teams
were 30% of the total, and as their scope was more
considerable than that of those of the tenantry,
there might well be some ⅖ of the total arable
in demesne ; also the bordars contributed to the
ploughs by the witness of Domesday (fo. 303*b*.,
two bordars with one plough*—no other tenants
named ; and often together with the villeins), and
as already shown the evidence from it is against the
teams being other than 8 oxen, that is to wit, whatever the actual mode of husbandry, the teams seem
to be reckoned in units of 8 oxen.

In the table of 9 counties, Taylor's Domesday
Analysis furnishes Glos'ter, and the rest are on
the author's responsibility ; all ploughs not in
demesne are counted on the other side, so that
ample correction should be made for the villeins†

Bordars
often had
plough
oxen, 1086.

Method of
*Table of
Nine
Counties.*

---

oxen, 71*a*, 206*a* ; *seven oxen*, 286*b* ; *eight oxen* (not found nor
to be expected) ; *nine oxen*, 359*b* ; and *ten oxen*, 366*a*.

* See note on p. 11 for instances selected from 20
counties.

† The following 64 references from D. B. illustrate the
Villani of 1086 : as *equated to sokemen*, 209*b* ; as *under sokemen*,

per plough, which, as they can seldom be dis-
entangled from bordars and sokemen, cannot be
done with precision. The casts differ somewhat

---

ii. 392 ; as *paying forfeits*, 17*b* ; as *chattels* (bore away a rustic *Villani*
who was remaining on 1 virg.) 30*a* ; as *holding land at farm*, illustrated
127*b* ; as *paying tithes*, 38*a* ; *freeman who had* $\frac{H}{2}$ *now a villan*, Domesday.
ii. 1 ; as *witnesses*, 44*b* (*de villanis et vili plebe*), and ii. 393 ;
as *rent payers*, 52*b* (10s. p. ann.), 182*a* (18 villans, 6 bord.,
and 1 priest render 18s.), 263*a* (1 villan, 8d.) ; as *fractional
persons*, 110*b* ($\frac{1}{2}$ a villan), 168*a* (7 half vill.), 196*a* (1$\frac{1}{2}$ vill.),
and 252*a* (4 whole, and 6 half vill.)—the partition seemingly
in reference to amount of services due ; as *paying relief on
royal Manors*. 30*b* (20s.), 181*a* (an ox) ; as *paying gheld*, 203*a* ;
as *rendering custom*, ii. 5 (a villan had $\frac{H}{2}$ and rendered custom) ;
certain villans quit from all thing of the Sheriff, 30*b* ; as *holding
or having held lands*, 26*b* (the villans held it T. R. E.) ; 40*a*
(the like) ; 41*b* (41 vill. hold and held it) ; 41*b* (28 vill.
hold and held it ; no hall) ; 73*b* (the villans hold it) ; 175*a*
(the land was of the demesne of the villans) ; and 273*a*
(other 3 carucates of land are of the villans) ; as *with specified
holdings*, 12*b* (30 vill. held 4 solins, T. R. E.), 29*a* (1 vill.
holds and held 1 virg.), 192*a* (8 vill., 7$\frac{1}{2}$ ac. each), 198*b*
(5 vill. hold 25s. worth of land), ii. 3 (1 vill. holds 30 ac.,
another 15 ac.), ii. 5 (1 vill. had $\frac{H}{2}$), and in Hanwell and
West Bedfont, co. Midd., are 3 vill. with 2 Hides each, the
highest amount writer has found (see p. 131) ; *as to Status*,
41*a* (a certain prefect held 5$\frac{3}{4}$ Hides, 2 of them as a villan),
41*a* (Aluric held 3 virg. as a villan), 68*a* (5$\frac{1}{2}$ Hides held by
men of the church serving as villans), compare 175*a* (making
services as other freemen), 269*b* (thanes working as villans),
and ii. 145 (6 free villans) ; as *to Servile work*, 17*a* (the
burgesses worked like vill. at the court), 166*a* (the reeve has
1$\frac{1}{2}$ villans), 182*a* (the men of another vill labor in this one),
246*b* (8 burgesses working as other villans), and 291*b* (the
work of the villans pertains to Saxebi in Lincs.) ; as *to
number of plough oxen* varying from none to 3$\frac{1}{2}$ pls. to 3 villans
(182*b*), which may be compared with 180*a* (1 bordar, 1 pl.),
—in certain cases it might appear the villan had 2 pls., but
such (21*b*, 317*a*, and 327*a*—Hugh has 1 vill. and 2 pls.)

from Prof. Maitland's, who claims no minute accuracy for his great industry ; at the same time let not his statement detract from their worth for practical ends, as his tables are of the utmost value, and based, so far as I have discovered, on a sound knowledge of Domesday's method, which entitles his work to the grateful acknowledgment of all interested in our ancient Record.

Yorkshire Agriculture from the 1297 Subsidy Rolls.

An example offers in the 1297 Subsidy (Vol. 16 Yorks Record Ser.) where from the editor's epitome in the Introduction are 1,044 oxen and 681 horses, against just under 5,000 qrs. of corn

---

seem to be instances where the lord is whole or part owner ; the following show extreme cases as found : 115*a* (1 vill., 1 pl.), 164*b* (15 vill., 15 pls.), 185*a* (1 vill., 1 pl.), 325*a* (1 vill., 1 pl.), 327*b* (1 vill., 1 pl.), and 323*a* (5 vill., with ½ pl.), 328*a* (10 vill. 2 bord. with 1 pl.), 353*a* (11 vill. with 1 pl.), and frequently with none ; as *to sowing the lords' land with their own seed,* 174*b* (*bis*), 179*b* (36 vill. 10 bord. plough and sow 80 ac. wheat, 71 ac. oats), and 180*a* (238 vill. ploughed and sowed 140 ac. ; now 224 pl. and sow 125 ac.), which Prof. Maitland gives as instances (p. 57, 'D .B., and Beyond') of the light work of the 1086 *villani,* omitting to observe that it is not the fact of ploughing the demesne (matter superfluous to record),but of sowing the ploughed acres with their own proper seed, which is worthy of note—thus in A.D. 1124 (A.S. Chron.) the acre's seed of wheat (2 bush.) sold at 6s., that of barley (3 bush.) at 6s., and that of oats (4 bush.) at 4s. in a very dear year, whereas the cost of aration would scarcely exceed 2d. per acre. That the *villani* did not till as much demesne land in 1086 as in the thirteenth cent. follows as a matter of mere necessity, by reason that they had fewer ploughs and less land (actually, and also relatively in proportion to the demesne) at the former period ; the demesne ploughs then were probably some $\frac{3}{10}$ of the total, and the lords' arable presumably $\frac{2}{5}$—of course these proportions would be quite inapplicable to the latter period (see p. 152).

and pulse, when a Michaelmas taxation was ordered to be made on all the goods in the house and fields; taking the oxen alone (on the 120 acre theory), there would be some 15,000 acres tillage, and if but 8,000 of them had been sown, a return of 5 bush. p. acre : as some $\frac{4}{5}$ of the crop was oats, 4 (of 5) bush. would have to be kept for seed, nor is it very unlikely that some of the horses were joined in the plough, which would further increase the area and lessen the yield per acre. There were but 370 qrs. (say $\frac{1}{13}$ of sown crops) of wheat (frumentum), 465 qrs. rye (*siligo*),* and 102$\frac{3}{8}$ qrs. of barley, which if all malted would but yield about 18 gallons p. annum per record man, and makes out but poorly in comparison with Prof. Maitland's 2$\frac{1}{2}$ gallons per day for same : in conclusion it may well be allowed that the tax-payers would probably better conceal their corn than live stock, but scarcely to the enormous extent needful for the above supposition.

In the E. H. R. (V. 9, pp. 417-439) Prof. Maitland has very handsomely recorded the results of a search in divers records relating to the Manor of Wilburton, with a result of perhaps the best Manor of article on Mediæval† Agriculture extant (at any Wilburton. rate known to the writer): this paper alone would prove the unreality of the 120 acre theory, and as

---

* The accomplished editor (Wm. Brown, B.A.) turns the rye into wheat, and then explains the absence of the former : the point is not what a word may sometimes mean, but what it represents in a particular record, taking into consideration the sense and date.

† Walt. de Whytleseye's *Hist.* containing extents of over a score of Manors, discovers their structure far more lucidly than the usual *modern* explication.

the evidence (quite unconsciously of course) is
given by an author who is at great pains to support
the opposite (*D. B. and Beyond*), an epitome of
the matter in aforesaid magazine is here appended.

In *1086* (D. B.) the Manor of Wilburton had
3 ploughs in *Demesne*, in *1277* there were 216
acres arable ; *t. Ed. II.* 4 ploughmen (*i.e.*, 2
ploughs), and 128 acres reaped ; in *1426*, 246
acres arable : as to the *Villeinage* in *1277* were
15½ full lands, of 24 acres each, total 372 *acres*,
which Prof. Maitland particularly notes as being
equivalent to statute ones ; *t. Ed. I.* for winter
and spring ploughing were due from each full land
one *ploughing* (the work of one man for one day,
but each 2 ploughings reckoned as 1 diet) per
week for 28 weeks (30 less 2 at Christmas)—total
by theory *434*, and noted as actually done in
4 consecutive years, 420½, 406, 377, 406,—say
400 winter and spring ploughings p. a. The
amount of ploughing not being given, let it be
supposed that 2 ploughings (*i.e.*, the work of
2 men for 1 day) yield an acre ; then (*t. Ed. I.*)
are some 200 acres (once ploughed) performed by
the villein teams alone, taking no account of
5 free tenants, who owe 5 days' tilling each. In
1381 the full lands each owed 1 day's *Somererthe*
(1 acre per day), 2 days' *Nederthe* (1 acre, as
½ acre each day), and *all* the tenants owed 2 boon
ploughings (bringing all the oxen they had), which
latter with almost certainty they may have been
said to owe *t. Ed. I.* ; in *t. Ed. II.* Prof. Maitland
states that about 5s. per an. (2d. a plough each day)
was expended as *regards*, for the boon ploughers

Details
from it
refute
scholastic
theories of
Agricul-
ture.

for their 16 (*sic*) ploughs : the above can leave no room to doubt that at least half of the 216 arable acres of the demesne was completely tilled by the tenantry, leaving at most 108 acres for the 4 hired ploughmen named *t. Ed. II.*, and further the husbandry here must have been far more thorough than that set forth in Walter de Henley's work on Agriculture, as each acre at Wilburton would on an average be ploughed twice or more, instead of the almost incredibly scanty aration of the *bailiff knight*.

The Kentish Manors of Rochester Cathedral (Custumal Reg. Roff. *1290-1320* A.D., publ. 1788) illustrate the note on p. 149 of this vol., and the following table demonstrates that in them (1290-1320) the demesne teams are practically the same as Domesday, whereas those of the villeins have more than doubled,

Great increase of ploughs of tenantry.

Ploughs (1086).		Manors.	Ploughs (1290-1320).		Rochester Manors
Dem.	Ten.		Dem.	Villeinage.	1086, and *c.* Ed. I.
1	12	Southfleet ... ...,	2	18	
5	11	Frendesberie	4	28	
1	1	Deintonia	1	$3\frac{1}{2}$	
2	4	Stokes...	$1\frac{1}{2}$	$4\frac{1}{2}$	
2	6	Wldeham	2	$6\frac{1}{2}$	
6	14 + (? 1)	Heddenham (co. Bucks)	7	48	
17 + 49 = 56			$17\frac{1}{2}$ + $108\frac{1}{2}$ = 126		

and further it may be noted that in *Southfleet*, 25 juga plough 50 acres, besides 2 precations (of 1 acre per plough), total 86 acres ; *Frendesberie*, 21 juga plough 21 + 16 acres ; *Deintonia*, 3 juga, 3 acres plough 6 acres and 6 *quartulas ; Stokes*,

Plough services due therefrom, at latter period.

9 juga plough 9 acres ; *Wldeham*, 10 jugas each 2 acres per plough, and 6½ jugas (of the 10) a further 6½ acres ; precations only noted in *South-fleet*, but perhaps demandable in the other Manors. 68 juga therefore possess 60½ ploughs, or *1 plough to 45 acres*, and in no case more than 4 acres recorded as done in addition on the demesne : that the *jugum* is computed at 40 acres is obvious from entries on p. 6, thus—2 juga pay 81d. *gavel*, ½ jugum 20d., 8½ acres 8½d., 3 juga and 14 acres 11s. 2d.,* etc.: from p. 10 it appears the reeve must be a virgater (Heddenham, co. Bucks), and during office has *4 oxen* in the lord's pasture.

Agricultural details of the 12th and 13th centuries. I would further submit that tenants of 2 virgates may easily be rated at 8 oxen, of 1 v. at 4 oxen, and of lesser quantities, in proportion (more or less), at any rate in the 12th and 13th centuries, and that these amounts were sometimes exceeded, in support of which as follows. In the Burton Chart. A.D. 1114 (p. 30 Wm. Salt Soc. Coll., Staffs) a note of 4 virgates *inland*, that is land of 2 pls. which are there with 16 oxen ; in 1189 custumal of Glastonbury (Roxb. Soc.) men of 3, 5, 10 acres, and ½ virgate all plough at precations (pp. 22, 61-2), a 3 acre man to join his ox if he has one (p. 28) ; 17 virgaters to plough each with 8 oxen (p. 123), and in a later custumal of

---

* The rate is of course 1d. per acre, but (as may be observed from the note on pp. 8, 9, in this vol.), the most simple agricultural arithmetic is apt to bewilder the erudite,—hence an explanation (deemed advisable to clear the morning mists from the *learned* mind) which for the ordinary reader would be esteemed entirely superfluous.

the same Abbey A.D. 1235-61 (Somerset Rec.
Soc.) 17 *three acre men* are each to come with
their plough and what oxen they have (p. 204);
18 *five acre men* each with one ox or more if
possessed (p. 78); 13 *ten acre men* each with a
plough and what oxen he has (p. 74); 9 *half
virgaters* are to plough and find 2 oxen each
(p. 130); 13 ditto each to join their oxen for
ploughing (pp. 149-150); 2 ditto each with 4
oxen if owned (p. 182), and 20 ditto each to
plough with 8 oxen if possessed (p. 210), 21 *virgaters* each if he has 8 oxen (p. 51), to find 4 oxen
(p. 82), 50 ditto each if he has a full plough to
himself (p. 108); 9 ditto each if he has a full
plough (p. 165), with 8 oxen if he has them
(p. 189), to find 8 oxen and himself with a rod
superintend his ploughmen (p. 210); a $\frac{1}{2}$ *Hide
man* (given $\frac{1}{2}$ acre man, an obvious slip) to come
with plough*s* (p. 133); and one with *2 virgates
plus 10 acres* to be beside his plough*s* at precations
(pp. 83-4). On p. 141 of the 1189 custumal
occurs as under : " Walter de Hennelea holds
1 virgate for 8s., and ought 9 times in the year to
plough on his lord's land, with a whole pl. if he
has it, and with $\frac{1}{2}$ pl. if he has not unless half, and
with 2 oxen if he has no more "—and three others
likewise hold and work as said Walter. It will
be observed the name is the same as that of the
Dominus whose exposition heads this chapter, and
whom Prof. Rogers was the (or one of the) first
to exploit ; this *find* seems to have had " no luck "
in its exponents, and the discoverer cannot but
have smiled at the discomfiture of his compeers in

their interpretation of " La Dite de Hosbanderye ";
as himself (p. 75, Six Centuries, etc., Rogers) remarks, " By this he means, not that a team is engaged in ploughing all the year round, but that if
it were so engaged, it would cover the space of an
acre a day," and further, the same writer assesses
the Manor of Cuxham, known to have 3 ploughs
at 250 acres or thereabouts (Hist. Agr.), and not
at 160-180 multiplied by three; nevertheless,
after pointing out the remark cited (p. 75, Six
Centuries) I have been informed that certainly
Rogers assumes 240 acres ploughing per team, the
truth of which must be left to the judgment of
any candid reader.

These custumals (Glastonbury as cited) show
the fallacy of supposing that the ploughmen spent
every hour of the week days in 44 weeks in continued aration ; and also the status of the *carucarii*
as being often 3-5 acre men (*passim*), and once
$\frac{1}{2}$ virgaters (p. 70 Som. Rec. Soc.) ; and the cessa-
tion of villein services for 3-4 weeks at Christmas,
Easter, and Pentecost, is matter notorious (Ramsey
Chart., Boldon Buke, St. Paul's Domesday), and
further, the teamsters had to work their own land.
Bad weather and frost stopped ploughing (it seems
necessary to make this statement explicitly ; see
Ramsey Chart.; p. 64 Roxb. Soc.; pp. 12, 65, 160
Som. Rec. Soc.), and in the later Glastonbury
record both holder and driver are noted to have
the private use of the lord's team for one day in
the week, by turns each (pp. 70, 94, 217) ; for
2 out of every 3 Saturdays (p. 63) ; further, the
ploughmen carry hay and prepare the lord's malt

*Demesne
ploughmen
had divers
duties.*

(p. 94), and work in the harvest field (p. 167 ; also in the appendix to Hatfield's Survey *circa* 1348, under Bailiff's A/^{cs}, and in the Manor of Gravesend, see Cruden's History of same), and thresh in the barn (Bailiff's A/^{cs} in Hatfield's Survey, Surtees Soc.), and by negative evidence of the last named reference, harrow and set out and spread dung, as these items are not burdened on the account.*

Nowadays broadly speaking every 100 acres of land (47 arable, 53 grass) has some 4 men, but in 1086 there were not unless 3·56 of recorded population per team ; if each ploughland really had been 120 acres arable, and if all those noted were actually manual labourers (an extravagant postulate), then would there have been but 3 men per 100 acres all arable, and none whatever for the work of pasture and meadow. Now altho' the crops then raised do not compare with the present yield, it must be borne in mind for each 8 and 4 ox plough 2 men would be engaged (all the year round as by theory), and if ploughs of 2 oxen are to be considered, at least at the rate of 4 men occupied in tillage per each 120 acres, which exceeds the 3·56 found ; whereas at this present one ploughman would (in the North at least) usually suffice each team ; and further the mowing machine surpasses the scythe, the reaper the hook, the steam threshing-machine the flail, and

Impracticability of the current School theory.

---

* Harrowing is sometimes noted, but where not accounted for, the presumption is that the servants of the Manor performed the operation.

so forth as to other labour saving economies unknown T. R.W. Then supposing 3·56 men really
aid work 120 acres arable *plus* the supplemental
grass land, it is difficult to conceive how at hay
time and harvest the $1\frac{1}{2}$ men (for by hypothesis
the other two are ploughing) even with the assistance of women, etc., would get in the crops, and
supervise the stock at pasture; whereas it appears
that in 1348-9 (Bailiff's A/cs Manor of Quaringdon) a harvest of some 160 acres was got in in
4 weeks (23 days) by 8 hired men in the 1st and
2nd weeks, 40 in the 3rd, and 20 in the last, at a
cost of 5d. and 4d. per day per man, with doubtless unnoted assistance from women, etc.

Manor of Cuxham.

In the Manor of Cuxham (7 Ed. I., Rot. Hund.,
and 26 Ed. I., Rogers' Hist. Agr. citing Survey)
were 2 carucates of land in demesne with works of
8 half virgaters in 1279, but in 1317 (Bailiff's
A/c), and 1332-1350 (Rogers' Hist. Agr. presumably from uncited A/cs) were 3 ploughs culti-
vating a varying acreage of some 170 sown acres,
which Rogers has extended by fallow as 232 ac.
(1332-3), and 258 ac. (1350-1), which of course
is an estimate.

Manor of Cotum.

In the Manor of Cotum (Bailiff's A/cs, 1348-9,
Hatfield's Survey) were in demesne 27 oxen,
4 horses, 6 ploughmen, and at least 3 pls. (six
or more noted in the A/c), 189 sown acres by
weeding, and by seed A/c 69 ac. Wheat, 110 ac.
Oats *plus* some 4 qrs. of Peas sown; in *c.* 1377-80
(Hatfield's Survey) the total arable is returned as
242 acres.

In the Manor of Quaringdon (same ref. date

1348-9) were in demesne 27 oxen, 3 horses, 6 ploughmen, at least 3 pls. (others named in A/^{c}) with 164 acres by reaping, and by seeding 66 acres Wheat, 88 ac. Oats, and 9 sown bush. of Barley but no fallow defined ; the gaps and omissions in these A/^{cs} do not give sufficient data for the other Manors. *(margin: Manor of Quaringdon.)*

The areal carucate as shown varied from 60 to 160 acres (H. R., 1279) in co. Beds, but in St. Paul's Domesday (Camd. Soc.) in 1222 are 720 acres in demesne by 3 pls., to wit 3 carucates of 240 acres each, that extent being possible by the large services owed by the tenants on some 5,000 acres on the old Manor of Adulfsnasa, of which Waleton was a portion, with Thorpe, Horlock and Kirkby. To the writer on ancient Agriculture it is perhaps all one whether a plough goes 60 acres or 240 in the year (or at best accounted for by lighter and heavier soils);* not so however in actual practice, nor yet in records, if read with care and discretion. *(margin: Manor of Adulfsnasa.)*

There appears formerly to have been consider-able variation in agricultural measures, and it is probable that a change in the quasi-standard quarter occurred *t.* Hen. III., in which reign it seems to have had 8 bushels, each weighing (for wheat) *c.* 64 lbs. Troy, such pound containing 7,680 wheat grains† " taken in the midst of the ear." This *(margin: Mediæval measures of agriculture.)*

---

* The comparative rainfall has a much greater influence under this head, as by the number of days in a year in which land can be worked. *(margin: Rainfall.)*

† *Vide* Statutes cited as *51 Hen. III.; 31 Ed. I.;* and *t. Hen. VII.*

lb. W. Chaffers* states to have been used by the
Saxons, and known as the Cologne pound; whether
or not there was a qr. of wheat in England composed as above prior to Hen. III. I may not pretend to discern, but certain it is that *t.* Hen. II.
and John, a quasi-standard quarter existed which
was of $\frac{1}{2}$ (or less than $\frac{1}{2}$) the dimensions of that
under notice.   Two writers on agriculture (see
Walt. de Henley, ed. *R. H. S.*, and the more
valuable anonymous *Husbandry* incorporated in
same vol.), both perhaps *t.* Hen. III. evidently use
the larger qr. [*vide* feeding rations and seed sown
in vol., *ut sup.*) ; and a like one occurs in the
Rules of Robert Grostete (who died *t.* Hen. III.)
as appears from the statement that 180 loaves
(white and brown *together*), each weighing 5 *marcs*
(25,600 grains), are made from a quarter of wheat
in his *Household* ; at this present an average qr. of
Wheat, Barley, and Oats may be taken at 500,
440, and 336 lbs. (avoirdupois, **7000** wheat grains
each) respectively ; this modern pound presumed
to be somewhat *heavier* than the older one of 64
to the bushel.   That the quarter from† **7680** wheat
grains was not *t.* Hen. II. and John the quasi-
standard one appears from divers entries on the
Misæ Roll (14 John), as to the travels of the
King's cart horses, which are each allowed 1 bushel‡

---

* *Hall Marks on Plate.*

† *Id est,* 7680 × 64 × 8 wheat grains per qr.

‡ It is, of course, not intended to convey that either
62 or 31 modern lbs. of corn was consumed *per* horse; in
1261-1270, the larger qr. seems to have sold (for oats) at
2s.: there is no particular occasion to suppose an overstrained
morality either on the part of King John's grooms, or on that
of the servants of the *hostels.*

of oats (price 1od. to 1s. per qr., and in some cases provably of 8 bush.); this smaller measure would appear [*vide* entries *Rot. Pip.* 17, 19 and 20 *Hen. II.*, where quarters are named] to have been somewhat an equivalent of the contemporary *horse-load*, always bearing in mind that the burden of a *sumpter* cannot be precisely equated with a measure of capacity, owing to the differences in weight of Wheat, Barley, and Oats (*ut sup.*). Taking the qr. of Hen. III. onwards as being of like capacity with the present (an assumption), its contents would have had rather less actual weight (the smaller grains being relatively lighter), and the other *much* smaller quarter of *Hen. II.*—*John* would more or less be the actual load of a horse, which is the "standard" measure in the *Pipe Rolls* of the former reign. The allowance of a *destrier* t. Ed. I. (*Wardrobe A|cs*), is $\frac{1}{2}$ bush. of oats (of course with sufficient hay), but a war horse it must be noted might have to carry a considerable weight of iron armour (up to 361 modern lbs.,* cited for a *barded* horse, 1560, in Scott's *Brit. Army*); for a cart horse (*W. A|cs*) $\frac{1}{4}$ bush., which bearing in mind that beans were not supplied, and that the bushel was probably somewhat light (as by modern weight) is not inconsistent with present practice ; the *professed* antiquary, however, should note that 1 bush. of corn per horse (14 John, *ut sup.*) in the measure of A.D. 1900, is just as inapplicable as the *120 acre plough theory*, merely proving the unlikeness of the quasi-standard (*t.* John) to our own. Walt. de Henley's allowance of $\frac{1}{6}$ bush. (*t.* Hen. III., hence rather short of modern weight) of corn with

---

* This includes the rider.

hay and chaff only, would be a defective winter ration for an average modern farm horse ; but, the anonymous writer on Husbandry (in same vol.) appears to give an intelligent record of the practice of his own district : his information can be extended, in matters like the gestation of animals, the terms in that item being nearly agreeable with modern averages. There must of course have been many ancient local variations of measure, not coincident with the quasi-standard : *horse loads* and *bushels* were used as measures *t.* Hen. I. [*Pipe Roll* and *Chron. Pet.*], and a *modius* in 1086 (*D. B.*), apparently of considerable capacity [*t.* Hen. I. app. *Chron. Pet.*] : the rendering of the term *seedlip* (1124, *A. S. Chron.*), as *bushel* in the note on p. 149 must not be taken as evidence of the *then* existence of a measure so called of like capacity with a modern $\frac{1}{8}$ of a qr., but it seems to demonstrate there was in 1124 an antecessor of the modern *bush.*, by whatever name called, of like dimensions—the curious *achersetum* (presumably seed, for one acre), of the Peterboro' Inquisition (1125-8) may also be noted.